THE MIND OF THE MINISTER

Restoring trust between
ministers and civil servants

THE MIND OF THE MINISTER

Tom Brown

Biteback Publishing

First published in Great Britain in 2024 by
Biteback Publishing Ltd, London
Copyright © Tom Brown 2024

Tom Brown has asserted his right under the Copyright, Designs and Patents Act 1988 to be identified as the author of this work.

All rights reserved. No part of this publication may be reproduced, stored in a retrieval system or transmitted, in any form or by any means, without the publisher's prior permission in writing.

This book is sold subject to the condition that it shall not, by way of trade or otherwise, be lent, resold, hired out or otherwise circulated without the publisher's prior consent in any form of binding or cover other than that in which it is published and without a similar condition, including this condition, being imposed on the subsequent purchaser.

Every reasonable effort has been made to trace copyright holders of material reproduced in this book, but if any have been inadvertently overlooked the publisher would be glad to hear from them.

ISBN 978-1-78590-933-7

10 9 8 7 6 5 4 3 2 1

A CIP catalogue record for this book is available from the British Library.

Set in Minion Pro

Printed and bound in Great Britain by
CPI Group (UK) Ltd, Croydon CR0 4YY

For Elodie and Miles

CONTENTS

Introduction ix

PART ONE: SETTING THE SCENE 1
Civil servants: The backstory 2
Ministers: The backstory 9
Special advisers: The backstory 16
Governance of the relationship 18
Ministers are people 23
Adversarial structure 27
Change always costs something 29
Trust and growth 31
Building trust 33
The ministerial lifespan 40

PART TWO: THE BEGINNING 43
The minister arrives 43
The role of private office 59
Building trust 65
Managing the ministerial team 75
The art of relationship building 81
Minister getting to grips 92
Ministers also need to know about… civil service hierarchy 99

PART THREE: THE MIDDLE — 101
Working together — 101
Politics — 111
Special advisers — 123
Difficult conversations — 135
Disagreement and conflict — 139
Differences — 153
What you don't see — 159
We are people — 166
Truth, impartiality and authenticity — 174
Blind spots and weaknesses — 195
Control — 212

PART FOUR: THE END — 223
Distraction — 223
The end — 228
Problems: What's gone wrong — 234
Problems: Boris Johnson and Dominic Cummings — 245
Making improvements — 250
How to be a better minister — 256

Conclusion — 273
Appendix: List of interviewees — 281
Notes — 287
Acknowledgements — 291

INTRODUCTION

On 29 February 2020, I awoke to the prospect of a birthday for the first time in four years. The discovery that I was born on a leap year evokes surprise and (to me, at least) strange reactions from other people; around the world, 29 February carries all sorts of mysterious connotations and superstitions. In Ireland, it has been considered the day that women may propose to men. Italian proverbs have warned that leap years make women erratic and they are urged not to make any big life decisions until the leap year has ended. Greek and Ukrainian folklore suggests that getting married during a leap year will ultimately end in divorce. It is a day that apparently both births and dooms relationships.

The day of 29 February 2020 was also the day that Sir Philip Rutnam chose, very publicly, to resign as Permanent Secretary from the Home Office, following a high-profile clash with Home Secretary Priti Patel. The moment marked a nadir in relations between civil servants and ministers and sent seismic waves through Westminster (the world of politicians) and Whitehall (the world of civil servants). In the pouring rain (under an umbrella), Rutnam opened with this statement:

I have this morning resigned as Permanent Secretary of the Home Office. I take this decision with great regret after a career of thirty-three years. I am making this statement now because I will be issuing a claim against the Home Office for constructive dismissal.

In the last ten days, I have been the target of a vicious and orchestrated briefing campaign. It has been alleged that I have briefed the media against the Home Secretary. This – along with many other claims – is completely false.

The Home Secretary categorically denied any involvement in this campaign to the Cabinet Office. I regret I do not believe her.

She has not made the efforts I would expect to dissociate herself from the comments. Even despite this campaign, I was willing to effect a reconciliation with the Home Secretary, as requested by the Cabinet Secretary on behalf of the Prime Minister. But despite my efforts to engage with her, Priti Patel has made no effort to engage with me to discuss this.[1]

In normal language, this might sound like a strong statement. In the language of government, these were devastating words which shook the foundations of minister–civil servant relations. Long before the term 'unprecedented' became commonplace, former head of the civil service Lord Kerslake described the nature of Rutnam's resignation as just that, stating that it would 'send shockwaves through the civil service'.[2] It was and it did.

Superstition might suggest that the leap year had struck again, ending another relationship in divorce. More likely is that we were witnessing another drastic moment of decline in Britain's most important relationship – that of ministers and civil servants. That sounds like an exaggeration, but it is not. Government exists to serve citizens, which it does through projects and services. These are underpinned by policy (a plan or course of action by the government), which is initiated by ministers and then developed and delivered by civil servants. When it comes to health, education, pensions, benefits, transport, police, national defence and security, protecting consumers, national energy supply and paying for all of those things, it is the most critical relationship for the country. And this was a drastic moment. There have been (few and far between) examples of senior civil servants being moved within Whitehall to get away from a minister who they were unable to get along with (including a couple of premature departures in the 1990s). But none at the level of Rutnam or in the manner in which he was forced out.

Trouble had been brewing in the years leading up to this moment. In 2018, one (unnamed) Permanent Secretary said the relationship was at its 'lowest ebb':

I think it was very low in the Francis Maude days [2010–14], but it's pretty low now. I think a number of things are making it worse at the moment … The default is that [civil servants are] to blame for everything. We're to blame for Brexit being difficult; if we say Brexit's difficult, we're blamed for being Remoaners.[3]

Things got worse. The Patel–Rutnam fall-out of 2020 marked a distinct low moment. Later that year, during the Covid-19 pandemic, the Department for Education faced a school exam grading controversy, where an algorithm designed to combat grade inflation ended up disproportionately benefiting private school students and penalising those from state schools. It was a major error and caused stress and anxiety for thousands of students. The Department for Education's Permanent Secretary, Jonathan Slater, and the CEO of exams regulator Ofqual, Sally Collier, were forced to resign. The Secretary of State for Education, Gavin Williamson, who should have taken responsibility (under the principle of individual ministerial responsibility), refused to. Slater only discovered plans to replace him after he was contacted by a journalist from *The Times* for comment. His sacking was widely seen as a way to shield Williamson.

In September 2020, the Permanent Secretary of the Government Legal Department, Jonathan Jones, resigned over the government's plan to use the Internal Market Bill to back out of parts of its withdrawal agreement with the EU. The Secretary of State for Northern Ireland, Brandon Lewis, had told MPs that the bill would break international law in a 'very specific and limited way' by giving UK ministers the power to override EU law in 'tightly defined circumstances' if border negotiations broke down. The government was asking civil servants to break the law.

The year of 2020 also saw a clear-out of other Permanent Secretaries, on a scale not witnessed before. In a very public war on Whitehall, government sources leaked that Sir Simon McDonald, Sir Philip Rutnam and Sir Tom Scholar (Permanent Secretaries at the Foreign Office, Home Office and HM Treasury, respectively) were on a three-person hit list of those they wanted removed from post.[4] Scholar managed to survive the 2020 cull of Permanent Secretaries but was later removed by Liz Truss during her short spell as Prime Minister in 2022.

Following widespread press reports that he was to be sacked, Cabinet Secretary Sir Mark Sedwill left in September 2020. *The Telegraph* said that Downing Street regarded Sedwill as 'too much of a Europhile and establishment figure' to be in post for its planned Whitehall reforms. Sir Richard Heaton left the Ministry of Justice (MOJ) at the

INTRODUCTION

end of his initial five-year appointment period, but he apparently only learned of his departure because it was tagged onto the end of a statement by No. 10 announcing the departure of Sedwill.[5]

Sir Simon McDonald had worked with Boris Johnson while he was Foreign Secretary and they appeared to have a tense relationship, including during Johnson's exit from the role. As Permanent Under-Secretary at the Foreign and Commonwealth Office (FCO), McDonald had subsequently criticised Johnson's handling of a row over leaked cables that led to the resignation of Sir Kim Darroch, the UK ambassador to the US, during the Tory leadership contest (which Johnson won). McDonald had expected to stay to oversee the merger of the FCO with the Department for International Development (DfID) in 2020 but was forced out early, in what some described as prime ministerial revenge.

The Covid era also brought about many more examples of a deterioration in the health of the relationship between ministers and civil servants. In November 2022, Adam Tolley KC began a five-month investigation into the behaviour of Dominic Raab, following accusations of bullying. Tolley concluded Raab's conduct 'involved an abuse or misuse of power in a way that undermines or humiliates' officials. Following publication of the inquiry findings, in April 2023, Raab resigned. Later that year, the Covid Inquiry produced damning findings, particularly Helen MacNamara's testimony of Prime Minister Boris Johnson's refusal to address misogyny, lying and 'nuclear levels' of overconfidence.

One senior civil servant, with over thirty years of experience, said of that time: 'There is a poisonous, horrible atmosphere – a feeling that retribution could strike at any time for offering the wrong advice to the wrong person.'[6] In December 2022, Jill Rutter wrote for the Institute for Government that 'Brexit, Covid and Boris Johnson have made existing tensions in relations between civil servants and ministers unsustainable'.[7]

Following seismic events and crises (like Brexit and Covid), there is often much analysis attributing the extreme circumstances to extreme actions. There is no doubt that the relationship between civil servants and ministers, and particularly Permanent Secretaries (as the top civil servant in a department) and Secretaries of State (the minister in charge of that department), reached its worst point during the periods of Brexit and Covid. But the basis of how the two work together, in true British institutional fashion, sits upon centuries of carefully constructed precedent and mutual understanding.

None of these periods marked the first occasion that civil servants had been asked, by ministers, to break the law. They did not mark the first occasion that a minister should have resigned but did not. We can be fairly confident that cases of bullying or intimidating behaviour from ministers occurred before 2016. But the intensity of damaging behaviour, the testing of civil service integrity and a scorched-earth approach to constitutional norms have left scars that need more than time to heal.

The relationship between ministers and civil servants is a subject about which relatively little is known, beyond those who have happened to have done the job themselves. In public consciousness, the reflection of how ministers and civil servants work together is somewhere between the TV shows *Yes Minister* and *The Thick of It*. Both are funny and provide glimpses into the workings of government, but neither presents the whole picture, not even in combination.

Civil servants are employed by the Crown (the state), which is represented by the executive (the government of the day). The political party with the most elected representatives in Parliament forms a government of ministers. Most civil servants work in government departments and are therefore employed by a government minister (a Secretary of State). However, the department itself is led and run by a top civil servant, the Permanent Secretary. The civil service (unlike the US system) is not politically appointed and is intended to remain as a consistent body of expertise capable of delivering policy ideas for ministers. Ministers, meanwhile, retain the democratic mandate for authority and decision-making. In the currency of power, ministers are paid the big bucks but at the price of public accountability – which is why they come and go.

Despite some forms of devolution (including Scottish and Welsh Parliaments, the Northern Ireland Assembly and Metro Mayors), the UK remains very centralised. The vast majority of decision-making still happens in a single postcode (SW1) between a maximum of 109 ministers[8] (roughly twenty-five to thirty of which form the Cabinet) and a couple of thousand senior civil servants. It is the relationship between these two parties that has soured so much in recent years and on which this book is focused.

In some ways, it is unfortunate that such an impactful element of public life sits with so few people, although that does mean we can be more targeted in trying to make improvements. It is a fallacy that time, alone, heals all wounds. Patience, behaviour change and consistency play much greater roles, as does acknowledging the history of past mistakes so we are not inevitably doomed to repeat them. In the end, it will be up to the individuals who fulfil those public roles to improve how they work together. If relations are bad, it is not enough for civil servants to hold their breath and wait or hope for someone to arrive who they get along with better; an amiable, favourable minister could be replaced at any moment. And it is not enough for ministers to simply decide that force of will is enough to bend and change the delivery machine of government. That approach forgets that the machine is, in fact, constructed of people.

Ministers, famously, begin the job with an hour's notice. There is an enormous amount to do and they are in at the deep end, often knowing very little about the department they've landed in but bringing energy, drive and optimism for change. Over time, these can be drowned by reality, accountability and crises. And then, eventually, by the distraction of promotion, demotion or a changing political landscape.

A minister evolves over their time in office and civil servants must seek to understand that changing person again and again over the minister's tenure. No minister is the same person on the day they leave as the day they arrived; but their mandate remains and so the onus is on civil servants to keep trying to understand the minister, attuning to different personalities and preferences. Experienced senior civil servants can quickly decipher whether ministers are more policy- or communications-driven (usually derived from a combination of their background, topic experience and ambition); whether they think in ink or through debate; whether they prefer detail or synopsis; whether they like having a smorgasbord of options or a strong recommendation; and whether they are efficient and well organised or… not.

Douglas Wass, Permanent Secretary to HM Treasury from 1974–83, captured the blurred nature of the minister–civil servant relationship:

> Ministers do not always define their political objectives, or if they do, they define them in terms which permit quite a lot of discretion in their interpretation. On the other hand, administrative methods are often highly charged political issues. The way a tax is

administered may greatly affect the political standing of the government; and the use of some administrative techniques may be anathema to Ministers. So in the real-world, Ministers and civil servants are inextricably mixed up with each other. And they can only function on the basis of a close and harmonious partnership in which each has the trust of the other.[9]

This conclusion seems clear and, to anyone looking at the issue, obvious. Perhaps the easy to ask, difficult to answer question is: how? How do ministers and civil servants build a close and harmonious partnership in which each has the trust of the other? Civil servants serve the government of the day and by their nature, they must be ready to adjust and support a minister of any political persuasion, or personality, and to provide options for any policy idea. How can a minister, of tribal political nature, trust civil servants who have been implementing the ideas of their nemesis (another political party)? The civil servant will say they are governed by a code and that they are committed to impartiality, honesty, integrity and objectivity. I have worked with thousands of civil servants, public officials and politicians in more than forty countries throughout my career, from policy and communications teams to Permanent Secretaries and Prime Ministers. Do I believe British civil servants are committed to impartiality, honesty, integrity and objectivity? Yes. But politics is about people and feeling and emotion and momentum. The commitments of the Civil Service Code are vitally important, but alone they are insufficient to establish trust.

Ministers are governed by the Ministerial Code. Except there is a catch: the final decision over whether a minister has breached the expected standards of that code rests with the Prime Minister. A Prime Minister simply needs to decide not to implement the standards of the code on their ministers for it to lose any potency of protection. If rule makers do not believe the rules apply to themselves, it is difficult for civil servants to know where they stand. Rules, guidelines and frameworks alone are insufficient to establish trust.

In the alchemy of governance, the trust between a minister and the civil servants around them is the most precious element, transforming policy visions into tangible realities. But it also aids navigation through crisis and makes the country a better place to live. A fundamental question this book asks is: How can ministers and civil servants build, and rebuild, trust?

Building genuine trusting relationships is an art form rather than a science, which is a frustration if you are in a hurry or have an agenda to get on with. The reality is that humans are individuals and different from one another. Life would, perhaps, be easier if everyone could fit into simple boxes, but if there was a fixed formula for successful working between ministers and civil servants, I suspect it would have been found by now. I am somewhat sceptical of 'one-man think tank'-style analysis (it is usually from men), which suggests everything is broken but, fortuitously for us, they have all the answers to fix it. I do not have all the answers, which is why I have drawn from a wide variety of people who have been on one side or the other of the minister–civil servant relationship. For this book, I interviewed, in depth and on the record, thirteen prominent former ministers and Permanent Secretaries to gain a much deeper understanding of how ministers and officials can work better together. I also spoke with dozens more in my research. Collectively, they bring reflection, experience and differing views: some of the base ingredients needed to improve something.

I've wondered, many times, while writing this book: 'Was it really

INTRODUCTION

that bad?' The intensity of examples of souring relationships between ministers and civil servants, particularly since 2016, is inescapable. But government still functions, a change of government can signal a reset and critics might label some of the fall-outs as overblown. It is tempting to think that a period of calm and the de-escalation of conflict is sufficient to see past the events of 2016–24. But the trajectory of change has taken place over a much longer period than that and the nature of British constitutional norms means that when something 'unprecedented' happens, it creates a new precedent that enables it to happen again. By definition, those things cannot be undone and so ministers and civil servants must now decide the future direction of the relationship.

As with all things, the relationships between ministers and civil servants are neither all bad nor all good (though some are considerably better or worse than others). But each time, I have come back to the question, 'How important is this relationship?' If you have any interest in government successfully serving citizens, then I would say it is critical. In which case, it needs all the investment and careful attention it can get – for the sake of the country.

PART ONE

SETTING THE SCENE

The period between 2016 and 2024 (and particularly during the Boris Johnson administration) does not mark the only time that ministers and civil servants have faced a strain in their relationship. But it did mark a particularly intense period of turmoil and sat within the context of two all-encompassing events: Brexit and the Covid pandemic. It was also a period during which several constitutional precedents, underpinning the way in which ministers and civil servants work together, were undermined. Those acts cannot be undone, and because of the UK's uncodified constitution, it's easy for such acts to set precedent and then become established norms. In other words, it is not possible to pretend nothing happened between 2016 and 2024 and simply return to old ways; those no longer exist. A new space has been created and decisions must be made about how these new precedents are governed or formalised. In order to step back and decide on the way forward, it is important to understand the context of the minister–civil servant relationship and its evolution so far.

CIVIL SERVANTS: THE BACKSTORY

The civil service is often referred to as if it were a single entity. That was once true. Today, in practice, it is a collection of organisations tied together by a series of threads, unified in their commitment to serve the government of the day and by a carefully established code and set of principles which have been honed over 170 years. The nature of the British civil service rests very heavily upon two reports:

1. The 1854 Northcote–Trevelyan Report established the core values which form the bedrock of today's Civil Service Code: integrity, honesty, objectivity and impartiality.
2. The 1918 Haldane Report emphasised the necessity for government departments to engage in ongoing knowledge enhancement and research to provide a solid foundation for policymaking. It also established a mutual interdependence between ministers and civil servants.

However, it is not only these reports that have shaped the working relationship between civil servants and ministers. There have been several other significant reports, rules and events which have carefully evolved the relationship over the course of more than 150 years.

THE NORTHCOTE–TREVELYAN REFORMS (1854)

The Northcote–Trevelyan Report laid the foundation for a professional civil service by emphasising merit-based recruitment. The reforms minimised political patronage, allowing civil servants to serve with increased integrity and impartiality and enabling them to offer unbiased support and advice to ministers, irrespective of political affiliation. Importantly, these reforms established the principles of integrity, honesty, objectivity and impartiality, providing the foundation for civil servants' professional ethos and the Civil Service Code's core values. The reforms heralded a new era where talent and hard work should define a civil servant's rise through the ranks, not who they knew.

THE CIVIL SERVICE COMMISSION (1855)
The establishment of the Civil Service Commission to oversee merit-based recruitment reinforced the professional barrier between ministers and civil service appointments. This allowed civil servants to function as objective administrators, focusing on policy implementation and efficient administration without undue political influence.

THE INTRODUCTION OF COMPETITIVE EXAMINATIONS (1870)
The introduction of competitive examinations for entry into the civil service helped ensure that civil servants possessed the necessary expertise and competence to effectively support ministerial directives and collaborate on policy development, enhancing the functional synergy between civil servants and ministers.

THE HALDANE REPORT (1918)
The Haldane Report underscored the need for robust collaboration between ministers and civil servants, proposing a model where both parties work closely on the basis of mutual respect and shared knowledge. This relationship was aimed at improving policy formulation and decision-making, recognising the specialised knowledge that civil servants bring to the government. The report introduced

the idea of mutual interdependence, with ministers providing authority and officials providing expertise.

Richard Burdon Haldane suggested that this collaborative effort should not be confined to a small group of officials around a minister, as was common in the nineteenth century, but should extend across entire departments, leveraging their collective expertise and perspectives. Despite enormous changes over the past 100 years, this remains the model on which ministers and civil servants operate.

Former senior civil servant Martin Stanley summarised the impact of the Haldane model well:

UK civil servants are intended to work so closely with Ministers that they know Ministers' minds so well that they take the same decisions that Ministers would take, given the law and the substance of the relevant government policy. This is the reason why civil servants are almost always present when Ministers meet their colleagues to discuss policy and when Ministers meet others in 'official' meetings. They listen in to ministerial phone calls, take notes of meetings and debrief those who need to know. Ministers may not reach decisions in private, with each other or with someone else – nor can officials.[1]

Professors Dave Richards and Martin Smith have added to this:

Constitutionally, the Haldane convention does not recognise any division in the personality of ministers and their officials ... The principles of both indivisibility and mutual dependence within the UK system are seen as providing both a practical and constitutional constraint to protect against the arbitrary (ab)use of power ... This convention became a bedrock of the Westminster model. It established the modus operandi that officials and ministers should operate in a symbiotic relationship whereby ministers decide after consultation with their officials whose wisdom, institutional memory and knowledge of the processes of governing helps to guide the minister. The official is loyal to the minister who takes the rap when things go wrong. Whatever the problems with this approach, democratic or otherwise, it at least outlined clear lines of responsibility and accountability.[2]

CENTRAL COORDINATION BY THE TREASURY (1920)
The move to centralise civil service coordination under the Treasury was designed to unify administrative practices across departments, leading to more cohesive support for ministerial projects and initiatives. This helped streamline interactions between civil servants and ministers, facilitating smoother policy execution.

THE CARLTONA PRINCIPLE (1943)
The Carltona Principle allowed civil servants to exercise power on behalf of ministers, underscoring the delegation and trust integral to the minister–civil servant relationship. This principle has facilitated efficient government operation by enabling ministers to rely on civil servants for the execution of their decisions, reflecting an operational aspect of their collaboration.

THE CRICHEL DOWN RULES (1954)
The Crichel Down affair involved a promise in Parliament by Winston Churchill in 1941 that requisitioned land would be returned to its owners after the Second World War, once it was no longer required for the purpose for which it had been bought. After the war, the land was handed over to the Ministry of Agriculture,

which increased the price of the land far in excess of the amount the original owners had sold it for. Mass outcry and a public inquiry ensued, following which the minister responsible, Sir Thomas Dugdale, resigned. That moment set a precedent for ministerial responsibility and a chain of accountability, whereby civil servants were accountable to their ministers, and ministers were accountable to Parliament. Ministerial accountability was subsequently established, whereby it is expected that a minister will protect a civil servant who has carried out an order by the minister. This includes a minister acknowledging and taking responsibility for a mistake made by a civil servant and not exposing them to public criticism.

The Crichel Down episode is important in constitutional terms because of the four categories drawn up by the then Home Secretary, Sir David Maxwell Fyfe, to distinguish the degree of accountability of ministers for their civil servants:

1. A minister must protect a civil servant who has carried out an explicit order by the minister.
2. A minister must protect and defend a civil servant who acts properly in accordance with the policy laid down by the minister.
3. Where an official makes a mistake or causes some delay, but not on an important issue of policy and not where a claim to individual rights is seriously involved, the minister acknowledges the mistake and accepts the responsibility, although he is not personally involved, and states that he will take appropriate corrective action in the department. The minister would not expose the official to public criticism.
4. Where action has been taken by a civil servant of which the minister disapproves and has no prior knowledge, and the conduct of the official is reprehensible, there is no obligation on the part

of the minister to endorse what he believes is wrong or to defend what are clearly shown to be errors of his officials. But the minister remains constitutionally responsible to Parliament for the fact that something has gone wrong, and the minister alone can tell Parliament what has occurred.[3]

The subsequent Crichel Down Rules improved the transparency and accountability of civil servants, particularly in the management of public assets, reinforcing the trust and reliability expected by ministers. These rules helped solidify a more accountable and ethically grounded relationship between civil servants and ministers.

THE FULTON REPORT (1968)
The Fulton Report highlighted the necessity for modernisation and specialisation within the civil service, leading to a more skilled and adaptable workforce capable of effectively supporting a range of ministerial needs and enhancing the overall responsiveness of civil servants to ministerial goals.

THE CIVIL SERVICE DEPARTMENT (1968)
The creation of the Civil Service Department was instrumental in elevating the professional management within the civil service, ensuring that civil servants were well prepared to meet the increasingly complex demands of ministers and to provide high-level administrative support.

THE ARMSTRONG MEMORANDUM (1985)
The Armstrong Memorandum detailed the ethical framework within which civil servants operate, emphasising their commitment to serve the government of the day efficiently and impartially. This

guidance ensured that civil servants supported ministers in a manner consistent with legal and ethical standards, fostering a stable and trustworthy governmental environment. Crucially, the Armstrong Memorandum was designed to ensure the confidence of ministers that civil servants will always support the government of the day.

THE 'NEXT STEPS' INITIATIVE (1988)
The 'Next Steps' initiative led to the formation of executive agencies (part of a government department that is managerially and budgetarily separate), which allowed civil servants to manage operational functions more effectively and with greater autonomy. This structure supported a more efficient collaboration with ministers by clarifying roles and responsibilities, thus enhancing the focus on achieving ministerial objectives.

THE CITIZEN'S CHARTER (1991)
The Citizen's Charter initiative placed a greater emphasis on service quality and responsiveness to the public, aligning civil service operations more closely with ministerial commitments to public accountability. This alignment helped ensure that civil servants were not only supporting ministers but also jointly accountable for the delivery of public services.

THE CIVIL SERVICE CODE (1996)
The establishment of the Civil Service Code legally codified civil servants' roles and responsibilities, emphasising integrity, honesty, objectivity and impartiality. This legal backbone supports the enduring values highlighted in the earlier history, ensuring that civil servants' conduct continues to meet the highest standards in support of democratic governance.

SETTING THE SCENE

MINISTERS: THE BACKSTORY

The formal history of ministers extends further back than the permanent civil service, but the evolution of the role has been less steady and consistent than for officials. Crucially, also, there has not been a continuous handover and building of institutional knowledge as there has been within the civil service. In a change of government, typically, the outgoing administration does not engage in a detailed handover with the incoming one, and civil servants do not disclose the plans of a previous government to a new one – as part of their commitment to serve the government of the day. In being politically impartial, civil servants may not disclose the advice they have given to ministers. That includes advice given to an incumbent's predecessor.

Many of the major events which have evolved the role of the minister tally with the milestones for civil service changes.

THE GLORIOUS REVOLUTION (1688)
The Glorious Revolution established the constitutional monarchy and Parliament's supremacy over the Crown, which led to the gradual development of a distinct ministerial role within the government. This was the foundation for the relationship between ministers and civil servants, emphasising the importance of accountability to Parliament.

THE NORTHCOTE–TREVELYAN REFORMS (1854)
Although primarily focused on the civil service, the Northcote–Trevelyan reforms also indirectly influenced the development of the ministerial role by professionalising the civil service. Ministers were now supported by competent and permanent civil servants, rather

than personal appointees. From this point, the relationship became rooted, more formally, in meritocracy and professionalism.

THE PARLIAMENT ACTS (1911 AND 1949)
The Parliament Acts removed the House of Lords' power to veto a bill (1911) and reduced its power to delay a bill to one year (1949). The Acts increased the power and responsibility of the House of Commons and, by extension, the ministers within it. This was important for the relationship between ministers and officials, as it increased the civil service's role in ensuring that ministers could meet their expanded legislative responsibilities, reinforcing the need for effective policy advice and administration.

THE FULTON COMMITTEE (1968)
The Fulton Committee's examination of the civil service also led to a re-evaluation of how ministers interact with their civil servants, advocating for better management and specialisation. This pushed for a more specialised civil service, which in turn required ministers to engage more deeply with expert advice and support for effective governance.

THE CIVIL SERVICE DEPARTMENT'S CREATION (1968)
Following the Fulton Report, the Civil Service Department was created, which aimed to manage the civil service more effectively, influencing how civil servants were allocated and managed in support of ministers. This led to more structured support for ministers, with improved allocation and management of civil service resources.

THE THATCHER REFORMS (1980s)
Margaret Thatcher's tenure saw significant changes in the ethos

of the civil service, pushing for a more businesslike, efficient government. The period also saw tensions emerge, as the roles of civil servants and the expectations of ministers evolved. This shifted the civil service towards a culture of efficiency and performance, affecting the dynamic between civil servants and ministers, often leading to stress on traditional roles and responsibilities. The launch and broadcast of political sitcom *Yes Minister* in the 1980s was (and is) responsible for several myths surrounding people's understanding of the civil service. But the show's release coincided with the exact moment the real-life relationship between ministers and civil servants accelerated away from this portrayal, as Thatcher's government tore through formalities of the 1950s and '60s and shifted the primary purpose of civil servants from being policy advisers to policy deliverers. These changes then provided a platform for further changes, particularly with a growing role for special advisers, during Tony Blair's tenure.

THE 'NEXT STEPS' INITIATIVE (1988)
The 'Next Steps' initiative led to the establishment of executive agencies, changing the operational landscape of ministries and the way ministers interacted with the civil service. This created a more focused and agency-specific approach to civil service work, altering the traditional broad-support model and requiring ministers to adapt to a new structure of civil service interaction.

THE INTRODUCTION OF THE MINISTERIAL CODE (1997)
The codification of a Ministerial Code provided clear guidelines on how ministers should conduct themselves in relation to the civil service, reinforcing standards of conduct and the relationship dynamic. The code introduced a standardised approach to interactions

between ministers and civil servants, clarifying expectations and roles.

THE CONSTITUTIONAL REFORM AND GOVERNANCE ACT (2010)
The Constitutional Reform and Governance Act codified many practices relating to civil servants and ministers, formalising aspects of their relationship, particularly around appointments and the role of civil servants. This strengthened the framework governing the interaction between ministers and civil servants, ensuring more transparency and fairness in their working relationship.

The evolution of the relationship between ministers and civil servants has happened slowly and over a long period of time. Mapped against major political events,[4] it's clear how changes have steadily taken place in line with the United Kingdom's own journey:

Evolution of relationship between civil servants and ministers	Major political events
	1801 United Kingdom formed by union of the kingdoms of Great Britain and Ireland.
	1815 Role in defeating Napoleon's French Empire leads to Britain becoming pre-eminent imperial power.
	1830s Electoral reform acts begin steady move towards primacy of House of Commons and universal suffrage.
	1840s British industrial power harnessing technological change boosts free trade and investment worldwide, reaching its peak in the second half of the nineteenth century.
1854 Northcote–Trevelyan reforms.	
1855 Civil Service Commission established.	
1870 Introduction of competitive examinations.	
	1880s Devolved government for Ireland becomes a major political issue, splitting Liberal Party and reviving a violent Irish separatist movement.

SETTING THE SCENE

	1904 Entente Cordiale with France marks Britain's return to European security treaties.
	1906 Liberal government lays foundations for later welfare state with pensions, work and sickness insurance and the expansion of secondary education.
1911 Parliament Act.	
	1914 Outbreak of First World War.
1918 Haldane Report.	**1918** War ends in November with armistice.
1920 Central coordination by the Treasury.	**1921** UK agrees to the foundation of the Irish Free State after the three-year Irish War of Independence. Northern Ireland remains part of the UK.
	1924 First government led by the Labour Party under Ramsay MacDonald.
	1926 General Strike arising from coal dispute.
	1929 World stock market crash. Unemployment begins to rise in UK.
	1931 Economic crisis. Millions are unemployed. National government coalition formed.
	1939 Germany invades Poland. UK declares war on Germany.
	1940 Winston Churchill becomes Prime Minister. Fighter pilots repel German air attacks in the Battle of Britain.
1943 Carltona Principle.	**1944** Allied troops invade France from Britain on D-Day (6 June).
	1945 Germany surrenders (8 May).
	1945 Labour leader Clement Attlee wins landslide election victory.
	1945 The UK becomes a permanent member of the UN Security Council.
	1947 The former colony of India becomes independent.
	1948 The National Health Service is established.
1949 Parliament Act.	**1949** The UK becomes a founder member of NATO.
1954 Crichel Down Rules.	**1956** UK intervenes in Suez Canal Zone but withdraws under pressure from the US.
1968 Fulton Report.	
1968 Creation of the Civil Service Department.	
	1973 The UK joins the European Economic Community (EEC).
	1975 EEC membership is endorsed in a referendum. North Sea oil begins to be pumped ashore.
	1979 Margaret Thatcher becomes Prime Minister and begins to introduce free-market policies.
1980s Thatcher reforms.	**1981** Government begins privatisation of state-run industries, followed by deregulation of financial markets.

	1982 Argentina invades the Falklands Islands in the South Atlantic. The UK dispatches a task force, which retakes them.
	1984 The IRA attempts to assassinate Margaret Thatcher in her hotel in Brighton. Several killed and injured by a bomb blast, but the Prime Minister escapes unhurt.
1985 Armstrong Memorandum.	
1988 'Next Steps' initiative.	
	1990 Margaret Thatcher resigns and John Major becomes Prime Minister.
1991 Citizen's Charter.	**1991** UK takes part in US-led military campaign to liberate Kuwait from Iraqi occupation.
	1992 John Major re-elected as Prime Minister.
1996 Introduction of the Civil Service Code.	**1993** Downing Street declaration on Northern Ireland – a peace proposal issued jointly with the Irish government.
1997 Introduction of the Ministerial Code.	**1997** Labour Party under Tony Blair wins landslide election victory.
	1997 Referendums in Scotland and Wales back the creation of separate assemblies, which are inaugurated in 1999.
	1998 Good Friday Agreement on a political settlement for Northern Ireland is approved by voters in the Republic of Ireland and Northern Ireland.
	2003 UK joins US-led military campaign against Iraq.
	2005 IRA announces formal end to its armed campaign.
	2007 Gordon Brown succeeds Tony Blair as Prime Minister and Labour leader.
	2010 General election: Conservative Party wins most seats but fails to gain an absolute majority. Conservative leader David Cameron heads first post-war coalition with the Liberal Democrats.
	2011 Referendum rejects plan to replace first-past-the-post electoral system for House of Commons with alternative vote proportional system.
	2014 Voters in a referendum in Scotland reject independence.
	2015 Conservative Party confounds polls by winning majority in general election for first time since 1992.
	2016 Voters opt to leave the European Union in a referendum. David Cameron resigns, succeeded as Prime Minister by his Home Secretary, Theresa May.
	2017 Early elections, called by Prime Minister Theresa May, result in a hung parliament and a Conservative minority government.
	2019 Boris Johnson wins convincing majority at snap general election after succeeding Theresa May as Prime Minister in July.
	2020 Britain leaves the European Union.

SETTING THE SCENE

This careful evolution has fostered a cohesive set of values, rooted in commitment to public service and serving the country. Crucially, it has also set layers of precedent on which the particular type of relationship between ministers and civil servants rests. Ministers should know what behaviours to expect from civil servants, have clarity on the chain of accountability and trust that civil servants will work with them on the basis of mutual interdependence.

While civil servants share similarities between them, not all departments are the same; each has their own culture, identity and preferences. After leaving office, Amber Rudd reflected on her periods as Secretary of State in two very different departments: the Department for Energy and Climate Change (DECC) and the Home Office:

> The difference really is a difference in character of two different departments. DECC is a department which is trying to do something noble ... It felt like the people there really believed in what they were doing, a sort of noble cause in terms of decarbonising and keeping people's bills down. All that felt quite interesting, contained, people would come up with interesting ideas. The Home Office – it's homeland security, it's a defensive position. It's a completely different environment really.[5]

When trying to understand why relations between so many ministers and civil servants have soured in recent years, it's important to consider these different cultures. But it is also an important consideration for an incoming minister as it is these embedded cultures which shape and form departmental lines to take (the established biases of a government department).

SPECIAL ADVISERS: THE BACKSTORY

While the nature of the relationship between ministers and civil servants has evolved carefully over the past 170 years, a third actor has emerged in recent decades. Special advisers in the UK trace their formal origins back to the 1960s, although similar roles existed informally before that. Until the 1920s, it was usual to have a small number of personal and political appointees serving in the Prime Minister's office, and there are several examples of informal advisers after that.[6] John Wyndham had joined Harold Macmillan's private secretaries at No. 10 (the Prime Minister's office) in 1957, but the first notable special adviser, in its modern guise, was Marcia Williams, appointed by Harold Wilson in 1964. Williams played a pivotal role for Wilson in both personal and political capacities and set a precedent for the integral role of special advisers in political governance.

The role of the special adviser was then formally recognised during Edward Heath's government in the early 1970s. Special advisers were instituted to provide ministers with advice that was overtly political, distinct from the non-partisan advice given by the permanent civil service. This differentiation was intended to enhance the political responsiveness of ministerial decisions without compromising the neutrality of the civil service.

Throughout the 1970s and 1980s, under successive governments, the number and influence of special advisers grew, reflecting the increasing complexity of government decision-making and communications. At this point, the roles of advisers diversified, ranging from policy specialists to media and communications strategists. It was becoming clearer that there was a separation between the political roles of special advisers and the administrative roles of civil servants. But the resistance to fully formalise the role continued to muddy the governance of advisers.

In 1978, the Committee on Political Activities of Civil Servants, chaired by Sir Arthur Armitage, concluded 'that the guidelines and rules for the political activities of Special Advisers should be laid down by the Prime Minister; and that these should be separate and distinct from the rules applicable to career civil servants.' This evolved in 1986, when the Treasury and the Civil Service Committee established a new position, stating that special advisers 'are civil servants and they are bound by all the conventions of civil servants'.

Margaret Thatcher then provided a written answer on the question of the role of special advisers on 10 April 1984, which stated that 'their terms of appointment are similar to those of other civil servants and they are subject to the same rules of conduct … apart from certain exceptions which reflect the special nature of their role'.[7] In short, there was still a way for special advisers to act as they pleased.

In 1997, after eighteen years in opposition, Labour re-entered government. But Tony Blair's government was cautious of a civil service which had spent so long working with, and delivering for, their opposite numbers, and came to rely much more on the network of advisers they had established in opposition. Trust had been built in adversity and the new government coming in relied upon the advisers who had been there for the long winter in opposition. The role of the special adviser changed dramatically, where their numbers and the scope of their influence expanded significantly. High-profile advisers like Alastair Campbell, who served as Blair's director of communications, were seen as pivotal figures in shaping government policy and public communications. Special advisers

(SpAds) became established as crucial players, greasing the wheels of government and providing a political buffer to allow civil servants to focus on policy and administration.

The Constitutional Reform and Governance Act 2010 was a landmark in formalising the status and functions of special advisers, setting legal boundaries and employment conditions and aiming to stabilise their roles within the governmental framework. In 2016, the Cabinet Office issued a Code of Conduct for Special Advisers, but the formal governance for SpAds still has many holes and there remains no training or preparation for the job.

GOVERNANCE OF THE RELATIONSHIP

The relationship between civil servants and ministers is governed by the Constitutional Reform and Governance Act 2010 and via the Civil Service Code (with the civil service's values of integrity, honesty, objectivity and impartiality) and the Ministerial Code.

The Cabinet Manual, published in October 2011 in the context of the coalition government, is a comprehensive document outlining the internal rules and procedures under which the UK government operates. Authored under the auspices of the Prime Minister and the Cabinet Secretary, its purpose is to be a transparent codification of the conventions that dictate government operations, aiming to make the workings of government more open and accountable. On how civil servants and ministers should work together, it says:

> Civil servants are required to act with honesty, objectivity, impartiality and integrity. Ministers must uphold the political impartiality of the civil service, and not ask civil servants to act in any way which would conflict with the Civil Service Code and

SETTING THE SCENE

the requirements of the Constitutional Reform and Governance Act 2010.⁸

The Act codifies the expectations and principles guiding the interaction between ministers and civil servants, emphasising the need for a professional and unbiased civil service. Civil servants should serve the government of the day while maintaining high standards of propriety. Meanwhile, the Ministerial Code's opening principle is that 'ministers of the Crown are expected to maintain high standards of behaviour and to behave in a way that upholds the highest standards of propriety'.⁹ More specifically:

> 1.2 Ministers should be professional in all their dealings and treat all those with whom they come into contact with consideration and respect. Working relationships, including with civil servants, ministerial and parliamentary colleagues and parliamentary staff should be proper and appropriate. Harassing, bullying or other inappropriate or discriminating behaviour wherever it takes place is not consistent with the Ministerial Code and will not be tolerated.

The Ministerial Code is primarily about minimum expectations for the behaviour of ministers (with what appears to be a fairly low bar) and procedural guidance. It has in-built weaknesses, one of which leads all judgement of compliance with the code to one person:

> 1.7 Where the Prime Minister determines that a breach of the expected standards has occurred, they may ask the Independent Adviser for confidential advice on the appropriate sanction. *The final decision rests with the Prime Minister.* Where the Prime Minister retains his confidence in the Minister, available sanctions

include requiring some form of public apology, remedial action, or removal of ministerial salary for a period.

The expectation is that if a minister breaches the code, they are removed from office, either through resignation or termination. Since the publication of the Ministerial Code in 1997, this process was consistently applied in several high-profile cases, with the most significant in-built weakness not showing itself to be a problem:

- Peter Mandelson (2001): The Northern Ireland Secretary resigned for a second time after accusations – hotly denied – that he used his position to influence a passport application.
- David Blunkett (2005): The Work and Pensions Secretary resigned after being accused of breaking the Ministerial Code by taking a job with DNA Bioscience, which could have led to a conflict of interest, while he was still an MP.
- Liam Fox (2011): The Defence Secretary resigned after it was found that he had given a close friend, Adam Werritty, access to the Ministry of Defence and allowed him to join official trips, despite him not having an official role.
- Damian Green (2017): The Minister of the Cabinet Office was found to have made misleading statements about allegations that pornography was found on his office computer in 2008. He was sacked after an investigation determined that he had breached the Ministerial Code.

But in 2020, following the resignation of Philip Rutnam, as detailed at the beginning of this book, this all changed. Prime Minister Boris Johnson's ethics adviser, Sir Alex Allan, began an inquiry into the behaviour of Priti Patel. After several months, Allan's report said that the Home Secretary's conduct 'amounted to behaviour that can be described as bullying' – noting instances of 'shouting and swearing' and finding that she had breached the Ministerial Code, 'even if unintentionally'. It was that final word which Johnson used to pirouette around the straightforward consequence of Allan's conclusion. The Prime Minister insisted Patel was not a bully, that the code had not been breached and that he had full confidence in her. He then urged colleagues in a WhatsApp message to 'form a square around the Prittster'.[10]

Sir Alex Allan, who had also served Johnson's two predecessors, issued a statement at the same time as the Prime Minister's decision, saying, 'I feel that it is right that I should now resign from my position as the Prime Minister's independent adviser on the code.'

Johnson had taken advantage of the Ministerial Code's flexibility and undermined its standing, demonstrating that rules, alone, are insufficient to establish strong, functioning, trusting relationships.

The civil service is in a difficult position. In 2024, the UK Governance Project, chaired by the Rt Hon. Dominic Grieve, sought to make practical recommendations to improve governance in UK institutions. About the civil service, it wrote:

> The ability of the Civil Service to operate within and uphold standards in governance has been the bedrock of much of the operation of our governance system. We recognise that, in 2024, the Civil Service is under strain as an institution. In private, in conversations with those who have experience as Ministers or senior Civil Servants, it is striking how much consensus there is on the need for a fundamental re-think.[11]

In tacit acknowledgement of the nadir of civil service–ministerial relations, it recommended legal changes to protect civil servants. In this, the Constitutional Reform and Governance Act 2010 would be amended to make explicit that civil servants have a legal obligation to act in compliance with their responsibilities under the Civil Service Code and therefore ministers could not direct them to act in opposition to the code.

Nearly everyone agrees that civil service reform is needed and that amending the rules to provide more protection for civil servants is a good first step. But that is only half the solution. While rules can be an equalising force, providing clarity and consistency (which is particularly important given that civil servants remain in post while ministers come and go), rules can also be a tool used to ensure a particular outcome – which gives considerable power to those making them. And rules can also be changed again in future, making them unpredictable and short-lived. Reform is needed in (and for) the civil service, but a shift in approach and mindset must also occur, to enable civil servants to work better with the government of the day and to allow ministers to get the best out of the civil service.

As such, to create effective reform, civil servants and ministers need to be better equipped with tools to understand each other. Ministers and civil servants should seek to show empathy, commit to building trust and work to find common good for the public. Of course they should, but this isn't enforceable in the white heat of government, and certainly not in the same way a rule change is (or should be). Therefore, the first step to helping civil servants and ministers navigate crises and journey through the ministerial lifecycle together is to acknowledge the human nature of each side.

SETTING THE SCENE

MINISTERS ARE PEOPLE

On the one hand, it seems an obvious statement that ministers are human beings. On the other, that may come as a surprise, particularly if you have witnessed a programmed government minister repeat the same scripted party line ten times during an interview.

A criticism sometimes levelled at Westminster and Whitehall is that they operate in an out-of-touch bubble. There is a story of an ageing member of the House of Lords who was so inspired by a debate on public transport that, immediately afterwards, he decided to take the bus for the first time in his life. Having flagged down the 87 bus, he boarded, loudly declared his home address to the driver and ensconced himself on the nearest seat. These types of anecdotes don't help with the 'out-of-touch' criticism.

There is also a wide public perception that all MPs and ministers are the same: greedy elites from privileged backgrounds. While the proportion of MPs with a university degree has consistently increased over the past forty years, every other form of homogeneity has dramatically decreased. The proportion of MPs from black and ethnic minority backgrounds (roughly 15 per cent nationally) was 10 per cent in 2019 (up from 2 per cent in 2005). In 1979, 36 per cent of MPs had been to Oxford or Cambridge University. The corresponding figure in 2019 was 22 per cent.[12] This doesn't seem dramatic (and is not representative of the population as a whole), but the number of Oxbridge graduates in Parliament has steadily decreased since 1997.

As an eagle-eyed reader, you will have already contested that diversity amongst MPs is not the same as diversity amongst ministers. But MPs (largely) form the pool from which ministers are drawn, and over time, we have consistently seen increased diversity in the House of Commons reflected in increased diversity in governments. In Keir Starmer's first Cabinet (2024), only 8 per cent of ministers had been privately educated, roughly in line with the national population for the first time in history. No doubt, more needs to be done. But some steady progress has been made. In my experience, MPs and ministers are all ambitious, highly driven and keenly aware of the importance of their role as a representative, but each has their own experiences, prejudices and deficiencies. These similarities and differences both unite and separate them.

I have found Westminster and Whitehall to be full of highly dedicated people who have committed their lives to public service and making the country better. Perhaps with the exception of a handful of high-profile cases (you, reader, can decide who that may refer to), MPs make enormous sacrifices to be in Parliament so they can make a positive difference. And nearly every civil servant I have worked with has been extremely committed, hard-working and underpaid. They are real people, also carrying the problems, stresses and traumas that life brings. And just like anyone else, they do not have infinite resilience or energy. The role of a minister is highly extractive to the individual who holds it. Tony Benn once said, 'New ministers come in with very little knowledge and a great deal of energy – and leave with a great deal of knowledge and very little energy.'[13] Having spoken to dozens of former ministers in the process of writing this book, I heard this sentiment echoed repeatedly.

Sir Geoffrey Holland, a former Permanent Secretary at the Departments of Employment and Education, adds to this picture:

> It is a constant source of wonder that any Minister fits it all in. It is easy to give intellectual assent to the fact that time pressures are

endless and constant. At first hand it means that Ministers are, mentally at least, switching from one world to another, from one topic to another, constantly, every day of the week for the whole of their career as Ministers. There is no let up. They are constantly on call, constantly expected to be accessible by the Cabinet Office, the Department, the party, the constituency. It is tiring; it is exhausting; it is a wonder that most Ministers do so well. And woe betide the Sir Humphrey or the Department who do not, at the interface with Ministers, recognise these pressures, allow for them, and allow simple humanity to break through. All Ministers need a break from time to time.[14]

Ministers are perpetually tired; it is an exhausting role with exhausting demands that would be difficult for anyone to keep up with. The job has undoubtedly got more difficult since the days of Sir Geoffrey Holland, as ministers are now under relentless surveillance, scrutiny and attack. For the level of responsibility they are required to bear, ministers are also underpaid. Forget comparisons with the private sector – charities pay considerably more for roles with even vaguely comparable requirements. And despite the confidence and charisma that they often ooze publicly, ministers are as prone to imposter syndrome and self-doubt as anyone else. Former Leader of the Liberal Democrats and Secretary of State for Business, Innovation and Skills Vince Cable, in his book *How to Be a Politician*, neatly encompassed what I had heard from nearly every former minister I have spoken to – that it is a baptism by fire:

> First exposure to a department is a real shock. There is a lot to take in. A new health minister said that coming to terms with the acronyms of the NHS was like learning the first 100 characters

of Mandarin. Yet, within days, there will be meetings with civil servants and 'stakeholders' who have been immersed in the subject for years and questions in Parliament or from the media on the new subject.[15]

Remarkably, ministers receive no formal training before starting in post. In fact, they usually only find out what job they are in hours before starting it (this is an exaggeration – it is often less than an hour). It is a strange quirk amongst (particularly British) politicians that the appearance of learning something formally is equated with a weakness – of not knowing it in the first place. As if it were an admission of incompleteness in one's skillset. It is a ridiculous notion which every individual disagrees with, when asked alone. But I have experienced, first hand, this being a major barrier to supporting ministers (and MPs, for that matter) when they first start; many ministers reflect on the shock of starting their first ministerial role. Mercifully, this attitude is appearing to shift. Parliament has started taking the training of Members of Parliament more seriously, recently employing a dedicated person to organise training for MPs, while we have also seen the beginnings of better support for ministers once they are in post.

The 2024 general election saw more than 130 MPs step down, deciding not to stand for re-election. Many cited the hostility of social media, and its negative impact on their mental health, as being a factor in their decision. Ministers are also not immune from this. Personal security concerns have also become much more frequent in recent years and I have spoken to many MPs and ministers who have been concerned for the safety of their families because of threats of violence from members of the public.

ADVERSARIAL STRUCTURE

To my mind, there is no doubt that social media has been a major factor in hostility more frequently turning into tangible threat for MPs and, by extension, ministers. But we have also seen the application of blunt worldviews and lazy absolutism which has stoked tribalism and polarisation. On nearly every topic, we seem to be presented with two sides: right/wrong, for us/against us, allies/enemies. A combination of Brexit and populism seem to have made that worse since 2016, but it has grown within an environment which has been deliberately constructed to encourage an adversarial approach.

In October 1943, following the destruction of the Commons chamber by incendiary bombs during the Blitz, the House of Commons debated the question of rebuilding the chamber. With Winston Churchill's approval, they agreed to retain its adversarial rectangular pattern instead of changing to a semi-circular or horseshoe design favoured by some other legislative assemblies. Churchill insisted that the shape of the old chamber was responsible for the two-party system, which is the essence of British parliamentary democracy, saying, 'We shape our buildings and afterwards our buildings shape us.'[16] In the House of Commons, the distance between the front benches of the government and the opposition is two swords' lengths, originally to prevent adversaries from crossing the aisle to throw punches or draw swords. These set-ups are supposed to encourage confrontation, an objective of which the weekly Prime Minister's Questions is a roaring success. But oversimplification of everything into *us or them* is not the answer to absolutely everything.

There is a basic human desire to understand things in their simplest form. On many occasions, this manifests as the construction of a line somewhere, in which one side is right and the other is wrong. In reality, there are many things which cannot be measured in this linear way. The challenges of government, generally, cannot.

There is a maturity in realising that most things are not binary. Not everything is only right or only wrong, one thing or another. This framing, the false dilemma or false binary fallacy, limits the options available and is a classic manipulative tool which provokes reaction and then channels people into one of two camps. It has become a standard feature of modern politics, exacerbated in the UK by the oversimplified nature of the Brexit referendum.

Marketing legend tells us that when Coca-Cola and Pepsi vending machines are placed next to each other, sales increase for both. This is because when someone walks past a single machine, the question they ask themselves is: 'Do I want a cold drink?' But when both options stand side by side, it can be reframed to: 'Which cold drink do I want?' When we are presented with two options, our natural inclination is to choose one of them. In fact, we should ask ourselves: 'Who does this benefit?' Something I've learned is that if someone clusters options like this, it's not for my benefit – they are trying to sell me something. In the vending machine example, the reframed question benefits Coca-Cola or Pepsi. In Britain's first-past-the-post (parliamentary) electoral system, there is a single winner in each constituency and voters are often presented with an uninspiring 'it's us or them' narrative. Historically, this has disproportionately benefited the two major political parties which end up then sitting two swords' length from each other in the House of Commons. In the case of Brexit, the absolute nature of the options provided (completely in or completely out of the EU) benefited hardcore positions on the extremities of the debate. This has been a major theme in recent times.

Complexity is everywhere and in everything. That includes the notion of being either in support of or a hindrance to ministers. Or the narrative of the civil service being an enemy – or a blob. 'The blob' might well be the laziest admission that public service is complex, in the modern era. The idea that inconvenient tasks are lost in a sea of bureaucracy is actually an attempt to simplify complexity into two sides, pitched against each other. The mandate of a minister against this thing we can't be bothered to understand, let alone articulate. This adversarial framing also tears at the foundations of the interdependency that civil servants and ministers have with each other. The civil servant isn't trying to undermine the minister. They are trying to understand the mind of the minister. The solutions to the complexities of government are often found in people figuring out ways to work together: finding common goals, listening to one another, understanding another's perspective.

CHANGE ALWAYS COSTS SOMETHING

When I arrived at university for the first time, I was asked, repeatedly, by other students what school I went to. I had gone to a non-fee-paying local school. Everyone in our area knew of it (it was a good school), but there was no real reason that anyone from further afield would have. On one occasion, someone had said they thought they knew it, but it turned out they had confused the name with another school. I remember thinking the question was strange. After several 'I've never heard of it' responses, I realised the question was not to learn about my educational experience but to determine my social status. In the drop-down list of acceptable answers to the question, populated with elite private and grammar schools, my answer was allocated as 'other – not important'.

While this question had, at first, seemed strange to me, it was perfectly normal for the people asking it. It is a question which has been asked for hundreds of years to quickly establish mutual connections and common experience. And it was part of the basis on which relationships between administrators and decision-makers in Westminster and Whitehall had historically been founded. The world of government, particularly at senior levels, feels like a small one, but it used to be smaller. MPs, ministers and civil servants all went to the same schools, were members of the same social clubs, inter-married and holidayed together. Relationships were built and strengthened in smoking rooms and cricket pavilions, rather than in meeting rooms and networking events.

Collectively, we have decided that this exclusive approach is unfair, unrepresentative and overlooked too much talent. Transparency, diversity and meritocracy have sought to replace the opaque, homogenous and often nepotistic ways of the past. This is the progressive path and, in my view, a positive change. But we must acknowledge that all change comes at a cost. For those who benefited, the old ways worked and helped those civil servants and ministers to build strong relationships. There was a consistency and shared experience in their upbringing, education and values. Diversity is not only fairer and more reflective of society; it is a powerful tool in combatting biases and group think. It provides more inputs and inspirations for creative policy solutions and helps policy-makers concentrate on fixing real human problems. But it also dilutes the ready-made social lubricants of common background and familial networks.

It is easy enough for me to say that ministers and civil servants should try to find common goals, listen to one another and understand each other's perspective. Perhaps those things were easier to do when officials and ministers were almost exclusively drawn from a very small pool of social elites with similar worldviews. If we are serious about societal progress, about transparency and meritocracy, then those things need to be acknowledged. One benefit of common understanding and background is that it builds a (shallow) level of trust. If ministers and civil servants are to work better together and improve on the relationships that the 'old ways' fostered, rebuilding and strengthening trust needs to be a priority.

TRUST AND GROWTH

The evolution of the relationship between civil servants and ministers rests heavily on trust. Trust that the other will continue to commit to the rules which protect the relationship. Trust that ministers will not publicly blame civil servants who have no right of response. Trust that civil servants will deliver government policy to the best of their ability, even if they privately disagree with it. Trust that each will tell the truth to the other.

For ministers, to get anything done, they need the civil servants who surround them. Ministers need to lead, they need to be clear, they need to be decisive and they need officials to know (and trust) that they will act within the rules and the law. There is a school of thought that codes and rules (and perhaps law) might need to be broken in order for civil servants to deliver any radical and transformative true will of a minister. The opposite is true. The strength and value of the civil service is in its continuity and institutional knowledge, which lies at the disposal of the minister. This is protected and facilitated by the rules and codes within which civil servants act and function; if these are broken, civil servants are compromised and limited in what they are able to deliver. The more civil servants know their governing code will not be compromised, the better they can be led to develop, implement and enforce the minister's policy idea. This is not to defend status quo or resist change – far from it. The Civil Service Code is about behaviours, not activity. The more confidence there is in the rules being upheld, the more radical and transformational civil servants are free to be. Mark Zuckerberg's famous adage was to 'move fast and break things', not 'move fast and break people'. Empowered civil servants can deliver radical, impactful and workable agendas.

Trust is the most critical element for the minister–civil servant relationship to function well and if either side is serious about working well with the other, they must be deliberate and strategic about building trust. Both ministers and civil servants need to think strategically about how the relationship between them can keep improving, how trust can be increased and what needs adjusting as circumstances change and, in the words of Harold Macmillan, 'events' happen.

Ministers should be clear and transparent with officials, including sharing their own current levels of trust in the department and those around them. This is different from whether they are happy with those civil servants or whether things are going well or badly; it is the degree to which the minister believes in the reliability, ability and commitment of those around them. There is often a degree of reciprocity in trust. If ministers feel their level of trust is low in their officials, they might consider how much that may be reflected the other way and what can be done to get things back on track. The more trust that there is in the relationship, the better the conditions are for ministers and civil servants to work as a team and combine the political mandate and the will of the minister with the expertise and delivery capability of the civil service.

It is much easier to diagnose and prescribe changes from the outside looking in than it is while you are in the thick of daily business; that is the basis for the entire management consultancy industry. This is why it's important to deliberately determine an approach to maximising working together in advance. The approach to building trust in the relationship must be deliberate and strategic.

BUILDING TRUST

Professor Frances Frei and serial entrepreneur Anne Morriss identified three core drivers for trust: authenticity, logic and empathy. For *Harvard Business Review*, they wrote:

> People tend to trust you when they believe they are interacting with the real you (authenticity), when they have faith in your judgment and competence (logic), and when they feel that you care about them (empathy). When trust is lost, it can almost always be traced back to a breakdown in one of these three drivers.[17]

Over my career, I have interacted with thousands of civil servants and ministers, and over the past few years, I have spoken with hundreds about the specific issue of civil servants and ministers working with each other. For this book, I interviewed, in depth and on the record, six prominent former ministers and seven prominent former Permanent Secretaries to gain a much deeper understanding of how ministers and officials can work together. In my research, I have spoken with dozens more. Almost everyone cited competence as a major factor in building trust between ministers and civil servants. A handful mentioned authenticity or empathy.

There are some other important factors which have made trust more difficult to establish. One is the contradiction of the enormous power a minister has within a department to change and redirect activity but their total subordination to the Prime Minister, should it be deemed that they must move to a different role. There is an expected churn in government and it is highly uncommon that a minister retains their post for a full electoral cycle (Vince Cable, who I interviewed for this book, is a rare example). But the turnover of ministers between 2016 and 2024, in particular, was farcical. It did not help that there were five Prime Ministers between the Brexit referendum result in 2016 and the general election of 2024, the most turbulent period for 100 years. But even at junior minister level, it was difficult to keep up with who was doing what. Between 1997 and 2016 (nineteen years), there were thirteen Housing Ministers – which is considered high. Between 2016 and 2024 (eight years), there were also thirteen Housing Ministers. This uncertainty, instability and inconsistency has made it considerably more difficult for civil servants and government departments to get to know the ministers in charge and implement any policy.

Another factor undermining trust has been a politicisation of the relationship, driven by outside interests and polarising narratives. Relentless right-wing media stories asserting that civil servants were trying to thwart Brexit or undermining the will of ministers combined with Boris Johnson's adviser Dominic Cummings's desire to reform and reorganise the civil service. Some media outlets railed against the undemocratic behaviour of unelected bureaucrats and a Whitehall blob which sought to undermine the will of the people.

Creating far more problems was Cummings, an unelected adviser accountable (it appeared) only to the Prime Minister.

In August 2019, Cummings sacked Chancellor Sajid Javid's press secretary, Sonia Khan, for allegedly leaking information – without Javid's knowledge. She later settled out of court with the government for unfair dismissal. Several months later, in February 2020, Javid resigned (on principle) as Chancellor after Cummings demanded his five closest advisers be sacked and replaced with a joint team of aides, managed from No. 10. After the humiliation of the previous summer, Javid said that 'no self-respecting minister would accept those terms'.

Secretary of State for Justice Robert Buckland was also told he must fire one of his aides if he wanted to keep his job. Peter Cardwell, Buckland's special adviser, confirmed that he had been sacked at the behest of No. 10, with Buckland delivering the news that his services would no longer be required without a specific explanation.[18] This wasn't simply a personal vendetta against Sajid Javid; it was a centralisation of power from ministers to No. 10.

Beyond undermining Cabinet ministers, Cummings retained a fabled 'shit list' of senior civil servants (mainly Permanent Secretaries) who he wanted removed in order to enact widescale reforms to how the civil service operated. Many of Cummings's criticisms were warranted. The civil service has not evolved to optimally respond to modern-day challenges, it has gaps in several areas of expertise and its relationships outside central government are not strong enough. But never before had an adviser been afforded so much power and decision-making authority. His role and approach undermined democratic norms, the interdependency between ministers and civil servants and the trust which underpinned the relationship.

Trust is more difficult to establish than it is to weaken. To strengthen the relationship between civil servants and ministers, both sides need to see trust building as a continuous activity. Within Frei and Morriss's triangle of trust, they establish authenticity, logic and empathy as its three main drivers. They say that when trust is broken, it is usually because one of these three areas has gone wrong in some way:

> People don't always realize how the information (or more often, the misinformation) that they're broadcasting may undermine their own trustworthiness. What's worse, stress tends to amplify the problem, causing people to double down on behaviors that make others skeptical …
>
> The good news is that most of us generate a stable pattern of trust signals, which means a small change in behavior can go a long way. In moments when trust is broken, or fails to get any real traction, it's usually the same driver that has gone wobbly on us – authenticity, empathy, or logic.[19]

I think this approach can be useful as we move from establishing that the relationship between ministers and civil servants has reached a bad place to looking at how things can improve. The nature of government makes for a stressful environment and we should take that as a given. There are always steps people can take to make their lives less (or more) stressful, but public service and public policy are littered with challenges, and the added element of politics means there will always be issues and crises to deal with. So we should factor in, as Frei and Morriss say, the fact that problems will be amplified.

For our purposes, I think we can use slightly amended definitions for the three drivers identified:

- Authenticity: I experience the real you and believe you are being truthful with me.
- Logic: I believe you understand what you are talking about and that you have some form of evidence behind your judgement and reasoning.
- Empathy: I believe you care about me and my success, you can understand my point of view and you can vicariously experience my feelings.

There are other areas to acknowledge, but using these three as a lens is a helpful way of establishing where things have gone wrong and how civil servants and ministers can find each other on some middle ground. Sometimes academic theory can feel too far from reality for it to be useful, requiring specific conditions and (frankly) forgetting that human behaviour is not rational or relentlessly consistent with a worldview. But I think these three 'drivers' sufficiently reflect the trust touch points in this important relationship.

Authenticity is perhaps the trickiest of the three to draw broad conclusions from. Every minister is different and so a sweeping comment about any of the drivers is not going to capture every experience. There is also a uniqueness in the situation of government, whereby civil servants need to understand the mind of the minister, what their preferences are and how they might like to do things. Ministers do not need to do the same in reverse. Where authenticity does manifest itself is in the level of openness and honesty between officials and ministers. What is appropriate? What is helpful? What is necessary? Do the answers to these questions change over time and in different contexts? We will explore the answers to these questions in more depth later in this book.

Logic is an area which, on the surface, looks to have the fewest wobbles of the three drivers. Most ministers who have spent any reasonable length of time working with civil servants appreciate the immense depth of knowledge and capability which is at their disposal. There are many criticisms of the civil service which hold water, but the vocal minority (and it is a very small number) of former ministers who think the civil service is useless and plotting against the will of ministers tend to be swimming in a soup of conspiratorial views that are quite difficult to follow through to conclusion; their interest is not in logic. Most former ministers acknowledge that the civil service is competent and logical in its approach. But the logic for civil servants is less complex than that of ministers. Ministers have multiple considerations and the complicated nature of politics to contend with.

Many civil servants are aware of the different hats that ministers wear. On the basis they are an MP (rather than in the House of Lords), they are a party member, an MP, a member of the parliamentary party, head of a department and a member of the Cabinet. They are also an individual with their own views and preferences. Politics considers each of these elements and often in changing orders of priority, which means the logic of decision-making can come with lots of different lenses. It can also change, considerably, depending on the point of progress in an electoral cycle or a parliament and the perceived stage in the lifespan of a ministerial post. This final point is complicated by the fact that the length of a ministerial lifespan is unknown to anyone but the Prime Minister – who themselves usually only know when they make a decision about the fate of the minister in question.

The third driver, empathy, helps people know that you care about them. But the nature of senior civil service and ministerial roles, as they are now, can frustrate empathy in its natural form. Ministers have often spent years posting leaflets, knocking on doors and hopelessly standing for election over and over again in constituencies where they have no hope of winning, just to have the opportunity to be picked for a winnable parliamentary seat. They then have to win that seat and hope their party ends up with the most MPs in Parliament and can form a government. At that point, they then need to foster connections with senior members of the party, the government whips and No. 10 to get noticed and hopefully become a PPS (parliamentary private secretary/unpaid assistant/bag carrier) to a minister. At that point, they've got to hope they've backed a winning horse (that they are allied to senior MPs who are in favour with the Prime Minister and will support them) and that an opportunity opens for a junior ministerial role. Even if all that happens and they manage to become a government minister, it could all be taken away, at any point, by a Prime Minister who decides to move people around. It is easy to see why ministers can become fixated on legacy and relentlessly redirected by the unpredictable winds of politics. It is easy to see why ministers can become self-focused in an unstable career that, any point, could become fleeting.

Meanwhile, civil servants see ministers come and go, and are there to impartially advise and deliver for ministers who might (incorrectly) see them as existing to act on demand. There is not equivalence in the relationship, and so while ministers make decisions driven by politics (and prejudices), civil servants must put their personal preferences to one side and discover the best way in which a minister's idea could be delivered. Evidence is collected and presented as a series of options, which the minister chooses from (or rejects). The need to provide evidence-based policy options can lead civil servants (in some departments) to assume a logical/rational view of a world that is often neither. It becomes easy to see how a distanced and impersonal approach towards a minister might feel simpler.

How does each find the other? Government can be a chaotic and pressurised place. How can ministers and civil servants find the space to really listen to, understand and empathise with each other? Or to care? To some people, this might sound soft. But it's a critical component of trust and it's part of the answer in addressing the relational and constitutional scorched-earth approach of the past few years.

THE MINISTERIAL LIFESPAN

In collating input for this book, I spoke to a large number of existing and former civil servants and ministers, gaining reflections and comment on the relationship between the two groups. But I felt there would be most value in spending more time on a select number of in-depth reflections representing different types of experiences to provide a range of insights, which included on-the-record interviews with six prominent former ministers and seven prominent former Permanent Secretaries (listed in the Appendix). I wanted to explore the major themes that seemed so apparent to me: that the relationship needs to be based on trust and ready for truth and transparency. But I also wanted to find the middle ground, where ministers and civil servants can find each other and understand each other better. Given it is the minister who comes and goes, and the ministerial role to which civil servants are answerable and accountable, it seemed to make sense to work through the stages of a ministerial lifespan.

The three stages of a ministerial lifespan reflect the way any story reveals itself:

- The beginning sees the arrival of a new minister. They are full of energy, optimism and ideas. They (almost certainly) don't know much about the department they have just joined, but they bring the excitement, momentum and drive that change can bring. This is their opportunity to create legacy and make a difference.
- The middle brings the onset of reality and accountability: the sticky mud of government business, the invasion of crisis and the blowing winds of political pressure. The minister knows more about the policy area and ideas are being turned into something that can be delivered. But the challenges of governing are now very apparent.
- The end is dominated by distraction. Crisis or changes in the political landscape can rapidly alter priorities and the business of the department can, all of a sudden, become unimportant. The career trajectory of a minister is always moving up or down – there is no flatline. In the good moments, promotion is around every corner, ready to embrace this rising star, this fearless leader. Opportunity beckons. In the bad moments, demotion hangs like a sword of Damocles. A fearless leader can quickly be seen as a useless idiot.

Ministers are people and people change over time, particularly as they become competent and confident in a role. Civil servants are the ones who must adapt and get to know the changing minister throughout the different stages.

Every person listed in the Appendix was included for a specific reason, each with a different experience in government from anyone else in the group. Most have worked with other interviewees in some capacity and, combined, they demonstrate how each minister is different and how senior civil servants vary their approach to working with different ministers. It also helps us see that the world of government decision-making is a small one, with overlapping experiences and complex relational networks. But that is not how things start for a new minister. At first, life in government is big, overwhelming and unfamiliar. It is there that we begin.

PART TWO

THE BEGINNING

THE MINISTER ARRIVES

I sat down with Vince Cable almost exactly fourteen years after the 2010 coalition was formed, when he became a government minister for the first time. As I pressed the record button for our interview, he drained his cappuccino, inhaled a solitary chocolate chip cookie and began recounting those first days as if they had been only a week earlier:

> I wasn't involved in the coalition negotiations, but within twenty-four hours, we decided we would go for it. I was Nick Clegg's deputy and he'd taken the view that neither he nor I should be involved in a hands-on way, but we would sit back and judge whether it was a good agreement. In retrospect, that was unfortunate, because I hadn't understood some of the things that we'd signed up to or the precise significance of some of the phraseology and the coalition agreement, and I should have.
>
> I was called in to see Nick Clegg on the day of the formation of the government to decide what job I should do, which we should

both have thought about further in advance. I said I should be put forward to be the Chancellor of the Exchequer. I'd been working for a long time on public spending and taxation and on the banking system and [before the election], I'd had a conversation with the Permanent Secretary of the Treasury, Mr [Nick] Macpherson, because it was assumed that I was going to the Treasury. [Macpherson] gave me a caricature Treasury lecture on the complete wastefulness of all government spending and that there was no such thing as government investment.

But Nick [Clegg] said, 'No, we've already allocated that to Osborne. The only thing we can get you is BIS [the Department for Business, Innovation and Skills]' – universities plus all the other things from the business department that I knew very little about.

I could have said to Nick, 'Do you realise that there's going to be a problem that I'm being sent to a department responsible for universities when you've publicly committed us to certain things which are almost certainly not deliverable?' But we never even discussed it.

So I was plunged into a department for which I had no preparation for whatsoever. I was absolutely and completely unprepared. I knew very little about the department and I knew next to nothing about university finance, which is very complicated and was going to be the big nightmare of the department.

In 1979 and 1997, at the previous two significant turnovers of government, roughly 40 per cent of shadow ministers had not secured the corresponding role in Cabinet. In 2010, it was 50 per cent. Until an hour or so beforehand, departments don't know, for sure, which minister is going to arrive, and ministers often don't know, for sure, where they are going. Vince continued:

THE BEGINNING

So I went round to the department and discovered that Mr Cameron had turned up at the front door and was already making a speech there. I joined him to say how wonderful it all was, but I wanted to get in the building because I knew that there were hundreds of very difficult decisions waiting to be made. And I also needed to find out where the loos were.

After that, I went to meet the top civil servants in my private office, six or seven of them with the principal private secretary. I was staggered to discover that there were that many civil servants handling my personal correspondence. It didn't occur to me that government was quite like that, this vast mini army of people around me, plus the Permanent Secretary and then the rest of the department. [The private office staff] were lovely and very welcoming. And they were obviously very tickled to be there, because it's a step on the career ladder as [the department] hadn't been a very high-profile [one]. Suddenly, they were celebrities because they've got a celebrity minister who's come in in a very unique point of history.

But there was an immediate awkwardness in that the Permanent Secretary and the principal private secretary (PPS) were great fans of Peter Mandelson and had a very strong personal loyalty to him. I got a sense fairly early on that they wanted to move on, which meant I didn't have the key people around me who were committed to making a great success of my role. I trusted them in the sense that they would be professional and honest and that they were highly competent and intelligent people. But I didn't feel they were invested in my making a success of the job, in the way that I wanted. They clearly wanted to move on with the change of ethos and government.

Vince had started in a role he had never done before, in a department he knew nothing about (missing out on the one he studied in opposition and thought he would get), only to then discover the key officials there to support him weren't really onside. Already he faced a challenge to part of the empathetic strand of our trust triangle ('I believe you care about me and my success').

On the same day I sat down to speak with Vince Cable, I also interviewed David Gauke, the former Tory MP for South West Hertfordshire. Two MPs from two different parties, both on the winning side of the 2010 election and expectant of a role in government. Both had occupied shadow Treasury roles in opposition (although Gauke in a junior capacity). But while Vince Cable had lost out in the spoils of the coalition negotiations, the victorious new Chancellor of the Exchequer, George Osborne, had included David Gauke in his team:

> There was a huge amount of excitement. I think we expected to win the general election, so it didn't come as a huge shock, but I had this moment of, 'Gosh, it's a coalition, clearly some of the ministerial berths are going to be taken up by Liberal Democrats.' I suddenly had this question of whether I was going to make the cut or not. So it was a great sense of relief to be in, but then suddenly you're doing the walk round the department and meeting the senior private secretary and your new private office.
>
> I was fortunate in the sense of having shadowed the role I got, so I was familiar with the subject matter. I had also given some thought as to what my priorities were going to be, so it was a case of immediately sitting down and being asked lots of very good pertinent questions and coming up with appropriate answers. I felt pretty comfortable with them and they were asking me all the right questions and successfully conveyed that they wanted to

understand our priorities and were here to help. I had good personal chemistry with the senior private secretary, who was very impressive, thoughtful and probing. And a few years later, I've left politics and he's left the civil service, but we're still in regular contact.

They were there to be onside because immediately you're meeting the private office who, unlike some other bits of the department, are on your side. I can remember a conversation with the senior private secretary who was talking about another official, saying he was very heavily involved in the Gordon Brown Treasury [immediately beforehand]. The culture there was one in which junior ministers weren't central to the running of the department. He very tactfully conveyed that quite a lot of the department was not, including this particular official, used to taking junior ministers seriously. But that sort of thing is not in the hands of the junior minister – it comes from the head of the department. In this case, the Chancellor of the Exchequer.

While Vince Cable had been plunged into a world unknown to him, David Gauke had received a relatively smooth introduction to government. His subsequent roles were not quite as serene: 'Starting [as Secretary of State] at the Ministry of Justice was fraught because I was doing an emergency statement, asking an urgent question on the first full day in the job. That was sort of bonkers and quite a good preparation for that department.'

Clearly, the existing culture of the department should not be overlooked. I returned to Vince:

There was actually a positive side [of the Permanent Secretary and PPS wanting to go], because it meant I could get people in who I felt were ideal for me. I particularly wanted a principal private secretary who had a Treasury background and understood how to deal with the Treasury. That was going to be the biggest challenge. From day one, I was angling to get a top-quality Treasury official to come and handle my private office and act in a mediation role, and a few weeks later, I did.

It had been a tough start for Cable, but it laid the groundwork for him to completely drive the BIS machine and in his own image. He was also prescient in prioritising the need for a Treasury insider on his team. I returned to David Gauke to understand his first engagements with Treasury officials:

The Treasury ministers of 2010 came in, collectively, with a sense that public finances were out of control, that we were borrowing too much money, and that debt was going up too quickly. Our position was that we were going to have to constrain those things and make some tough decisions on tax and public spending. Institutionally, I think the Treasury was absolutely with us on that. For example, when we saw the initial shared overview of the state of the economy in 2010 and the challenges that we faced, we were quite aligned [with the Treasury], whereas I suspect if you went to other departments, there was a feeling that lots of the spending was very important.

In that moment, there was a clean alignment between Treasury ministers and officials on what needed to happen regarding government spending. David was on top of his brief, there was a clear plan that the department was fully on board with and he could get going straight away. George Osborne's team announced, almost immediately, that they wanted nearly all government departments to slash an average of 25 per cent from their annual budgets before the next election (plus a two-year pay freeze for all public sector employees) to save £83 billion by 2014–15. Ministers across the board faced an immediate challenge in reducing costs, including Vince Cable:

> I was being told to cut up to 25 per cent of the costs of the budget. [I was asked]: 'What do you want to cut, Minister?' I hadn't a clue! BIS was a very big, complex department, and it needed people at the top of it who really had a grounding in the issues. And I had none. The coalition committed to taking urgent action on the deficit within days of the formation of the government, and that required getting to grips with the financing of BIS, which was an absolute nightmare. The technicalities of the funding of university places, higher education, hundreds of projects which are being supported in one way or another, which I had never heard of.
>
> [Peter Mandelson's] Permanent Secretary [Sir Simon Fraser] and staff had these lists in front of them. They would say to me, 'Well, your government has said it wants to cut 25 per cent of the budget. What do you want to cut?' I finished up by accidentally cutting two industrial projects in Sheffield, which I should have realised were going to have very bad implications for Nick Clegg [then MP for Sheffield Hallam] because he was then hounded for five years by the local government and the local newspaper for withdrawing help from a very popular local company.

BIS had a complicated start as Permanent Secretaries moved around Whitehall. When Sir Peter Ricketts left the FCO, Sir Martin

Donnelly took over as Permanent Under-Secretary. Sir Simon Fraser (Permanent Secretary at BIS) then effectively swapped roles with Donnelly. Sir Philip Rutnam held the fort at BIS in between.

Vince highlighted:

> The first few weeks were like that. I felt I could have been helped a little bit more around the spending cuts and the issues around the different options for dealing with the university crisis, rather than just saying to me, 'There's a problem, you've got to deal with it' – I think we could have had better advice there.

By this point in our interview, Vince had warmed up. In the early stages of our conversation, he had given me the impression that he was a little distracted, although I quickly learned he was listening to every single word I said. But now he was leaning forward on his chair and was captivating as he moved quickly onto bank reform (words I never thought I would write):

> The big issue I was really concerned with was bank reform, and I was determined that the government would act decisively on several fronts, most notably by making the banking system safer. I had a clear idea how it should be done. One of my unhappinesses [sic] with the civil service in the early months was that they didn't see the banks as a problem, whereas we saw them as a terrible problem. And in BIS, the philosophy was 'We're here to represent business. Banks are businesses. We're here to represent them. We're not here to beat them around the head.' Civil servants responsible for banking lived in a different universe to me and I found that very hard. I think eventually they understood what I was trying to do, but there was a culture where they thought they

were there to deal with their stakeholders, which included the banks. And I made it very clear that wasn't my view. [The banks] needed drastic reform and change, and there was enormous resistance to that. The Treasury were opposed to what I was trying to do, but the officials weren't helpful either.

They realised that I had strong views on the subject; they read the newspapers and knew what was going on. But I think they felt conflicted because they'd obviously spent years building up good relationships with the banks; they saw that as part of their job. And here was a minister coming in trying to smash crockery. That was the one case, I think, of all the subjects I dealt with, where they didn't get it, although they did come around in the end and were eventually helpful.

Despite both ascending to government on the same day, victorious and ready to enter the corridors of power, David Gauke and Vince Cable had very different experiences beginning ministerial life. David's smooth entry into the Treasury, engaging with like-minded officials and a clear strategy from day one, contrasted with Vince's plunge into an unknown world that included responsibility for everything from universities and regional economic development to postal services and outer space. Both ended up serving long, stable terms in office but with very different approaches. Vince Cable was Secretary of State for BIS for five uninterrupted years and refashioned the department in his own image. David Gauke spent seven years as a minister in the Treasury, eventually leaving, very much a 'Treasury man', to become Secretary of State for Work and Pensions. A relatively orderly ascension to office followed by a long uninterrupted spell in post is not that common for ministers. More likely is a chaotic change of personnel, as I heard from Caroline

Flint, former Minister of State for Europe: 'When I found out [I was being offered a ministerial role], I was coming back to the UK on a plane from Kuwait having been to Basra [Iraq] a few days earlier.'

Caroline's ministerial tenures stretched back much further in time than the other interviews I was conducting. But her recall was immaculate:

> I was on the plane back with some other MPs, while the reshuffle was going on. I had been doing the armed forces parliamentary scheme and there was a lot of joking about whether I was going to get anything. When we touched down at Heathrow, my husband had been trying to get hold of me and said, 'We've had No. 10 on the phone, where are you?! You've got to get straight to Downing Street.' So I rang up No. 10 and they said, 'Get here as quickly as you can.' I was wearing a great big backpack, chinos and a khaki T-shirt, but I didn't have time to change, so I just dropped the backpack in my office and then walked straight to Downing Street. There was another new minister in front of me who was in a smart suit and the media were shouting at him, asking what he thought he was going to get. Nobody thought I was an MP; I looked like somebody turning up to fix the pipes and they totally ignored me.

Vince and David had won an election and dived immediately into the deep end of government. Caroline had become an MP in the Labour landslide victory of 1997 but had to wait until 2003 before becoming a minister in the Home Office:

> When I came into Parliament, I had no presumption that I should immediately become a minister. I didn't really want to because

I thought I had so much to learn, serving my apprenticeship on the back benches. I was a mum and I felt so humbled to represent the constituency and all the people in Don Valley. Before I joined the Labour Party, I had never even met an MP and never in my life did I think I would become one. So I felt my duty to the constituency was really enormous. I know a number of other MPs didn't have that view. Some thought they should become a minister straight away, and I learned later on, they were having quite a lot of tantrums with the Whips' Office about why they hadn't been promoted quick enough.

I also realised that it wasn't about your merits. It was about whether you had a big beast in your corner, a member of the Cabinet who was going to try to make sure you were in their team next time they moved on, so there was a lot of horse trading. That's not just a Labour Party thing; it happens across the political divide. But when I first started, I was focused on working hard, doing the job, putting in the hours, setting down markers, then trying to learn what worked for me.

Its uncommon for a minister to come into post based on merit or subject matter expertise (although this trend was partially bucked by Keir Starmer in 2024). But Robert Halfon was one of those, having served as Minister for Skills and Apprenticeships, then chair of the Education Select Committee (after being shuffled out of government), before reclaiming the same ministerial role (this time including higher education). I met with him while he was still an MP, in his office in Parliament, and had to weave my way through loud and busy pro-Palestine protests to enter the building. When I finally got there, Robert's office was quiet, adorned with his memories in pictures and photographs and home to two very comfortable armchairs. He offered me a drink, opened a Diet Coke for himself and began recalling his own first day in office:

> It's very hard because, within a millisecond of being appointed, you get a call from an ethics person and then straight after that from the private office. The private office are very welcoming and do everything they can – they ask if you would like a cup of tea etc. But then you get bombarded with paperwork and appointment meetings all day long. And if you don't manage that, it becomes all you do. There is nothing that prepares you for being a minister apart from the few months of being a minister.
>
> I was a much better minister the second time because I knew what happens and I was better able to manage time and understand the way to do it. I only learned that halfway or three quarters of the way through the first time I did the job. The second time, I had a meeting with the head of the private office straight away and I said, 'This is what I want done: I want only a few box items a day. I want them to be very small, but I also want box surgeries.' Where there were complex things, rather than sending me thirty pages to read late at night making big decisions, I wanted a short summary, and then I wanted to sit down with the key people who knew about it – a box surgery. I would have box surgeries two or three times a week for one to one and a half hours, where groups of ten people would come in for fifteen minutes at a time and we would question it out. And then I said [to the head of private office] that I also wanted a directors' meeting where all the directors come in and we check the progress of our key priorities. I knew what I wanted to do the second time. I knew what I wanted to do first time, to be fair, but I'd grown a bit wiser and, I hope, a bit more mature.

It is usual for a minister's first appointment to be overwhelming. It combines a rapid establishment of their own preferred ways of working with understanding a new and alien structure and a portfolio of policy areas which are simultaneously ongoing and require the minister's own stamp and thinking. David Gauke had told me that his first days at the Treasury were his most memorable first days in any ministerial role, because he had to establish his personal preferences and connect with a new world of working. There might be many first days in different ministerial roles, but there is only one first day as a minister. Robert Halfon was unusual in that he had the opportunity many would crave: a second bite of the cherry. He knew the role, he knew the subject matter and he was able to apply the benefit of hindsight.

While ministers are carried in the whirlwind of an election or a reshuffle to their new role, they are welcomed by a calm and experienced team of civil servants, who are ready to establish the minister's preferences and the direction for the department. Dame Sue Owen, as a Permanent Secretary at the Department for Culture, Media and Sport, worked with six, and welcomed five, Secretaries of State. I asked her about what day one would look like when a new Secretary of State arrived. She replied:

> My approach was to meet a new Secretary of State, which I did five times, immediately and be very welcoming. Then try to talk to them about what kind of person they were, find out how they absorbed information, whether they were comfortable with not knowing anything about their brief and being public about that, or if they would need to hide away for a week while we brief them. Then whether they are happy to say, 'I'm thrilled to have this job and I've got a lot to learn,' or would rather come out in a week's

time with a lot of knowledge and ideas. Just occasionally you get a Secretary of State, if it's an election and it's a change of government, who has shadowed the role, then they already know quite a lot about the brief. And then that's much more about the relationship, about how they want to work and managing expectations about how quickly things can get done, and how they want the cadence of the week to go etc.

It is uncommon for a minister to arrive knowing a lot about the subject matter of the role. Occasionally, when there is a change of government, ministers enter roles they have been shadowing and therefore enter with a great deal of subject knowledge. But that can also become an issue, as the minister may have years of statements (made in opposition) on record. Governing is more complicated than life in opposition and some ministers have told me that shadowing a ministerial role can be restrictive when taking it on in government. Critics stand ready to brand you a hypocrite and civil servants (doing due diligence) can research the minister's historical comments and feel like they have gauged priorities before the minister (now in post) establishes them.

Many people, including ministers, have questioned why existing expertise is not utilised better when allocating ministerial roles. Why do politicians with experience as local councillors so rarely become ministers in the local government department? Why do those with professional health backgrounds or representing rural communities so infrequently end up as ministers for health or rural affairs? Caroline Flint's recognition that politics trumps merit is a major factor, but there is also the unpredictable nature of circumstance. In politics, things tend to happen quickly and reality quashes theory.

THE BEGINNING

I had been keen to speak with Dame Clare Moriarty (Permanent Secretary at DEFRA and DExEU) about her experiences working with ministers. We had to reschedule our conversation several times, because of changes in circumstance, and when we did finally speak, we had a total failure of 21st-century technology and had to revert to the ancient practice of a phone call. I asked her about her experience of quickly building subject matter understanding with new ministers when they first arrived. She highlighted:

In terms of building subject knowledge, there's a theoretical version which says every department produces wonderful briefing packs for a new minister and thinks about things which are the highest priority. The civil service is generally very good at these high-performance moments of condensing and presenting content. But the reality is that the first-day briefing never gets read because of the circumstances in which people become ministers. Whether it's after an election or in a reshuffle, it happens fast and there are other things on their mind. You've got twin tracks. The theoretically beautiful way introduces a minister to their portfolio, taking chunks at a time: What needs to be done today? What's the first week? What's the first month? What is the slower time and how do you work through the different areas of the portfolio? That's the theoretical bit. But the reality is that things happen very quickly. As a minister – as, indeed, I remember doing when I became a Permanent Secretary – you learn very fast about the stuff that is on the agenda right now. I remember when I first arrived in DEFRA, in the space of a couple of weeks, we had a milk prices crisis, something to do with neonicotinoids poisoning bees, an air quality issue and badger culling. Ministers have to focus on those things immediately. What you then end up doing is creating islands of subject matter expertise that the minister has built up quickly, then you have to find ways of filling in the gaps or working out which of the gaps are important enough to need filling in.

This hurry and scramble are part of the fabric of the process. Ministers might only receive an hour's notice of their new role, but that is also true for the civil servants who prepare for their arrival. Every minister is different and the Permanent Secretary and private office are adjusting and learning the moment their new boss walks through the door. In times of high ministerial turnover, as was seen between 2016 and 2024, these adjustments become second nature. One Permanent Secretary told me that their day-one briefing had not gathered dust for years. But on occasion, for example during a general election, there may be a little more foresight on who might arrive.

When I met with Simon McDonald (Permanent Under-Secretary at the Foreign and Commonwealth Office 2015–20), he was warm, charming and inviting. I suspected I had received a glimpse of what a new Foreign Secretary might have experienced entering their new headquarters on King Charles Street and meeting Simon for the first time. He had worked with four Foreign Secretaries (Philip Hammond, Boris Johnson, Jeremy Hunt and Dominic Raab) as Permanent Under-Secretary, adjusting to four completely different personalities and ways of working. Simon had also been principal private secretary to Jack Straw, who had been given ten minutes' notice that he would be Foreign Secretary 'with absolutely no preparation for the job'. Simon reinforced the idea, which so many Permanent Secretaries had told me, that the best preparation is to be ready to learn and adjust when the new Secretary of State arrives.

But he also recalled a single occasion when he and his team had prepared for a particular individual ahead of time:

> The only time I was conscious in advance, and we did a (not widely trumpeted) bit of work, were the elections when Jeremy Corbyn was Leader of the Opposition. [Corbyn winning] would have had major impacts on our foreign policy. And so there were two things that I thought an awful lot about during those campaigns. Even though it did not look likely that Corbyn was going to win either of them, he was one of only two people who could be Prime Minister after the election. I thought it was worth doing some work on nuclear and the Chagos Islands because he was very hot on both of these. So we did some small-group thinking about what we thought the Prime Minister needed to know before taking irrevocable decisions about important policies.

Perhaps some ministers can be prepared for. Arguably, however, the most learning and adjusting has to be done by the team of civil servants attached, specifically, to the minister: the private office.

THE ROLE OF PRIVATE OFFICE

Following the surprise discovery of which department they are now running, and being greeted by the Permanent Secretary in charge of it, a new minister also meets their private office staff. The private office consists of a small team dedicated to managing the minister's diary and acting as a communication channel between the minister and the rest of the department; for Secretaries of State, this can vary from five to more than fifteen people. Nearly every minister I have ever spoken to has told me how important their private office is, with many describing the team as their eyes and ears, helping to understand what is happening in the department – as well as what is not. When I asked former special advisers about the importance of the private office, they described it as 'phenomenal' and 'essential'.

The private office learns the preferences of the minister, manages their diary and is a dedicated support team which prioritises the interests of the minister. A minister's first day often includes establishing day-to-day preferences: how they like their tea, go-to lunch options etc. One private secretary told me how he had just got used to buying an egg and cress sandwich for his minister when the news broke that the minister had been caught in a sex scandal and was moved immediately. The incoming minister didn't have a favourite sandwich but hated egg and cress.

Another private secretary told me of a time when a minister moved from International Development to another department but was away on an overseas visit on what should have been her first day in the new role. So, the new private office worked with her previous one to set up her office how she liked things to be, which included acquiring her favourite cup. She liked them from day one.

Crucial to the smooth running of a private office is the principal private secretary (PPS – not to be confused with a parliamentary private secretary, who is an MP that acts as 'eyes and ears' for the minister in Parliament). The PPS is in charge of the Secretary of State's private office and also oversees the junior minister's private offices. Ministers tend to describe their principal private secretaries as talented and ambitious and many end up becoming Permanent Secretaries.

While the PPS is in charge of the private office, it is ministers who have the final say on the appointment of their private secretaries. One private secretary I spoke to was given the job by a minister because he always wore socks with a 007 logo and the minister was a James Bond fan; not all ministers are experienced in good recruitment practice. Private secretaries work to the preferences of the minister and are often asked, when interviewed, whether they would be happy to carry out all manner of tasks, such as buying a pizza or going shopping for a new shirt. One told me they were asked this question with the particularly awkward phrasing, 'Would you be prepared to do anything for the minister?' Fortunately, it was not misinterpreted.

Jonathan Slater (Permanent Secretary at the Department for Education) was not a career civil servant, having joined at a senior level from local government. He had also never been a PPS, and I wanted to ask him about his observations on their importance, as I had known of him as being thoughtful and straight-talking. When he arrived at our interview, I offered him a cup of tea. I also confessed to him one of my professional weaknesses: I do not drink tea myself and have learned to make it only from observation and other people's feedback, rather than from taste. Jonathan smiled. I boiled the kettle and we quickly fell into deep conversation. As we sat down, I realised he was taking the first sips of a tea that I hadn't made. Alongside being thoughtful and straight-talking, I had witnessed his expertise at subtly managing and taking control of a process which held an inherent high risk of a bad outcome. He shared his thoughts on the importance of a good PPS:

> The really simple thing that I learned was to get the right principal private secretary. The principal private secretary is the civil servant who the Secretary of State is going to be seeing more of than anybody else. And it makes an enormous difference to your life as a Permanent Secretary if the principal private secretary is

one [the Secretary of State is] happy with. Equally, if the principal private secretary is great for the Secretary of State but you don't trust them, that's hopeless. It's a difficult job to do, but getting the right person in place in that role was the thing that made the single biggest difference to me.

Other former Permanent Secretaries echoed these sentiments, and particularly that wiser ministers they had worked with created a good atmosphere in their private office and chose their PPS carefully. Vince Cable agreed:

> The private office were the key. I liked them and I think they like me. And they were trying to be helpful. There will be half a dozen friendly faces in the private office and they would do their best to get through these crises. So I think the point I always make to people is that the private office is a lot more important than is normally recognised relative to, say, the Permanent Secretary. The Permanent Secretary is an important figure but the *Yes Minister* story is that the Sir Humphrey figure is not actually as important in practice as the private secretary.

To some degree, it is natural and obvious that the private office would feel so important to a minister. The private office staff are the ones paying attention to specific needs and preferences, and they are the ones whose primary interest is the minister's interest. I asked Caroline Flint about the considerations that a private office would make. She replied:

> My portfolio was divided up between my private office team, and they were the ones who were really trying to get to know me as

a person and what my needs were. That wasn't just my political view and instinct on things but also understanding more about the pressures on me, not just as a minister but as an MP, my work–life balance, my family. There's a difference between an MP who lives in London and one who has to travel back and forth, which was my case. My family were in the constituency as well, so I wasn't going up just for a Friday and coming back. That meant in recess periods, we would have to have arrangements for sending [red] boxes up to Doncaster. I had good relationships with my private office, so I had confidence and trust with them that they were going to have my back. But they are also able to ask questions of policy experts in the department and say, 'Hang on, what would Caroline like?' When they got a submission, they would sometimes send it back and say, 'She won't be happy with this because you're not answering the question.' I would often write on the submission, 'What's the answer?' They all knew I hated anything which didn't answer the question being asked.

This intimate understanding of a minister's needs and preferences is the lifeblood of their success. Without it, a minister is stuck and can become isolated in a machine that is capable of carrying on without them.

I sat down with Lord Andrew Lansley, smartly dressed, on his way to the House of Lords for a bill. He is best known for his NHS reforms as Secretary of State for Health, but in his early career, he was a civil servant, which included time as private secretary to Norman Tebbit. Having worked on both sides of the fence, Lansley was able to offer a unique insight:

What is often neglected is that in addition to the relationship between the Secretary of State and their Permanent Secretary, there is the relationship the Secretary of State (and all ministers) has with and through their private office with the department. It is terrifically important. There are former ministers who lecture and say, 'Well, the first thing I did when they gave me this red box is open it up and turn it upside down to look at the stuff at the bottom, because the officials put the most important things right at the bottom.' When I hear that sort of thing, I think to myself, 'This person has never understood how it works.' If you can't trust your private office, you might as well not be doing the job.

Many private offices are now in a very delicate situation, because they're hanging on to the fact that you can put submissions in a red box. I don't know how they do it now, but I [as private secretary to Norman Tebbit] used to have a treasury tag, and I put an A5 piece of paper on the top with a treasury tag through it on which I would write 'SOS' followed by something the submission doesn't tell them about what the officials really think or what really needs to be said. At the end of that, on basically every submission, I would say, 'Do you agree?' So all [Tebbit] had to do was write yes or no. He didn't have to write anything else. Hopefully, I would have captured what I thought his approach would be, but I've also given him private information about the issue, which may have come from the conversations that I had had with senior officials. Then it goes in the red box, and it comes out of the red box and the note on the top disappears. And it is never a part of the long-term list of things. If the world out there knew this was happening, they'd say, 'Oh, no, we must see it all.' But this is why red boxes survive, because if you put everything onto digital formats, it will survive for ever. And it must not. In order to overcome this problem, ministers have to have a seriously competent and trusted private office. And if they don't, they're stuck.

Vince Cable had had a tricky start with an inherited Permanent Secretary and PPS who he felt were overly loyal to his predecessor Peter Mandelson and who subsequently moved on. Andrew Lansley, once he had taken a Cabinet role in 2010, had a different experience:

> I had a private secretary who had worked for Andy Burnham and then worked for me and stayed with me all the way through. They are still a friend. I remember I said to my principal private secretary after a short while, 'So, how are things different?' And they said, 'Well, of course, Secretary of State, I obviously can't breach any confidences from your predecessors, but what I can tell you is that, firstly, meetings run to time and secondly, there is a lot less swearing.'

BUILDING TRUST

Before meeting him for the first time, my understanding of Sir Philip Rutnam had been formed by his dramatic resignation in 2020, the subsequent media furore around him and his reputation for sticking very well to his lines when he was senior civil servant. He arrived fully suited and I recognised his navy-blue tie, speckled with white dots, from the Sky News video of his resignation. As we sat down, he removed the tie and carefully folded it away. My exaggerative mind wondered whether this was a profoundly symbolic moment, removing a traumatic proverbial millstone from around his neck. In fact, I wasn't wearing a tie and I suspect there was simply an aspect of mirroring, getting comfortable and adjusting to the surroundings. Or he was too hot. Whichever it was, he was immediately engaging, perceptive and astute.

If there is a thesis to this book, it is that trust is the foundation upon which the relationship between civil servants and ministers rests, that those foundations have been damaged and that both sides must consistently and deliberately seek to rebuild trust with the other. Given Rutnam's very public breakdown in relations with Priti Patel, I wanted to get a better idea of what had happened and whether there were changes that could be made to reduce the risk of something similar happening again in the future. In an intense period of examples where trust had broken between civil servants and ministers, Rutnam's resignation had been a significant moment. But Philip had also enjoyed a successful career before that point, working with several other Secretaries of State as a Permanent Secretary at the Department for Transport and the Home Office. He had welcomed many new ministers and Secretaries of State, and I wanted to know, typically, how he would begin building trust. He highlighted:

> Firstly, spend time with him or her and talk. Obviously, you've got to focus on what the agenda for the department is, so preparation is important. Then you need to be ready to talk about the things that he or she is likely to want to achieve and about the things that he or she may need to know, even if they're things that they're not particularly interested in. You've got to make judgements about how much of that to introduce and when. And you need to find ways of pleasing them, or enabling the department to please them, in the early days to avoid frustration. It's like the start of any

new relationship: where you know you're going to need to work together, you want to get it off to a good start.

It's not just about preparing yourself; it's about preparing the department. In the first few days, the people who will spend the most time with the Secretary of State, particularly the first forty-eight hours, are the Permanent Secretary and the principal private secretary. There's a really, really important task of acting as a bridge with the rest of the department, with the [director generals] and with the whole of the senior civil service. You need to *communicate* and act as a bridge, so that the rest of the department is falling into sync and adjusting.

Every former Permanent Secretary (and PPS) that I spoke with agreed that the early stages are about listening, communicating and spending time together. But another theme which came through was demonstrating competence and establishing credibility to build confidence. Clare Moriarty mentioned the importance of getting the small things right, in order to build trust:

> I always used to talk to my teams about what I call the pennies in the jar. You build trust through lots of tiny individual things that give the minister confidence that you understand what it is they're trying to achieve, that you are aligned and that you are working towards it. Whether or not ministers believe that comes down to their accumulated experience with lots and lots of little things. Every time we got a new minister, I used to say, 'Think about it in terms of putting the pennies in the jar. Everything you do potentially is putting your penny in the jar.' But the thing you have to bear in mind is if somebody knocks the thing over, all the pennies come out of the jar and you go back to the start. It's all

about recognising that in every interaction, there's that sense that we [civil servants] are listening and we're understanding what you want. We are going away and doing the thing you want – ideally, at the pace you want it – and you can see that happening. We're being honest about the things that can't be done. But that's not because we've got our own agenda or we don't want to do this for you. All of that needs to be seen by the minister.

There are some basic things [for civil servants] to avoid, like talking about what the previous government or the previous minister did. Or saying, 'This is the way we've always done it' or 'This is the department's policy.' Those are red flags that will make ministers think that you aren't listening to them. Then there are more subtle things like playing back to them the kinds of things that they're talking about and are interested in. But this needs to be authentic. It's got to be genuine, trying to get alongside them, understand what they're trying to achieve, help them to navigate spaces and help them to get decisions out of the system.

It starts with listening very carefully and then trying to make sure that you're trying to maximise the opportunities to demonstrate alignment, competence and delivery. And avoid the occasions when people accidentally say something that brings the whole penny jar crashing over.

Sue Owen helped build on this:

One of the first things the minister has to believe is that you're on their side and that you want to help show them in their best light and help them deliver their policies. That is what the civil service is there to do. So figuring out for each different person you work with what kind of person they are and how you can best serve them is incredibly important. It's as much about, if not more, emotional intelligence as it is IQ, because you can always find people with the IQ to give ministers the facts and analysis. The whole relationship is built, with some narrow exceptions, on them trusting you.

Sue had picked up on a thread I had been interested to pull on. Throughout the process of speaking to different people with civil service and ministerial backgrounds, I had been thinking about the components of the triangle of trust: logic, authenticity and empathy. It seemed to me that there has been an established commitment to logic, as a basis for trust; a desire to be authentic (although substantially undermined, in practice, for various reasons); and patchy understandings of what empathy is. Working with our understanding of empathy in this context ('I believe you care about me and my success, you can understand my point of view and you can vicariously experience my feelings'), I had tried to gauge understandings of empathetic leadership from different former ministers and senior civil servants (including many not named in this book). I found significant variations in understandings of what empathy (and emotional intelligence) was and also its value – particularly when compared with analytical thinking and logic. In a disappointing stereotype (and perhaps predictably), I found that the women, far beyond my named interviewees, I spoke with understood (more consistently) and valued empathy and emotional intelligence in the context of government much higher than the men did.

This was not completely universal, but in trying to find a space between ministers and civil servants, where they can meet each other and understand one another better, this seemed to be an area that would benefit from greater attention. In distinguishing between the civil service (as a whole) and civil servants who work more intimately with ministers, Andrew Lansley helped narrow down the specific space which would provide opportunity for better mutual understanding and empathy:

> Most Secretaries of State assume correctly that other members of their [wider] civil service are operating professionally and working to the objectives of the government of the day. But on a personal level, they wouldn't trust them, because it's not their job to be their friends. It's a bit like journalists and sources; it's not their job to be their friend. It's not their job to try to help them to do things differently. It's their job to do what the Secretary of State says their objective is and to help them to achieve it. Whereas with the Permanent Secretary, they are genuinely trying to help them to create the strategy, along with special advisers.

Andrew Lansley worked with two Permanent Secretaries at the Department of Health. One of them (for the majority of his tenure) was Dame Una O'Brien. I asked her about how she tried to build trust and foster a productive relationship with ministers:

> As Permanent Secretary, you have to be present and proactive in tracking what's going well and what isn't and then ensuring problems get addressed (judging when to get personally involved). In reality, most Permanent Secretaries are incredibly busy with running the department, interacting with other parts of Whitehall and all manner of governance and accountability and so will focus their personal attention on the Secretary of State. Which means when it comes to junior ministers, after the initial 'get to know you' meetings, it's the working relationships between the

Permanent Secretary's private office and the offices of each of the ministers that are very important – it's a sort of intel network, keeping you abreast of what's going on in a dynamic way.

One certain way to foster a good relationship with any minister is to be visible, to be curious about how things are going for them and to pick up and rapidly sort any problems they might be experiencing (for example, with the quality of advice coming from officials or with unblocking getting a decision from elsewhere in government). I found it was important to be open to each minister as an individual and to use available sources to understand the journey they had been on politically. What did they do before they were an MP? What constituency do they represent? What have they already done/said as an MP? What are their motivations? This helped shape my approach to building rapport and trust with ministers.

With this in mind, I asked Jonathan Slater how he built trust with ministers. He replied:

You try to look at things from their point of view, try to put yourself in their shoes. How would it feel being a new minister without any preparation? I imagined that they would be feeling a bit anxious. They've got a load of civil servants who know a lot of stuff and who might not be particularly enthusiastic to pursue some new direction. If you've been working on something which you're proud of and some new minister comes along wanting something different, how happy will they be to jump to it? You have to think about it from their point of view and try to make the process of engagement with the department as easy as possible. Try to make sure that everybody is listening as carefully and being as respectful as possible but also that the people you put in front of them know what they're talking about.

That builds the confidence of the Secretary of State, that if they want a conversation with X or Y person, all the people understand the subject but will not harangue or patronise. You lead from the top, spending a lot of time with the Secretary of State in the first few days, in most of his or her meetings to try to make sure that happens – and then learn yourself!

Credibility is established by having the right people in the room, who know what they are talking about. This credibility enables the logic aspect of our trust triangle but also provides a platform for questioning and challenge, which itself encourages authenticity (experiencing a real truthful engagement with the other person). Robert Halfon confirmed this was also the case at junior ministerial level:

I would like a situation where you had more opportunities for junior people to meet ministers. I found some reluctance for that to happen. Over time, I came to know who the really good ones were, at which point I would ask to have X person in the room because he or she knows this stuff inside out. But as they get to know you, they challenge you and I also challenged them back. I would say, 'I'm going to argue with you about XYZ' and they would come back explaining why the status quo was in place. It's absolutely essential you are challenged, but you have a right to argue back vigorously. They also want to know that you've read the stuff; that's important too. You don't need to read thirty pages, but they want to know that the minister has a grasp of the subject and cares about it. I think where they lose respect is when they see a minister hopping from one department to another and it's obvious he or she doesn't really care. They'll still do what that minister wants, of course, but if you have a grasp of the subject and if you tell them to challenge you, you build a better relationship. It makes such a huge difference.

Creating conditions where challenge is encouraged also enables better transparency and fuller versions of the truth. It is possible to tell the truth without sharing every aspect of the truth and that is unhelpful if a minister is trying to make important decisions quickly. Caroline Flint expanded on this from her own experience:

> I never wanted to hear that things weren't working or that there was bad news, late in the day. I never wanted to be caught out by something that had been bubbling away but no one had told me. And then next thing you know, it's going to be on the front page of one of our major newspapers, but I wasn't even aware of what was going on. I didn't want any surprises. Even if it was a small thing, I didn't need to be in the detail, but I wanted them to keep me posted.

There is an immense risk in creating an environment where those that are aware of dangers and pitfalls feel unable to share them. These are the conditions which brew political catastrophe, at best embarrassing a minister, at worst ending their career. David Gauke was aware of this. When he arrived at the Department for Work and Pensions (DWP), he had inherited the implementation stage of the behemoth policy Universal Credit (UC):

> When it came to the implementation of UC, there was this sense

that [civil servants] wanted to give good news stories, not bad news stories. Initially, I found that frustrating because I wanted to know problems sooner rather than later and I wanted to be able to give a balanced account and balanced assessment of what was good, what was bad and what we needed to fix. And for things which some people thought were bad, establishing whether it was a feature or a bug. I wanted to know which was which. It took a few instances of things going not entirely to plan, then me finding out about it and not hammering them with 'This is unacceptable etc.' but more 'OK, that's fine. You know that's the problem now, so what can we do about it? Is there a solution? Can we fix it?' I think that developed a greater sense of trust that they could be open with me. It's another issue winning the trust of civil servants. Lots of the focus is on how civil servants win the trust of politicians. The minister is important in that. But it's worth also considering the flip side, because I think you get the best out of civil servants when they trust ministers themselves.

I asked David how he built and gained the trust of the civil servants he worked with. We discussed reciprocity and that in showing openness and transparency, a minister might encourage and elicit openness and transparency. With assured humility, which I was learning to be his style, his example was one from one of his own bosses, rather than himself:

I went to goodness knows how many meetings chaired by George Osborne, my ministerial boss for six years. And I was always struck by the way in which George would be quite indiscreet. Not blurting out state secrets, but in a meeting full of civil servants, including some that he didn't necessarily know that well, he'd be quite open about what he was thinking. He might even be quite open about what he thought of some colleagues. There was a strong sense of openness about it. Perhaps it was partly a natural predisposition, but I also think there was a conscious effort of saying, 'I'm putting you in my confidence and you're part of my team.' And I think civil servants responded well to that.

Most civil servants are desperately interested in politics and interested in political gossip. If you are prepared to share a bit of gossip with private office, they can feel on the inside and that you're trusting them. I think reciprocity helps. There are downsides with being too guarded in front of civil servants. I generally wasn't and learned a bit of that from George [Osborne], who I don't think was particularly guarded in front of civil servants. It also means that civil servants know where the minister is coming from. They are asking: what's motivating him? Why is he doing it this way? What's driving a particular course of action? If they understand that, then they're able to advise accordingly.

The central focus of this book is the relationship and trust between civil servants and ministers, but another relationship which has an enormous impact on this is the one between the Secretary of State and their junior ministers. It is that one which needs to be looked at next.

MANAGING THE MINISTERIAL TEAM

I first spoke to Rory Stewart – former Secretary of State for International Development and co-host of *The Rest Is Politics* podcast – when I was making my way through arrivals at Budapest Airport, and he was about to go on stage to lecture in western Canada. We eventually managed to coordinate time zones and spoke again via video call. Naturally, he walked throughout the conversation. Rory's experiences of being a minister, and Secretary of State, have been well documented and I wanted to understand more about where he felt the importance lay in terms of their relationship. I asked him whether it was an imperative for a junior minister to have the Secretary of State onside to implement an idea. He replied:

Yes, 100 per cent. Because any significant change that challenges the way the department does business requires very big levers to be pulled. And you can only get there if you've got the Secretary of State, you've got the money and, ideally, a manifesto and No. 10 as well. It's not sufficient for the Secretary of State to agree with you. The Secretary of State has to be actively pushing it. In the case of [being a minister at] DfID, Priti Patel absolutely agreed with what I was trying to do. There was no sense in which she was blocking my attempts to try to transform language training, improve the quality of programming or improve our inspection regime. She was onside with all of that, but she wasn't able to put her full energy and commitment behind those things. With the Africa strategy [as a minister at the FCO], I presented it to the Foreign Secretary [Boris Johnson] with [Permanent Secretary] Simon McDonald and a lot of the director generals in the room and got Boris to formally sign off on the strategy. But that, again, was not sufficient unless Boris was really driving it. A Secretary of State can only really empower a junior minister to do something radical if they call in the civil servants, almost weekly, and reinforce the message that they're to do what the junior minister says. It's not sufficient for them to say, 'I've delegated to you. I trust you,' and to say occasionally to civil servants, 'Listen to Rory.

Do what he says.' That's not enough. It would be enough in the military, for example. There you can delegate to people and say, 'This person is in command, you have to follow their orders.' But this doesn't work in the civil service.

In his book *Politics On the Edge*, Rory had provided an example from when he was Prisons Minister at the Ministry of Justice, with David Gauke as the Secretary of State. In this, Rory had proposed changes to improve standards in ten prisons, with Gauke ensuring civil service support by scheduling regular updates and monitoring. In our interview, I had suggested there might be a spectrum between Gauke (with consistent monitoring and regular engagement) and Boris Johnson (agreeing but then retreating). 'Yes, exactly,' Rory replied. 'Gauke didn't just say, "I believe in this," but actually demonstrated that again and again, requesting updates every week on exactly what civil servants were doing to implement my plan.'

I had not encountered this feeling towards civil servants from every former minister I had spoken to, but this was clearly the approach (from a Secretary of State) that enabled Rory Stewart to perform most impactfully in a ministerial role. It seemed I should return to David Gauke to understand some more of his own experience, particularly from his earlier career working in the Treasury. He said:

> Over time, George [Osborne], I think, successfully sent signals that some of his junior ministers were key parts of the team and not just there to deal with the press and Parliament but for policy formation. It was helpful as a rookie minister to have an understanding that that's not automatic. One bit of advice I would give to any junior minister going in is that if you want the department

to take you seriously, they've got to believe that your Secretary of State or Chancellor of the Exchequer is taking you seriously. There is a degree of core politics in that. Unless you can do that, there is a risk that you will get the less senior officials come to you, and your office and influence over policy will become downplayed. You can end up in either a virtuous or a vicious circle. I've seen ministers do both.

Winning over the confidence of civil servants is important. People talk a lot about civil servants getting the confidence of ministers, which is also very important. But particularly for a junior minister, you sometimes have to fight hard to be taken seriously, and that, to a large extent, does depend upon the Secretary of State or Chancellor of the Exchequer.

A Secretary of State has the complex task of implementing a government agenda using a department which is being run by somebody else (the Permanent Secretary). They have a team of ministerial colleagues to help them deliver this agenda, but those people also need managing and leading. Politics doesn't allow for fixed or minimum time periods to implement an idea, and a Secretary of State may not even have much control of the composition of their team. It's worth noting, again, that there are some fundamental differences between the role of the Secretary of State and a CEO. But many of the elements which executive leadership programmes focus on still form the core structure of capabilities Secretaries of State need to manage their ministerial team: strategic vision and decision-making, building high performance within a top management team, persuasive communication and negotiation and leading change in an organisation.

Secretaries of State also need to develop trust with their own ministerial team. It is a problem within that team if they cannot, but it also causes problems in the relationship with civil servants. The example set at the top is reflected elsewhere in the organisation. Philip Rycroft's final role in the civil service was as Permanent Secretary of the Department for Exiting the EU, but he had worked with more than ten Secretaries of State (and other top ministers) before that. He noted the impact of mistrust amongst ministers:

> The hardest interaction [I had] was when we were in a context where the government machine was hobbled by this great ideological divide amongst ministers: around Brexit. Trust was at a premium because there was a loss of trust across the piece. I think I got on all right with David Davis, but Dominic Raab and Steve Barclay both came in after a crisis [following resignations], so there was a sense of instability in the government and very little trust between ministers. That was then reflected in the relationship with civil servants. That sense that we're all pulling in the same direction just wasn't there, so we had to work a lot harder to, metaphorically, just be in the same room.

My observation is that junior ministers perform much better when they are being led well by their Secretary of State. Nearly every junior minister can vividly recount the best and worst experiences they had working in ministerial teams. Each example, nearly without fail, related to how well they were led and managed by their Secretary of State. I asked Robert Halfon about his experiences as a junior minister. He replied:

> I've worked with several Secretaries of State. Gillian [Keegan] was amazing. I work well when I'm motivated by people, and she

was an incredible boss and very decent; she involved ministers hugely. I was asked to attend a lot of Secretary of State meetings and she would genuinely want your opinion and would delegate, including some key decisions, because she was passionate about apprenticeships and skills. That was tough but also so helpful to me, because she knew what she was talking about on this area [apprenticeships and skills]. She would, rightly, challenge me, but she also trusted me and delegated a lot to me. That made a huge difference because I felt a sense of empowerment and that the boss valued me. That then shows and tells the civil servants that it's really important, too.

Sometimes there were such big decisions that had been delegated to me that I referred them back upwards because I wanted a second opinion, perhaps from the SpAd. I had more interaction with the special advisers the second time [2022–24] than the first time [2016–17]. I would see them all the time, which was a lovely thing because although their primary duty is to the Secretary of State, I felt we were part of a team and I could call on their advice. They were very good and they worked well with the civil servants and I felt like they knew their stuff and I could refer things to them. Gillian made a huge difference and, as a result, I'll always be utterly loyal to her. My view is if people are good to me, I'll always be good to them. I was very sad to tell her I was going, a few days before I left.

Most people perform better when they feel valued and supported. A cohesive, well-performing top team also tends to instil more confidence in the rest of an organisation. Much of good leadership is not grand gestures but the small things that are personal and impactful to team members. Caroline Flint told me:

David [Blunkett] was the best Secretary of State I ever worked with. The whole ministerial team would say that we had meaningful team meetings. And there would be little things he did which made a difference. You would be on the *Today* programme and have had some grilling on something or other, then very soon after you finished, you would get a phone call from David, saying, 'You did well. Don't worry about the tricky bits, it's fine.'

Those sorts of things just meant so much. It gave me confidence to be able to speak to him if I was worried about something.

I heard many examples of Secretaries of State who were distant and did not engage their junior ministers, which in turn made those junior ministers feel disconnected from the priorities and mission of the Secretary of State. Across my conversations with more than twenty former ministers, my observation was that of every Secretary of State mentioned, for being either 'excellent' or 'terrible' to work with, it was the 'excellent' ones who had notable policy achievements to speak of. The 'terrible' ones did not. There may be a correlation.

THE ART OF RELATIONSHIP BUILDING

Once the new minister has arrived, met the Permanent Secretary and their private office and established their ministerial team, civil servants within the department need to start building a relationship with the person who now occupies the role. From the outside, ministers are often perceived (largely because of the media) somewhere between a broken robot parroting a government line and an incompetent moron flailing around in a moral vacuum. In fact, ministers are real people with the same basic needs as everyone else. The first step for civil servants in building a relationship with this person is to get to know them. Philip Rutnam and Clare Moriarty told me about how they approached those first stages of relationship building with a new minister. Philip began:

As a Permanent Secretary, you want to get to understand as quickly as possible where the individual is coming from, what is most important to them, what they want to achieve and [what they want for] the organisation of business, of the department/sector. And then why that matters to them and what they're like as a person. You want to get onto the same wavelength and start creating some kind of human bond.

One important distinction, which tends to get underestimated in the outside world, is between the Secretary of State and the rest of the ministerial team. In a department of state, the Secretary of State is the key figure, politically. It's he or she who is, legally, the embodiment of the department. It's he or she who sits in Cabinet as a full member. It is he or she who, in truth, matters most by far in a department. In the outside world, it can look like the other ministers are almost on a par. They're not. They have, at best, quite confined roles. So you want to understand the whole ministerial team, but if you're a Permanent Secretary, it's the relationship with the Secretary of State that matters most – by far. And it's the Secretary of State who should, and usually will, set the tone for the department: both the substance of the business and the tone of the organisation – demeanour, conduct, behaviour etc.

Spending some informal time together is helpful. Most ministers, in my experience, want to approach the job of working with the civil service quite formally. Almost all ministers see it as a very significant public duty which needs to be exercised properly. And that leads to, necessarily, a degree of formality and distance, which I think is right on the whole. But you're going to need to work with this individual closely, so if you can find a way of spending some informal time with them – I would generally try to have lunch or dinner with ministers that I work with, not just the Secretary of State, but other ministers too. There might be a trip coming up, perhaps to a factory in Britain or an international trip in the first few months. If you can do something like that, inevitably, it helps. I think with just about every Secretary of State I worked with, although some of them weren't around that long, we found some opportunity to have a bit of informal time, perhaps talking about family and finding points of connection. A senior minister's job is really tough. In some cases, I even ended up talking to ministers about individuals, about personal resilience and how to support them in some way through a tough time.

Clare Moriarty built upon this:

Everything comes back down to listening carefully and spending time with them. Particularly for the key roles of the Permanent Secretary and principal private secretary – and I did both of those roles – the thing you have, which is really valuable to you and to the whole of the department, is the opportunity to spend the time to listen and to be there to pick up on whatever it is that's going on. You pick things up quite quickly. Ministers will often come in and say, 'What you need to know about me is XYZ. I do like slide packs or I don't like slide packs. I like meetings. I absorb information in this way.' Sometimes what they tell you will turn out to be exactly what you find in practice. And sometimes what they tell you turns out to be slightly different. But if they tell you, then you've got a starting point to measure against.

And you certainly see quite quickly what irritates people. You are then trying to steer the ship towards doing more of the things that are helpful and less of the things that are unhelpful. In the early days when a minister arrives, departments will have daily meetings of the senior team to share the intelligence about what we are learning about this minister and their preferences and how we adapt to that, which is an informal intelligence-sharing process. Then, quite often, there will be a more formal process where the private office will send a note around to everybody saying: these are dos and don'ts for this particular minister. Over time, as people have more interactions with them, it gets refined because some of the things turn out to be more nuanced and other things need to be reinforced because people didn't quite believe them the first time, but they really are true.

The Permanent Secretary and PPS are able to spend a great deal of time with a minister, in order to get to know them better, but there are other civil servants who need to get to know a minister, too. Simon McDonald had told me about one of his early roles as a speechwriter:

The first Foreign Secretary I got to know really well was Douglas Hurd, because I was his speechwriter for two and a half years. The thing I worked out very early on was that he didn't really need a speechwriter because that was one of his talents and indeed one of his earlier jobs. He had been speechwriter to Edward Heath in the 1970s, so he knew the trade very well. What he needed was somebody to draw together, in gobbet form, the arguments and facts under the speech title, whether he was talking in Parliament or in the United Nations, to a foreign audience or to a British audience. And over two and a half years, I worked out how he ticked and I did that job for him longer than anyone else. One of the keys was spending as much time in his company as possible. It was the way the Foreign Office worked that there was generally a space in the Foreign Secretary's office, during a big meeting, for a relatively junior person to sit in if the topic was relevant. If there was a UN speech coming up and my subject might feature, I would ask if I could sit in, and they let me. So I was in a lot of meetings with Douglas Hurd, and then I went to as many of his speeches as possible. I saw how he both used and ignored my material.

Simon and Clare had highlighted, for me, that spending time with a minister helps you to understand not only their likes and dislikes but also indicators of how they work, their self-awareness and their strengths. I asked Jonathan Slater about what he found to be the most distinct differences between ministers. He replied:

Each person is different, but as you would expect, someone who's already been a Cabinet minister will be more confident than someone who's doing it for the first time and will give quicker direction. Someone who's newly in the role will be lacking confidence, so your task is to build their confidence. They are in charge. The department looks to the Secretary of State to set direction, and they've got to do it. So your job as a Permanent Secretary is to encourage the Secretary of State to say what they think. Sometimes you might have somebody who's very confident or has been preparing, for example in 2010, there were shadow Cabinet ministers like Liam Fox and Andrew Lansley who had been shadowing for some time, and they were pretty confident they knew what to do.

A big difference is whether somebody is confident or unconfident. If they're confident, then the job of the Permanent Secretary is to hold back a bit because they might be wrong. Whereas if they are lacking confidence, it's the opposite: you need to push them up a bit. They're in charge now. If you've got an incoming Secretary of State who's confident they know what needs to be done, that is a risky time, because they might be wrong, in the sense that they might not have thought through the consequences of what it is they want to do. And you haven't had the time to build the relationship yet. Telling them that's a stupid idea is not the best way to start building the trust. So that's when there is the most significant risk.

Justine Greening was someone who had already been a Cabinet minister and was confident [when she became Secretary of State for Education]. She was, and remains, all about social mobility and had thought quite a lot about the role, which is untypical in advance. Working for a confident Secretary of State with an agenda was a good opportunity for the department and what we needed to do was to demonstrate that we got it, and then put our best people to work with her on how to make that a reality.

I had put together a good team of people to help her achieve that objective and I let them get on with it. But I realised, after a while, that Justine wanted her top person in the team [to be there]. It didn't really matter whether my personal engagement in the meetings would make any difference, but it sent a message that 'if it's the most important thing for me [Justine], it's the most important thing for him [Jonathan]'. I was a pretty new Permanent Secretary when I was working for her and had only been in for three months when she arrived. I believed in the importance of distributed leadership and empowering my people, but I suddenly realised, 'Blimey, she wants to know that I'm involved.' So I did. That was a tricky balancing act, because it's important to empower your people to get on with stuff but I had to do that in a way that demonstrated to the Secretary of State that I was on it as well.

Sue Owen had a reputation for developing strong relationships with ministers at the Department for Culture, Media and Sport (DCMS). She highlighted to me some of the different preferences that ministers came in with and how the department makes adjustments:

Each of the Secretaries of State I worked with were very different. One point is whether they know anything or not, but then there are issues like how they absorb information. Some like to have a lot of written material, but others prefer to get their information through in small chunks. Sajid Javid, when he came in, immediately said, 'No meeting should be more than half an hour. I'll have the half-hour meeting, I'll go away and think about it and then if I need another meeting, I'll have another meeting.' So that was very clear. John [Whittingdale] already knew the stuff, but he wanted a lot of meetings.

Matt Hancock was promoted to be Secretary of State from a junior job in DCMS, but he had been moaning quite a bit about the length of briefings. We still had the [first day] chat, even though I already knew him, about how we could help him do this much bigger role. And he said he couldn't cope with the briefings because, and he'd never told anyone this, he was dyslexic and he couldn't really cope with more than one or one and a half pages of written material. He could cope with a lot of charts and diagrams but not the lengthy written documents. So I persuaded him that, now he was in the Cabinet, perhaps he should come out about it and tell people. He agreed to, and it was completely transformational because everybody then got it. And the dyslexic staff adored him. From then on, nobody wrote a brief more than one and a half sides. Now the whole public knows Matt, but at the time, it was quite a big and brave thing for him to do. It really made a huge difference.

In DCMS, there were a lot of events to go to in the evenings. So an early question was: how much were they prepared to do? One Secretary of State came in saying, 'I'm a morning person,' so we could see straight away they weren't going to be at many evening events. You then even get down into details like what do they like for lunch? How they like their coffee or tea etc. But it's about understanding them as a person. If you look at a Secretary of State and think of them as a person, it's a completely nightmare job because you've got to know the brief and you've got to know what you want to do. You've got to know what the party wants to do and you've got to manage junior ministers. You've got to work as a team – which very few of them have ever done before – and you've got to be in Cabinet. The party politics, your constituency, your family and the nightmare of social media. It's all there. It's a very stressful role and I used to see my role as helping them navigate all of that.

I always said to my ministers, in the very first meeting, 'Occasionally, things will go wrong. People are humans and everybody is there to help, but sometimes things go wrong. It's very rarely deliberate, more likely some cock-up or someone's stressed or it's an outside factor. But if something has gone wrong, we [the civil servants] will tell you immediately. And the deal is that we will tell you immediately but you will not shout at anyone. If you want to shout at anyone, you can shout at me [Sue], but you will not shout at staff because we have a no-blame culture in my department.'

And they always got it. So when something went wrong, usually the minister would say, 'Oh, that poor person, they must be mortified. How are we going to handle it?' I found that approach worked well because it gave people the confidence to take risks and think more broadly.

That civil servants are risk-averse and narrow thinkers is a famous criticism amongst politicians. It struck me that Sue's description would be exactly the environment many ministers would like to foster amongst the civil service, and one way to encourage broader thinking and a slightly higher risk appetite might be to establish clarity and openness (both of which are authenticity traits) early on. Building a genuine relationship and getting to know another person is built on the notion of authenticity. If a minister is not able to be authentic, then it is difficult for civil servants to know them and their priorities and therefore to be able to care about their success.

Authenticity and empathy (caring about their success) form two sides of the trust triangle, but the third (logic) rests on having faith in the other person's competence and judgement. I asked Sue about how she would demonstrate the competence of her teams early on. She told me that connecting and demonstrating competence in those early stages had a lot to do with adjusting to the minister themselves:

One way you built trust with them was by knowing what you

were talking about and answering their questions, and if you didn't know the answer, you would go away and find out. It never seemed to me to be a problem in those encounters that I had [as a civil servant] in the Treasury in the 1990s. It got more difficult when Labour came in. Gordon Brown proved to be such a difficult person to work with and the Treasury had to rapidly re-establish a way of working that would work. With him as the Chancellor, the expected behaviour was that engagement with junior ministers became more normalised. But what I learned from that was that the nature of the person who is the Secretary of State is incredibly important. And you cannot change them. Anybody who tries to go with a model of how they think a minister ought to be, not how that person actually is, is doomed to fail.

There was an occasion where I learned a great deal from observing a case where it went disastrously wrong. When I was in DfID in 2008 and Gordon Brown had become Prime Minister, Hilary Benn moved from being Secretary of State and Douglas Alexander came in. The Permanent Secretary at the time treated Douglas as though he was Hilary. But he was a completely different kind of person, and he absorbed information in a different kind of way. Douglas was a solicitor and he hated not knowing facts. Whereas Hilary was a more humble kind of character, who was a blank canvas willing to learn and would say, 'I don't know anything.' The mistake there was to expect everything to carry on the same, just with a different person at the top. But the relationship between the Permanent Secretary and Douglas broke down on about day three. And it was really very serious. It was a dreadful period, but I learned a lot from that about how you need to start again with a new Secretary of State and really find out what kind of person they are and what they are like. In return for doing that, you can then ask them to behave in a decent way towards civil servants.

Ministers are individuals with their own styles, preferences and goals. It is civil servants who must make the first adjustment as a new ministerial lifespan begins but also as the minister changes over time. These first days of building a positive and constructive relationship are led by the Permanent Secretary and, like all relationships, will be slightly different every time.

Una O'Brien was different to a lot of Permanent Secretaries in that she was, by and large, a policy subject specialist. Having worked in the NHS and then in several senior roles within the Department of Health, she then became its first ever female Permanent Secretary during Andrew Lansley's tenure as Secretary of State. After Lansley's departure, Una welcomed Jeremy Hunt as the new Secretary of State and highlighted some of the conditions that help with building a relationship with a new minister:

Jeremy Hunt came to the department with strong backing and trust from the PM and the Chancellor of the Exchequer, something that was perceptibly draining away from his predecessor [Andrew Lansley]. This immediately strengthened the department's standing within the government and enabled us to get things done. It was really a case of listening closely to what the new Secretary of State – Jeremy Hunt – wanted to do and pivoting rapidly to his priorities. In many respects, Jeremy was an easy person with whom to build trust because he was very clear about his expectations, priorities and how he wanted to use his time – surprisingly, something ministers can be quite poor at!

I never felt that his not having a health policy background

was an impediment. In my experience, MPs are very clued up about the NHS within their constituency and the surrounding area and health is a top subject of constituent concerns. So they do bring a lot of knowledge. At the level of the national system, of course it does take time and effort to grasp the complexities. Jeremy was very good at asking pertinent questions, disciplined and hard-working, and he developed his understanding at quite a pace.

Lots of people will resonate with the experience of starting a new job and feeling like an imposter. That feeling is usually not because they are the wrong person for the job but because they don't immediately know what they are doing. It is in those early days that building good relationships with surrounding colleagues helps with settling in, navigating new systems and understanding the workplace culture. Eventually, those feelings of insecurity are replaced with growing confidence and competence as the new employee stops being new and starts getting to grips with their role.

MINISTER GETTING TO GRIPS

After a few months, a new minister settles into the rhythm of government office and becomes more confident in providing direction and making decisions. It is often at this point that they begin to establish the bigger things they want to achieve in the role and master the smaller things which make them more effective. Having served as a minister in several departments, Caroline Flint was the ideal person to ask about when she felt she had moved out of the 'beginning' stage of each role:

It takes at least six months in a department to find your own voice and to suss out which civil servants are the most reliable to talk to. But also to discover the voices outside the department that are really useful as another sounding board. When I was a minister, there were these delivery boards, led by civil servants. My office would say, 'Oh, the board of officials are meeting, it would be really great if you could just pop in and say, "Hi."' It cost me nothing, really, but that sort of thing is important. It shows the minister is interested and it means a lot [to civil servants]. It would mean a lot to me if I was in that circumstance working for someone.

Part of getting established also involves identifying any loose ends from the previous minister. Many experienced ministers say that speaking to one's predecessor about any outstanding business is a major lesson they learned (sometimes the hard way). Civil servants will not share the content of previous privileged conversations with a new minister and Caroline told me she had been caught out by this:

> In one role, I had a situation where a particular scrutiny committee in Parliament met on a regular cycle, and the ministerial job I was doing had regular reporting back into them. I had just come in and inherited the diary and there was another meeting coming up of this committee. When I got the information for it, there was this long list of things that were meant to be followed through since the previous meeting and that hadn't been done. And it was me who was going to have to answer to the committee. In that instance, there wasn't enough leadership from the management

to impress on their team that despite it being a pain, this committee was really important. If the previous minister has made commitments to progress on particular areas, you can't send the new minister in with nothing done. Me having to go to this committee and report to these backbench MPs simply wasn't seen as enough of a priority.

If that's the culture set by the management, it gets fed down throughout the chain and no one else prioritises it. So I was suddenly a week away from the meeting and nothing had been done. In that particular case, the parliamentary unit within the department had been asking for the list to be looked at but the policy civil servants didn't prioritise any of it. I ended up getting in touch with the chair of the committee and had a private conversation apologising for the situation, then committed to rectifying it and to get answers to them, even if a bit late. I got a bit of a rollicking and a slapped wrist at the committee, then I had to have some serious conversations with the interested civil service parties to say, 'I don't want this happening again.'

Robert Halfon experienced the luxury of being able to use the benefit of hindsight, when he returned to the Department for Education. I asked him what he applied the second time around which helped him to get into a rhythm quicker. He said:

> I had to be ruthless about appointments and meetings; otherwise you can just end up doing those all day. I carefully went through the schedule, determining who I should see, who I shouldn't and which stakeholders to engage with. If you don't do that, you get submerged in meetings all day long with officials who want to brief you on anything and everything. We had a [civil service]

director's meeting which was 25 carat gold and they were about thirty to sixty minutes.

The first time [as a minister], I allowed myself to have what they called 'teach-ins', which take up all of your time and then, in essence, you've done nothing all day. It's important to tell the private office early on, 'This is how I like it. This is how I like the folder done' etc. Civil servants have a tendency to produce forests and forests of paper, although I was lucky I had a tablet, so I had very little paper given to me. But I said that I wanted just a few pages at a time, even preparing for [Department for] Education questions or a select committee, which is an enormous amount of preparatory work for a minister – it's like preparing for a court case. I remember I was once given a folder of about 150 pages and I said, 'This is crazy, I'm going to be overloaded with information. I don't want more than twenty or thirty pages.' And I was really good in committee because the [civil servants] then did the most incredible briefing for me. But there is a tendency for them to give you everything there is to know, the *Encyclopædia Britannica* of information, about whatever you're appearing on. When what you really need to do is work out what they're going to ask you and have roughly a page on each question. You know there's going to be fifteen questions from committee, so you have thirty pages max.

I had been [Education] Select Committee chair for five years [between the two ministerial posts], which gave me an incredible grounding in understanding the department and how civil servants work, as we questioned them a lot in committee. But it also gave me good grounding in the issues and that helped me to go in there with an agenda. I had the ladder of opportunity, which we worked on with officials early on. Each ladder had rungs, and there was a policy behind every rung and pillar. Setting priorities made a huge difference – everything then works much better. If you go in there and you don't have priorities, then the system sucks you in.

I found the officials I worked with, especially the second time [2022–24], to be outstanding. Most of them, and especially the directors, were there on a mission. This rubbish about 'the blob' is complete nonsense. If a minister goes into a department with clear priorities, the civil servants will do it. There's always going to be someone who is not as good as they might be, but then you just have to identify the really good people and say those are the people you want in the room. I ended up with really good people who knew the answer to everything and were excellent in the room. The people who go on about 'the blob' are the people who are justifying their own failures – a bad workman blaming their tools.

The idea of setting priorities is one that I had heard many times from various former ministers and Permanent Secretaries, far beyond the named interviewees in this book. Andrew Lansley had said Norman Fowler taught him that a Secretary of State should only have one big thing as a priority, if they wanted to achieve anything. But whether it is one or a couple of priorities, the most successful ministers, and the ministers of whom civil servants spoke most highly to me, all take this approach. Jonathan Slater overlapped with Robert Halfon at the Department for Education, and he echoed this:

The Secretary of State having clear priorities is the crucial thing. I didn't work for Michael Gove, but when I've asked people what it was like working for him, people comment on his special adviser

Dominic Cummings and also that he only had two priorities. One was to academise schools and one was to reduce the length of time it took for people to get adopted. No doubt it was more complicated than that, but that's what they remembered, and the department could respond to that. It's actually quite rare for a Cabinet minister, however experienced, to be able to prioritise like that.

Some of Michael Gove's policies provoked strong reactions from opposition and the public, but he was an extremely competent minister. Those who worked with him closely described to me his concentrated focus on the department for which he is responsible (his fiefdom) and his ability not to be distracted by events and behaviours elsewhere in government. He was also empowering of good ideas, from both advisers and civil servants, triangulating confidence and trust in the competence between the roles of the minister, civil servant and special adviser. On this topic, David Gauke said:

> You want to have a sense of direction and generate ideas. Ministers can, should and need to provide political direction and the idea that officials dislike that is not true. I think officials like Secretaries of State who will drive them in a particular direction and provide a sense that they can go into work each day knowing what their Secretary of State wants in clear, simple primary colours. That gives a sense of direction and that things are getting done. That's why Michael Gove is widely seen to have been a very effective minister in every department he's gone to. There seems to be this sense of: this is what we're doing, this is the journey we're on, come along for the ride. And officials have generally liked working for him.

Having clear priorities not only increases the likelihood of a minister achieving something while in post; it also helps provide clarity and direction for civil servants. With those, the relationship can be built on firmer foundation as everyone can start to pull in the same direction, reducing the likelihood of miscommunication and frustration. Priorities are an important tool in establishing a successful ministerial posting but also in acknowledging a political reality: legacy. The reality is that having worked so hard to make it to the top of a political career, most politicians want to achieve something which made it all worthwhile. Vince Cable shared his own experience of this realisation:

> There was a defining moment in the middle of the coalition government, when things were pretty bad for the Lib Dems. We were doing terribly in the polls and I was being talked up as somebody who should replace Nick Clegg. I had a much better public rating and a better rating in the party, and I don't know about him, but certainly his advisers suspected that a lot of plotting was going on. So we had a heart-to-heart meeting in his office, and his basic message was: you've got to decide, are you here campaigning, commentating, trying to set the terms of the debate or are you delivering a legacy? And I remember thinking that having a legacy of things you've done is more important than winning debates or storming out – which I was tempted to do on many occasions – about particular issues. So the latter part of the administration was about trying to create a constructive legacy. People who go into a ministerial job need to sort that in their mind first: what are they there for? Are they there to deliver something which they can pass on? Or is it to go around making statements and striking

up positions? Looking back at the last Conservative government [to 2024], there seemed to be an absence of legacy thinking and an obsession with simply finding a useful thing at a particular moment. I think of Grant Shapps when he had five ministerial roles in a year. That is exactly how not to run a government.

MINISTERS ALSO NEED TO KNOW ABOUT... CIVIL SERVICE HIERARCHY

By the end of the 'beginning' phase, a minister will likely feel they understand the brief, know more about how the department functions and will have settled into the role. That's not to say things become easy – far from it. The initial shock and anxiety on arrival may have been replaced by a growing confidence and some assuredness, but the optimism and momentum of the early days will also meet the reality of accountability and the sticky mud of governance. This is the end of the beginning and the beginning of the middle of a ministerial lifespan.

But as we move between these phases, there is something else that several former ministers mentioned to me as being something which confused them in their early days of ministerial life. The civil service is fervently against all, and makes inspiring effort to combat, discriminatory isms: sexism, racism, classism, ableism and many others. Except one: gradism. Hierarchy matters in the civil service and it is an area that many (many) ministers have navigated the hard way. There have been concerted efforts to tackle gradism, but the reality is it still exists in the system and having a basic understanding of the grade structure will help with ministers' early interactions and relations with top civil servants.

Several departments specify levels starting with A at the top and working alphabetically downwards; others start with A for the most junior roles and work alphabetically upwards, but the nomenclature (as below) is broadly consistent.

Rank		Short name	Full name
Most senior	Senior civil service	SCS	Permanent Secretary
			Second Permanent Secretary, Director General
			Director
			Deputy Director
		G6 & 7	Grade 6
			Grade 7
		SEO/HEO	Senior Executive Officer
			Higher Executive Officer
		EO	Executive Officer
Most junior		AO/AA	Administrative Officer
			Administrative Assistant

The grade structure, to some civil servants, is viewed more as a reflection of the rigidity of ranks in the army, rather than flexible levels of a corporate structure. Where the hierarchy is as upright and linear as the table above, it is not supposed to be this way (at least in modern times), nor would this be publicly admitted. But recognising a working practice in reality delivers better results than relying on promises and narratives to try to understand the system. And it is the recognition of reality that helps mark the transition from the beginning of a minister's tenure to the middle.

PART THREE

THE MIDDLE

WORKING TOGETHER

Once the excitement of gaining office has settled and the minister has their head around the brief, the maze of governance becomes more apparent. Occasionally, a minister decides the department is not for them or feels they should be somewhere more aligned with their ambitions. All is not lost in this instance, but this type of situation does require intervention, as Una O'Brien shared:

> One of the most difficult occasions is if a – usually junior – minister accepts a role and then a few weeks later comes to you as Permanent Secretary and says they hate it and want to leave. This happened to me, and I handled it by making a time-out with that person outside the department to understand more deeply what was going on and explore the options. Subsequently, we put in place more comms support and changed some ways of working and he ended up staying for two years!

On the basis that the minister has decided they will actually commit to do the job, one way through the maze is, as many have advised, to choose one or two priorities to achieve. But governance is also full of sticky mud and distractions and ministers need to work well with officials in order to achieve any degree of measurable success. That is true of achieving policy priorities, but it is also true of difficulties and crises. However well a government is set up, politics has a habit of shuffling the deck when you least expect it, which means everything can change at any moment. I asked Philip Rutnam about his experiences of having to adjust to fast, politically induced change. He replied:

> When I was appointed Permanent Secretary at [the Department for] Transport, Justine Greening was Secretary of State. I was getting on very well with Justine, but after a few months, No. 10 decided to change its approach to airport expansion. Poor Justine, who had been MP for Putney, had been elected on a platform absolutely opposing the expansion of Heathrow and was committed at every level to not supporting airport expansion. Suddenly, she found the ground shifting beneath her feet and it was really quite a difficult last forty-eight, seventy-two hours of her time in office, because it was clear that No. 10 were going in a different direction. And she risked being, bluntly, stranded by it. So I needed to provide her with some support there. But then she was moved to [the Department for] International Development and I had a new Secretary of State, Patrick McLoughlin, who came in with a different mandate from No. 10. So we had to shift the whole department's approach. Not the details of the issue, because that was going to need months and years of work, but on the orientation, outlook and demeanour. We had to lean into this new question, work out how to take things forward and look at whether there

was a need for airport expansion. So you may have to shift on a sixpence within a day. Political events, they can happen glacially slowly or they can happen incredibly fast.

In government, working together in fast-paced situations also comes in the context of crisis. These moments of intense pressure can, in fact, be fast builders of trust. Every senior person who has worked in government, in nearly any capacity, has been involved in a crisis at some point; some are battle-hardened by them. Vince Cable described his first year in government as full of constant crises (including with bankers, tuition fees, Rupert Murdoch), all potentially politically fatal. I've not included all the different crises shared with me, but I found one of Robert Halfon's examples a good one for giving a flavour of the speed and steps which a minister, and their team, might usually need to take. Robert said:

> The *Sunday Times* did a big exposé on agencies who were getting international students into UK institutions. [The *Sunday Times*] said the agencies were getting them in on the cheap and with poorer qualifications than British students. It looked like a terrible story and international students was a hot political potato. Because I'm a saddo, and I read all the papers on a Saturday night, and I saw this at midnight.
>
> So I am thinking, 'Oh my God, this is going to be murderous. We've got Education questions on Monday and there will probably be a UQ [urgent question] about it.' As it happened, there wasn't. So I had to deal with it straight away. I spoke to the private office head, who was incredible, and I said, 'We've got to deal with this immediately.' Then I spoke to Universities UK and we agreed to meet the vice chancellors that Sunday afternoon, and I asked

them about it. Then we discussed it with the officials and agreed that we were going to announce the investigation into agencies and how it can be done the next morning, Monday. That was a big thing. That kind of thing happens all the time and you never know from day to day if something big is going to happen. You often think there's going to be a UQ and there isn't one. And then there's some minor thing and suddenly there's a UQ on that or a debate or whatever it is, and you have to be quick. The speed is critical. I could have just done nothing and waited till the Monday, but we'd have been monstered. Five years ago as a minister, I might have thought, 'Oh, I'll discuss it with them tomorrow morning.' When you become a minister the second time, you know what to do. We dealt with it straight away and the officials had a very can-do attitude. This stuff about the blob and all these insults are nonsense. I absolutely hate it because the people I worked with were can-do and immediately worked to deal with the problem. [Secretary of State] Gillian [Keegan] also had brilliant special advisers, who I worked very well with. Potential crises happen all the time, but luckily, the media doesn't find out about a lot of them.

It's not easy because you have to come out with a series of measures pretty quickly, but there is also just so much you have to process and deal with. If it was really big, I would refer it to Gillian or the special advisers, after which Downing Street would have to approve everything and say yes or no. One of the really important things is that you need to know the right people to speak to when a crisis starts, so you have the right people in the room who can deal with each problem. The officials I worked with were excellent.

Civil servants are crucial to a minister in dealing with a crisis but also in achieving their priorities. Each minister I spoke to could pick out individuals whom they had worked really well with, including Robert:

> As a parliamentary candidate, I met some disadvantaged kids from the Prince's Trust and Catch22 who wanted to do skills [qualifications], but there were no opportunities. I wasn't an MP at that point, but I said, 'If I get elected, I'm going to make this my major issue' and I made my first speech about apprenticeships. I was the first MP to ever employ full-time apprentices in Parliament and I kept my promise to myself and made it clear from day one that I was going to be a social justice minister; I wanted everything that we did to embed that. There was a brilliant official, a genius, called Stephen Wan, who devised the 'ladder of opportunity' with me, with rungs on the policies and so on. One of the sides of the ladder was social justice and opportunity.
>
> Just to give you an example of the impact it had, I think on the Turing Scheme there were about 30 or 40 per cent of students who were from disadvantaged backgrounds. We got that pushed up to 60 per cent. We got the care leavers' bursary up from £1,000 to £3,000, when there was no money, and a mentoring scheme set up for disabled apprenticeships. All kinds of ladder [of opportunity] things. For every policy, I asked, 'How is it helping the disadvantaged?' because I believe this area [skills] is the greatest answer to social justice. And [the civil servants] got it because they realised it was my top priority. It would always be part of the submission without me asking for it because they understood what my priorities were. Adult community learning, for example, is something I'm very passionate about and often had to fight to champion and make sure it was funded properly because it's an

easy target to slash money from. That's somewhere where you get often the most disadvantaged people with difficult backgrounds. That was a priority for me and the [civil servants] got it and we worked well together. If you don't say anything, the system just kind of exists and carries on with the broad government priorities. But if you're very clear with the priorities, it makes a huge difference.

For a minister, having the right people around them and forming a top team who can work well together are critical for any sort of success. Strong, settled relationships not only help deliver success but also last. Vince Cable told me about how his Permanent Secretary (Martin Donnelly) supported him in getting the right structures in place to lead BIS:

> Once I'd got a good set-up, which included having a top-class principal private secretary and two political advisers in place, I felt much more confident, learned by doing and got a strategy in place for the department. I was guided by the Permanent Secretary to have an annual speech to all of the department – at the time 4,000+ people. We filled the Methodist Central Hall and then had regular meetings with the top 200 [civil servants] every quarter, and then with the top ten officials. The challenge each time was to say, 'This is what we want to do in the next year or quarter and this is what we've achieved.' Once we had got into that and given the department a structure to work within, things worked much better.
>
> Because I was a long-standing Secretary of State, they knew what I was trying to do and we were getting good results and good outcomes. If I made a mistake, it was towards the end, just

thinking everything's fine, when actually it wasn't and there were [coalition] problems bubbling up. I periodically meet up with some of my former civil servants for a drink or a meal, and one of my [former] special advisers organises a little drinks party every six months or a year. There were good memories.

It is important to note that civil servants and ministers can (and sometimes should) disagree. That is part of working well together in this unique dynamic. David Davis (former Secretary of State for Exiting the EU 2016–18 and Minister for Europe 1994–97) described his opening lines to his senior civil servants:

> I said, 'You and I are going to disagree on lots of things, but there will be no penalties for disagreeing with me. The whole point of this process is that you will disagree, up until the point at which we make a decision. Nobody will be punished for disagreeing with me. Indeed, just the reverse, I want you to challenge the argument until the moment of decision. Then you just do it. Do we understand each other?' When I left after Blair won the election, a number of them – Stephen Wall is the one that comes to mind – wrote me a handwritten note saying, 'It all worked brilliantly. We really enjoyed it.'[1]

I asked Philip Rycroft (who worked as Permanent Secretary to David Davis at DExEU) whether this had been his experience. He said, 'We did disagree with him a lot. Sometimes his opinion would adjust, sometimes it didn't. But he'd been around the block before and he's a very self-confident, ebullient sort of character. We had a robust relationship with him.'

The ability to disagree but still work well together is important.

Clare Moriarty took over from Philip Rycroft as Permanent Secretary of DExEU when he retired from the civil service. I asked her whether there had been any ministers she worked with where this dynamic had worked well. She recalled:

> My all-time favourite minister to work for was Stephen Dorrell, when I was the principal private secretary in [the Department of] Health and he was one of the Secretaries of State. The thing that I found really good about him was that he was confident in his politicalness. He was happy being a politician, which meant he would disagree with civil servants. Civil servants are really happy to be disagreed with by politicians who know that they're doing it for political reasons. The difficulty comes when ministers feel a bit insecure and feel that they can only be comfortable if the civil service is telling them the thing that they would like to be the answer. That's when you get into more difficult to manage conflict. But Stephen Dorrell was very sensible.
>
> When he took over as Secretary of State, we had previously been providing his predecessor with five red boxes at night because they wanted to be across everything. When Stephen arrived, I asked him, 'How many boxes would you like?' He said, 'I'll take one box. I will trust your judgement about what goes into that one box. And if it turns out that something which I wish afterwards I had known about and I haven't, because there's only so much you can put into one box, I will take responsibility for that.' He trusted my judgement and took responsibility. It was fantastic. There was an occasion when we were having a long meeting about something and the officials came in and they presented all their stuff and had a robust discussion with him. At the end of it he said, 'I've heard everything you've got to say. And now I'm

going to do the exact opposite, because politically that's what I need to do.' And everybody said, 'That's absolutely fine.'

Politics is an important element in civil servants navigating the relationship with ministers.

A policy implemented by one government may be amended or reversed by the next one, more often than not for political reasons, and it is difficult to implement policy which, essentially, becomes irreversible because it has been weaved into the fabric of life. Aside from needing to gain public buy-in and time things right, government policy demanding mass behavioural change often requires a web of stakeholders and sometimes multiple government departments involved. It is difficult to find a more successful major example of this than (what has come to be known as) 'the smoking ban'. In 2007, the Labour government introduced a ban on smoking in enclosed public places, radically accelerating a denormalisation of smoking in public. Caroline Flint was Minister of State for Public Health, tasked with realising what initially had seemed to be a fanciful idea:

> One of the biggest things over my two-year period [as Minister for] Public Health was Smokefree England. It was a policy I inherited that I didn't think would really work when I arrived. The policy of the Labour government wasn't in favour of going smokefree in closed public spaces. So I had a situation where I had to hold the party line in public while trying to, behind the scenes, explore what would happen if we did X and Y, and then at the same time had health professionals pushing and saying you've got to go further. We worked really hard in the department. I appreciated what [the civil servants] were trying to do and I think

they appreciated what I was trying to do, politically, to change the narrative on it. It was incremental but we did a huge amount of work, and then when we got the vote in favour of moving to Smokefree England, there was a huge amount of work again on getting the legislation right. We really tested ourselves and stress-tested every idea we had. We had a sounding board for pretty much every part of the private sector who would be affected by this, particularly the hospitality industry with pubs, clubs, working men's clubs, cafes, the whole sector. And we had fantastic relationships with the environmental health officers in local authorities who were on the ground making sure that every cafe, pub and establishment had the right signage and understood what the law was. We put money into training environmental health officers and played out all the possible scenarios to cover all the bases. So it wasn't just thinking about the legalistic framework of policy but also imagining how it would be interpreted. Would all those agents that were so important to making a success in local communities really understand it? There was a huge amount of really collaborative work that went on within the department and with me supporting my various teams involved in delivering it.

It seems obvious, given civil servants are supposed to implement government policies, that teams of officials and ministers need to work together well in order to successfully turn ideas into tangible activity. And yet so many ideas from ministers either never happen or do not stick. There are lots of reasons that the smoking ban was so successful, and the fact that so many different teams across different departments managed to work so effectively with ministers and other stakeholders is a major one. Another reason is that the politics and the timing were right.

THE MIDDLE

POLITICS

'The one thing I pushed back on near the end of the process was about the date we went live,' Caroline said.

I had asked her whether there had been any disagreements with officials in implementing the smoking ban. She replied:

> Scotland had already gone live [with smokefree enclosed public places] and Wales were working towards it as well. I think the Welsh Assembly at that time had decided to go earlier and I had a submission come through saying, 'They're going earlier, do you want to go live on 1 January 2007?' And I was like, 'Oh my God, honestly, people had just had Christmas, it's New Year's Day, it's the coldest time of the year and we're going to send them all outside.' I decided against it and went for 1 July because I thought: it's warmer and it gives us a bit more time. The fact Wales will go before England just wasn't a big enough deal for me. It was about this working. I said [to the civil servants], 'I know it might get a headline for the New Year, but politically this is better.' A big part of that was about understanding how the public received policies from the centre and how policy translates from Whitehall to communities. You have to ask: how will it be received? Should you do it on potentially the coldest day of the year, when everyone is feeling a bit jaded after Christmas? No. I don't think that civil servants always think about these things. And I have to say, I don't think a lot of politicians think about it either. But as a politician, you are always out there, hearing day in day out from the public what they think is wrong and what's going wrong. You become attuned to it and sometimes that can be helpful when people are in the midst of policy and logistics. Injecting some political reality into the process is important.

Politicians know politics. And, eventually, in government, politics prevails. Speaking to Caroline, I was reminded of something Helen MacNamara (former Deputy Permanent Secretary in the Cabinet Office) said in her Covid Inquiry witness statement: 'Elected politicians (in my experience) are much more likely to offer wider perspectives and can spot from a long way off when what they are being told does not make sense when translated into real life.'[2]

This is often the case and is important in the strand which links logic and empathy in the trust triangle. Political logic might differ from administrative logic. 'Ministers decide,' as the saying goes, and so civil servants have to be able to put one foot in a minister's shoe to understand the political lens they are using, while keeping the other foot in their own shoe to translate that political understanding into implementation. Rory Stewart had told me about an occasion at the FCO where he wasn't afforded this understanding:

> The civil servants wanted to shut all the nice staff accommodation in Kenya. I went to Kenya and we had a big budget. I said, 'Listen, the staff want to stay in those houses, they're family-friendly and I can pay for them. So can we just keep them open?' And the response from the equivalent of head of admin was: 'It's politically impossible, Minister, in the twenty-first century for staff to live in these kinds of houses.' I said, 'Wait a second. I'm the politician. I'm telling you it's fine.' He replied that it wouldn't pass the *Daily Mail* test. And I said, 'Listen, I'm the minister. Boris Johnson is the Foreign Secretary. He's happy for these things to stay open. And he can handle the *Daily Mail* better than any of us.' He could simply write a jolly article saying Britain needs to have decent accommodation for its staff abroad and everyone would swallow it.

So don't tell us, the politicians, what's politically possible or what does or doesn't fail the *Daily Mail* test. At least leave that to us.

Ministers with good political antennae are also good at navigating politics to get good policy outcomes. David Gauke had convinced me this was an area in which civil servants should trust their ministers:

> I was only at DWP for seven months, but I quickly took the view that I had one big task: implementing Universal Credit. That was partly about going to the Treasury and persuading them to be supportive of a few things. I had just been Chief Secretary of the Treasury and knew how it worked, so I wasn't going to turn around and say, 'We need more money.' Therefore, my strategy involved asking the department questions first and seeing what was really necessary. Then by the time I did bid for money, I got it. It was helpful, for me, to initially show resistance to spending more and demonstrating credibility with the Treasury, rather than rushing into the queue [for more money]. That's precisely the same approach I took with the MOJ.
>
> The way to do it is not to go for everything that's in view. You have to demonstrate control and establish to the Treasury that you're trying everything else. Then you can say, 'Look, we're the model department. I'm the model minister and I'm prepared to take some political heat around spending.' My wider MOJ agenda was one that the department were happy with. Had I gone in and done a Chris Grayling, asking, 'Why are we letting these people have books? Can we toughen the regime?' etc., then it would have been more difficult. I felt like my approach gave the MOJ

confidence and that we were setting an agenda that the department sort of secretly wanted but daren't voice.

Politics is the constant in the background of government. It can have quiet moments and loud moments, but it is always there, between the ruling party and its adversaries and within the government itself. In recent years, the civil service has had to make significant adjustments in a rapidly changing political landscape. Helen MacNamara reflected on the nature of Boris Johnson's government during the Covid period:

> I think I underestimated how difficult it would be to change the way of operating when decision-making would remain so centralised and political and so much a product of the imprint of the Prime Minister's approach to decision-making. If anything, the latter got a lot worse once Dominic Cummings had left. The Prime Minister rarely accepted that to govern is to choose. He really did want it all and changed his mind often.[3]

It is clear that the state of the relationship between a Secretary of State and their junior ministers will have an impact on the relationship between the ministers and the civil servants, and this is also the case with the Prime Minister and their Cabinet. If the Prime Minister does not display trust in their Cabinet, those ministers will act from a position of insecurity. Civil servants advise and ministers decide. It is difficult to make decisions within a context of uncertain and changing politics – and when your boss is indecisive.

Jonathan Slater raised a further point which civil servants should consider, particularly when decision-making is heavily centralised:

> It's worth bearing in mind that it's not that typical for a decision

to be within the power of one Secretary of State on their own. These are government decisions involving the Prime Minister and the Treasury. Quite often, ministers are having to do things they don't really want to do. You could often find yourself actually allied with the Secretary of State on this. They're doing it because they've got to, not because they want to.

To provide an idea of the change in intra-government politics which the civil service had to adjust to, the coalition government, only a few years before, was not nearly as centralised. It also introduced a new complicating factor in the operating politics of government: two ruling parties. Vince Cable helped to provide an overview:

> One of the strange things about the coalition was that we didn't have very much intervention or interference from No. 10 at all. You hear now about all the issues around Boris Johnson and [Dominic] Cummings, but we didn't have a Cummings figure in the coalition at all. The Prime Minister [David Cameron] had a kind of hands-off approach. I think he didn't particularly want to get involved in spats with me, and so they sort of left us alone. There were occasional issues that became quite difficult, but for the most part, No. 10 was not an issue. Treasury was a big, big issue because almost everything we wanted to do involved money. And we got into some quite vigorous arguments with the Treasury about the banks, public spending and public investment. I was trying to set up the Green Investment Bank with Chris Huhne, and we got into some really quite bitter arguments with the Treasury about whether this should be allowed and the public borrowing requirements for it. So there were some tough interactions with the Treasury. But not with No. 10.

We would have weekly meetings with the ministers or sometimes one-to-one meetings with Nick Clegg, which sometimes felt like a multidimensional game of chess. It didn't get easier over time. More difficult in many ways. As the Lib Dems became very unpopular, partly because of the tuition fees and partly because of the public spending cuts, there was an undercurrent as to who was to blame for all this, and what we should be doing and not doing about it was a major preoccupation. For civil servants, it was this mysterious issue that they knew was in the background, but they didn't quite know how to treat it. But there was one big issue where a clash between what we, as the Lib Dems, thought was a government policy and what the system, including the civil servants, interpreted differently. And that was over the immigration cap. I'd taken the view, which I still think is correct, that it was a [Liberal Democrat] commitment [in the coalition agreement]; we had agreed to differ on it, essentially. It was a Conservative policy, nothing to do with the Lib Dems.

So whenever we had bad immigration numbers, I would often say something different from the Home Secretary, which meant I had endless problems with Theresa May. I think there was one celebrated occasion when the immigration numbers had gone up substantially and this was treated by the government, including the civil service, as a great problem. And I'd gone to the media and said, 'This is great, we've got all these good people coming into universities and being useful workers. What are people complaining about?' And so I think the civil service was confused as to who was the government. Was I speaking as an individual or on behalf of the department or the Lib Dems or some combination? Nobody was quite clear. That was a particularity of the coalition.

In this environment, the political logic might not necessarily have been that easy to follow for civil servants. But also note that the political conflict was between two Secretaries of State (Cable and May), rather than with No. 10. I asked Vince whether he felt there was a successful navigation of the politics in government. He replied:

> There was a shift during the general election campaign when the political advisers, particularly this guy from Australia [Lynton Crosby], told Osborne, Cameron, Sajid Javid and the others involved, 'You've got to change tack and just concentrate all your fire on the Lib Dems.' I don't think it occurred to them in government that they were going to do that. They were told that was the way to conduct the election campaign, and all of the Lib Dem MPs, including me, were targeted with completely disingenuous literature. Everybody in Twickenham was getting daily letters from 10 Downing Street saying, 'The Prime Minister says you've got an excellent MP. However, we don't want the country run by the Scottish nationalists, so you're going to have to vote Conservative.' And people believed it.

I suppose the answer to my question was either yes or no, depending on your viewpoint. Andrew Lansley was also in the early coalition Cabinet (although as a Conservative). I asked him about his experience navigating this new type of politics within government. He recalled:

> It happened in the most unusual way. We didn't form a government in order to implement our manifesto. We formed a government in order to implement the coalition programme, which

in significant respects, including the health service, was radically different from what was in the two manifestos. There were parts of the health policies in the coalition programme that had no antecedents in either manifesto. Somebody, somewhere, is going to write a proper examination of quite what happened, but it didn't happen because I thought that should be the health policy. I was handed it. The Liberal Democrats wanted elected PCTs [primary care trusts] and I wanted GP-led consortia like the kind that was emerging. The coalition programme ended up with a very complicated relationship between local government and the clinical commissioning groups, where the clinical commissioning groups were no longer what I envisaged and the local government role was not what the Liberal Democrats really wanted. But they all had to be meshed together, which made it very complicated. Afterwards, many people assumed that I had written all this into our manifesto and I hadn't at all. I had something completely different. It was all worked out elsewhere.

To give you an example of what the politics would have done: it would be like John Prescott coming into the Department for Transport in 1997, having fought the campaign on the pledge to have an integrated transport policy and saying he wanted a White Paper on an integrated transport policy. The civil servants then ask whether there are any particular specifics he wants and he says, 'No, I just want a White Paper on an integrated transport policy. Go away and write one.' Because he didn't care as long as it was integrated, because 'integrated' was a word, a thought, a theme, an idea. Whereas I had written the Autonomy and Accountability White Paper, effectively, before the election, and I'd even written the legislation. The problem was the civil service took what I thought was a simple piece of legislation and turned it into a 300-clause monster. Why? Because they thought that they needed to write the legislation to tell everybody in the NHS and related organisations what the answers were to absolutely every single question. And so they ended up writing hundreds of clauses. We managed to write them all in the space of six months, which in itself was a remarkable achievement from [the Permanent Secretary] Hugh Taylor. But it was a monster. And it was not my monster. It was the result of a series of major discussions where I would say what I wanted, and then the civil servants would lay out every problem they could think of. And I would then respond with how I thought we should do it. And then they would take it away and rewrite it, adding more and more.

That said, we [with the civil service] managed an anticipated reduction in the administration costs of the NHS, by the end of the parliament. In fact, we exceeded the reduction with a £1.6 billion saving in administration costs over the period. That was partly because in 2009, the year before the 2010 election, the administration cost of the NHS had increased by 25 per cent. [Labour] had been fattening the pig before market day.

I wanted to understand the degree to which Andrew Lansley's agenda, crafted over years as shadow Health Secretary, was changed because of the coalition. He replied:

Not completely, because some of it was not the coalition but because No. 10 wasn't interested. I wanted the department to give the NHS operational autonomy while being accountable for the outcomes. [I also wanted] autonomy and accountability through the [NHS] mandate and to focus the department much more on the creation of a substantial public health agenda. Hence the public health White Paper in December [2010]. But getting anybody other than Oliver Letwin interested in public health just didn't happen. Once I'd left, the Cabinet subcommittee disappeared, the agenda disappeared and the Treasury took the money away. And Jeremy Hunt let them do it. The story that the [Covid] Inquiry isn't telling is that a significant proportion of the money for local government public health was taken away in the Budgets of 2015 and 2016, and they were just ill-equipped, which caused significant real problems. Strangely enough, the select committees when they talked about this didn't mention it. Guess who the chairman of the select committee was?

Jeremy Hunt was chairman of the Health Select Committee at that point. There will always be moments when ministers disagree with each other, and ministerial careers tend to attract ambitious and competitive beings. Una O'Brien (Permanent Secretary to both Andrew Lansley and then Jeremy Hunt) had already mentioned to me the higher degree of support from No. 10 that Hunt appeared to have, compared to his predecessor (although Lansley may dispute that). The stories of individual occupations of ministerial roles come and go, but a tension that often remains was one that David Gauke and Vince Cable had already raised: the relationship between the Treasury and (pretty much) everyone else.

David Gauke (a Treasury man) had already mentioned his successful approach to getting the Treasury to say yes. But, on the whole, ministers of spending departments (which is most of them) express frustration at the Treasury's tight grip on the public purse strings. The Treasury has a long history of producing and nurturing very talented civil servants. The department often has its own version of civil service talent programmes, separate to the rest of government, and for many, working in the Treasury is as much a career choice as it is a job. It is generally regarded as the most powerful department in government, and yet has come under criticism (as have other parts of Whitehall) for not thinking broadly enough, despite now having a campus in Darlington (in addition to headquarters in London). An Institute for Government report noted: 'As one interviewee for our research into Darlington put it: "In London, we [HM Treasury] read what Torsten Bell thinks. Up here, we're talking to different people, hearing different things."'[4]

This comment was made when Torsten Bell was in charge of the think tank Resolution Foundation and before he became an MP, but it paints a picture. I asked Andrew Lansley about civil servants adjusting to ministerial politics and whether the Treasury differed, given its powerful status. He said:

> I think the Treasury is a bit different. In the Treasury, civil servants are not partisan, but they have an unusual degree of intellectual arrogance that makes them believe they know about politics. And they don't. Politics is very different. It doesn't behave in an intellectually accessible way. It behaves in an emotionally accessible way. Civil servants in the Treasury think they get politics, but they don't. They also are much more likely to have been reading newspapers, journalists and commentators and thinking that by doing that, they've understood politics. No disrespect to our journalistic friends, but even journalists don't get politics. Not really. They are constantly saying, here we are, and this is that, he said that, she said that and this is where it's going. And I read it and think, 'It's not going there.' Because they haven't understood

where the balance of the issue really lies and where the politics is on this thing. They've just been told something by somebody. Journalists are constantly being manipulated. And Treasury civil servants read all that stuff and think that's where it's all going. I've always found Treasury civil servants much more likely to offer what they regard as a political analysis of something that ought, technically, to be an economic analysis.

I returned to David Gauke, to see whether he had a different perspective, given how long he had spent as a Treasury minister. He told me:

> The Treasury has to be the department that says, 'No, we can't spend this money.' And more often than not, that's a politically unpopular thing to say, at least in the eyes of the government department that's keen to spend the money. Very often there is a conversation where a department says, 'Look, unless we get this money, it's going to cause all sorts of political problems.' And the Treasury says, 'That's true, but you can't have the money.' Now, is that the Treasury being unpolitical? At one level, it is. But if political means doing the popular thing every time, then the country soon becomes bankrupt – and that's not very popular either. Of course, there will be times where the Treasury will get this wrong, whether it's the Treasury saying no but then a politician looks at it and calculates that the political costs very obviously massively outweigh the sums of money involved. And therefore we have to be more political and spend the money. Will Treasury always get it right? No. But the Treasury is set up to be unpolitical and do the unpopular thing. And if unpopular equals unpolitical, then there's no escaping that. That's their job.

SPECIAL ADVISERS

I should have had effective political advisers in place sooner. I did have one in fairly quickly who was very intelligent, but like me, she was struggling to get her head around everything and wasn't able to steer me away from the problems. The political adviser system is a very good one, but it assumes that your system is in place from day one when you need it most. And we hadn't.

I had asked Vince Cable about his experience with special advisers (SpAds). The role of the SpAd is one of the fastest evolving elements of the civil servant–minister relationship, with new precedents set during the Johnson/Cummings era, and in building trust and better working, SpAds have become an inescapably important element. There can be a temptation in government and politics (as in life) to get caught in a present-day narrative and struggle to see past the events of today continuing indefinitely. Looking at the trajectory of change, it is fairly safe to assume that the role of SpAds is likely to change further. Typically, change challenges status quo, which in itself creates friction. Vince continued:

> Alongside others, I had a *sort of* political adviser, Lord Oakeshott, who had been very helpful when we were in opposition. He was part of our [shadow] Treasury team and I tried to sign him up as a kind of ad hoc adviser, somebody who could just come in and give me personal advice. The civil service were very hostile to this and did everything they could to make sure it didn't work. I wasn't quite sure what the problem was, but I think that they had a view that there are civil servants and there are political advisers who are on contract, and that's it. So having people just wandering in

and out was something they were very uncomfortable with. They effectively stopped me being able to use him much, and I just had to drop the whole idea.

When I was dealing with banking reform, I was in quite a weak position and we had to give a lot of ground. It was one of the areas where the absence of Lord Oakeshott was a problem, because it was a subject he knew a great deal about and was going to help guide the policy with me. But he wasn't around. I occasionally had telephone conversations, but I was pretty much on my own dealing with hostile banks, a hostile Treasury and a department who clearly hadn't got the heart of what I was trying to do. We made some progress eventually, setting up the British Business Bank, but it would have been easier if Lord Oakeshott was able to help more.

One special adviser I had who was very good eventually became quite a big figure. He actually wasn't very political and he was very useful in dealing with the Treasury because he was respected by [George] Osborne's SpAd, Rupert Harrison, who was our main Treasury interlocutor. Once we'd got over the first year, relations with the Treasury were very good, and that was partly thanks to him acting as a linkman.

The other big problem I had with special advisers was not having anyone with a real interest in public relations in the early stages. I was getting a terrible press and that wasn't being properly answered. So I needed a special adviser who had some awareness of journalists, treating them properly and looking after them. For the last three years, I did then have a very good media-aware special adviser. It's an important job, which I don't think everyone adequately appreciates. I also needed people in the press office who were politically savvy and eventually I got some people doing that. But for a minister, if you're being attacked every day in the media, you can't do the job properly, so you really do need a good media presence and people who can manage that for you. Very often I think we don't show enough attention to that. I eventually got a good set-up, but it was after a lot of hitting and missing.

Bringing in good special advisers requires a degree of self-awareness from a minister. SpAds often have the greatest impact when they can complement the skillset and capabilities of the minister, bringing additional strengths and enhancing the implementation of the minister's will. Their role is a political one and the most effective (and successful) ones tend to have a strong grounding in and understanding of politics, with a good political antenna for navigating changing situations. Caroline Flint told me how impactful gaining a SpAd was for her:

> What made the biggest difference when I went to housing and planning at [the Department for Communities and Local Government] was getting a special adviser. Special advisers all work for the Secretary of State and divvy up the different parts of portfolios between them, then check in now and again, but I hardly ever saw them. Having a special adviser who understood the politics and could go and do a bit of checking out if I was worried about something or have a chat with a civil servant to fix a problem was a massive change. They also developed their relationships with the civil servants as well. I was very lucky that my special adviser was not interested in becoming a name in themselves. They were there to help us deliver on the policies, rather than do the comms, and that was really helpful. I think a good special adviser isn't there as someone to go into battle with the civil servants. You

don't want to put any civil servant in a position where they are stepping outside the boundaries of what is appropriate for them, and special advisers are a helpful conduit for some of that, where they can look at things more through a political lens.

But also it was good to have another person who could help get to the bottom of things and do some of the legwork for you, so that you can have a better understanding when you come to make a decision. I really think that most ministers should have access to their own person to help make that happen. I disagree with criticism that there are too many special advisers. Yes, some are there causing trouble and mischief, particularly the ones with the comms briefs. But the ones who are there to help you with your portfolio, to understand it better, to understand what the civil servants are doing better and to be that conduit are really very helpful. I found such a massive difference having that resource to be able to support me, but also I think it was good for the civil servants too.

The increase in communications-focused (comms) SpAds has been notable in recent years and is likely the source of much anonymised criticism of civil servants from within government. One special adviser pointed out to me that the background and career history of a SpAd is often important in establishing how they are likely to act. Those without a political party background (and who have perhaps worked only with one MP, who has become a minister) are more likely to prioritise building the profile of their minister. Those with exposure to a broader range of political roles may well have sharper political acumen.

Several former special advisers I spoke to emphasised the mutual respect between SpAds and civil servants within No. 10. Some described it as feeling like they were one team, with one telling me that 'the work ethic of civil servants in No. 10 is phenomenal'. Andrew Lansley suggested there are also considerations for ministers to make on this closeness:

> The number of political appointees in No. 10, relative to the number of civil servants, is quite large. In my view, civil servants in No. 10 become susceptible to the political imperative, rather than the policy imperative, partly because they're in an environment substantially consisting of political appointees. Everybody says every No. 10 [the Prime Minister's team] is exactly the same. Advisers arrive there and are given some space to apply their worldview. And soon their prejudices turn into the Prime Minister's prejudices in their minds. I was so often told No. 10 wants X and Y – and by extension the PM wants it. I'd say, 'Oh, does No. 10 want that? OK. Does David [Cameron] think that?' David used to work for me at the research department, so I would just go and see him. On every occasion, what I had been told he thought was not what he thought. Nobody should underestimate the influence of special advisers in No. 10. They play a significant role.

All ministers soon learn it is essential to identify *who* in No. 10 has said or instructed something. The institution itself, of course, cannot think or speak – any instruction is coming from a person. Ministers and civil servants need to know which person. Andrew continued:

> Interestingly, I was responsible for the Transparency of Lobbying bill as Leader of the House [of Commons]. I was responsible for it because Nick Clegg wouldn't do it. It was his ministerial

responsibility and he wouldn't take the bill through. So as Leader of the House, I had to take it through, despite having no ministerial responsibility for it at all. But what it didn't include was transparency in relation to the contacts between third-party lobbyists and special advisers, where there is still a gap. It's a big loophole.

The governance of SpAds continues to be spattered with more loopholes than for either civil servants or ministers. Perhaps the fluid nature of the role makes this necessary, but it does mean that there is greater possibility for variation in quality and consistency of behaviour of special advisers. The background and ambitions of SpAds is an important consideration, for both ministers and civil servants, in establishing how best to work with them. Sue Owen shared her experience working with special advisers:

> SpAds can be very different from each other. Some of them are political advisers; some are aspiring MPs. Sometimes they're subject matter experts and sometimes they're all those things. Iain Duncan Smith, for example, had Philippa Stroud, who subsequently stood to become an MP and then entered the Lords. But she really knew her stuff, from the Centre for Social Justice [which she co-founded]. And there was an expert SpAd, Stephen Bryan, who was the guy that would do spreadsheets on holiday. I always tried to be nice to the SpAds and get to know them as individuals. That was transformational because they then didn't criticise the staff and that kind of thing, if you were treating them seriously. If I were still in government now, the last five years [2019–24] may have been more difficult because the stock of SpAds, I think, has been a bit depleted. It's far more young

hopefuls of about twenty-three [years old] who are running around and don't really know anything but can keep tabs on the politics and what the party is thinking. But I liked the SpAds I worked with. One of them was Carrie Symonds. She and I had to help John Whittingdale through a quite difficult bit of publicity at one point, and they were both surprised I was being so helpful. Whereas my view was that we needed this little bit of publicity to go away as soon as possible because that was the best thing for the department, so it was best to try to help.

The current trajectory for special advisers is that there are increasingly more of them and they are increasingly involved in the running of government. It's very unlikely, particularly while things remain sufficiently uncodified, that the present-day situation is the final destination for the role of the special adviser. I asked several of the former Permanent Secretaries where things should go from here, based on their experience. Philip Rutnam started:

> I think special advisers potentially have a somewhat bigger role to fill than most civil servants would historically have thought. It's probably right to recognise that, around the Secretary of State, you need a group of political advisers who can help with this intensity of pressure which didn't exist thirty years ago.
>
> It needs to be thought through and structured appropriately, with clear definitions of roles and responsibilities and clear accountability. We've somehow evolved slightly haphazardly into a world where ministers are under intense pressure, and they've responded to that by increasing the complement of political advisers, but the definition of roles and responsibilities of the civil

service are unchanged. The fact that it's not been properly defined to create a resilient system with clear roles and responsibilities, I think that's a bit of a weakness.

Jonathan Slater went further:

When people ask: what's the point of the permanent civil service? What's it for? They would tend to say to provide expert advice without fear or favour of whoever the politicians are and then to implement it wisely. That's what they tend to say. They don't tend to say the point of a permanent civil service is to serve up things that make the ministers popular, whatever the implications are on the ground. But the civil service has spent quite a lot of time on that second thing, because that's what their ministers want them to do. And that's OK, so long as it's not being done in a way that breaks the Civil Service Code – and there's no reason why it should. But if I were designing a system from scratch, I would suggest that ministers should be entitled to employ quite a lot more people to help them with that task.

I think this is part of the idea from [Michael] Gove and [Francis] Maude, of extending ministerial offices: employ more people, essentially helping them do the politics and leave the civil service to focus on the other task. If you've only got a couple of SpAds, then inevitably the civil service spends quite a lot of time on announceables [announcing something in order to have something to say] because who else is going to do it? But a smarter system would be one in which we focus on what the civil service is supposed to be for. The model that we've got now is essentially the same model we had before the advent of 24/7 news and social media. Thirty years ago, staying on top of the news cycle and having something immediate to say didn't exist. It wasn't being done by anybody because it didn't need to be done. Now it's a really big part of the job, and so we [civil servants] do it, but it's not what we were set up for. And it might be a lot better if one recognised the world has changed and established a group of people whose task is to do that, beyond the couple [of SpAds] that each Secretary of State has. Because in practice, that is not the balance of the role.

There is, of course, not uniform agreement that the role and scope of the special adviser should continue to grow. Simon McDonald suggested it might be time to refine the number of SpAds in operation:

I remember a circular going around when Francis Pym was Foreign Secretary, in the 1980s. We got this political adviser and everyone was reacting quite oddly to this brand-new concept, and it was clearly a big issue because this is someone with very frequent close access to the boss and therefore very influential but not in our system. And so there was an issue. The SpAds I worked with early on in my career were fantastic. When I worked for Douglas Hurd, David Lidington and Maurice Fraser were the two SpAds and they were both excellent, very nice to me personally and very helpful to me professionally.

When I was PPS to Jack Straw, it was Ed Owen and Michael Williams who were fantastic. Roll the story forward and when I was Permanent Secretary, things were changing. Firstly, there were many more SpAds and when a minister had run to the end of his spadly allocation, they would try to get political advisers, 'polads', appointed. When [Liz] Truss was the Foreign Secretary, she had a group that were there because she was Foreign

Secretary, a group that were there because she was Minister for Equalities and a group who were polads. And she moved them all into the private secretary's office next to her own. So it did feel as though the SpAds were taking over. I think the numbers matter.

But also because they were greater in number, they could do more for the Foreign Secretary, and they began to behave more like a French '*cabinet*', taking on chunks of work rather than feeding in advice on top of work that others had done. That's not the way the British system works. I don't think the French system works particularly well with the *cabinet*. Why would we want to replicate that?

And, of course, with more numbers, the traditional tasks got bigger and bigger. The traditional tasks were around relations with the party, relations with Parliament, relations with the media and, very importantly, knowledge of the boss. Ed Owen was fantastic with helping people understand how to make a case to Jack Straw, because he'd known him for years. That kind of SpAd is very easily integrated into the system. Latterly, lots of SpAds seem to be fresh out of central office, very young, not very experienced and not actually very knowledgeable about the boss they're working for. What were they bringing to the party? And yet they are all over the place and throwing their weight around the system and gumming up the works.

The old way of a small number who are doing clear tasks is something, I think, that could be recaptured. Two or three seems a much better number than teens. Also in parallel with what I'm setting out was Cummings in No. 10 regarding the SpAds as his network for running the country. Explicitly. He needed more people and they needed to be personally loyal to him. What was that about?

The Dominic Cummings model of special advisers prioritised the delivery of a centralised government agenda over the idea of ministers collectively driving and deciding policy. Advisers were to report to Cummings, as No. 10 representative, ahead of their minister; an issue over which Sajid Javid famously resigned. There is rationale that this could improve delivery and outcomes. Advisers would be less personally loyal to a minister (and therefore able to prioritise policy being implemented rather than simply promoting the holder of their destiny), the government agenda could be tighter and better managed and the quality of SpAds could be more consistently monitored. He also wanted to 'change the No. 10 and 11 system so it's essentially one team, not two rival power centres', according to the book *All Out War* by Tim Shipman.

One SpAd who worked within Cummings's team told me:

Dom ruled with an iron fist. There was a lot of shouting and he would suddenly spring questions on you. It was… tense. But at the same time, he had a clear vision for what he wanted. He had expectations of people, and if he didn't think those were being met, people were fired. I think that clarity actually created quite a productive environment.

This approach may well deliver better outcomes for the government agenda, but it presents a major challenge for ministers. I asked David Gauke for his reflections on the considerations for ministers regarding SpAds. He replied:

We need to step back and work out what SpAds are for. Lots of SpAds, over the [recent] years, have had a reputation of being young, very political and straight out of the Conservative

Research Department. There's a reputation where they see the role as a stepping stone towards a career in politics and so don't necessarily have much knowledge of the department, subject matter or how Whitehall works. It's been portrayed as a super glamorous job where, particularly on the media side, they've got to be pushing their boss out there and getting anonymous quotes into every Tim Shipman and Steve Swinford piece. And if that means having a feud with another minister, a colleague, then so be it. My sense is that we need SpAds who have got a bit more wisdom about them. Not necessarily older, but they've got to be more mature and less hyper-macho and briefing anonymously using lurid language. It's an important, useful role and that type of behaviour doesn't help.

I also don't see how it works if SpAds are appointed from the centre. It's so much about the personal relationship with the Secretary of State, and for them to work effectively, the Secretary of State has to trust them. The Secretary of State should be appointing people who are collegiate and know how Whitehall works, rather than measuring success on how many anonymous quotes they get into the newspapers.

Obviously, there have been some brilliant SpAds who tick those boxes, for example George Osborne and David Cameron. They were intelligent and had political savvy as opposed to some of the ridiculous partisanship we have seen. SpAds should be the sort of people who you could imagine being ministers.

My own view is that SpAds should support the political implementation of the minister's will, and so if government is to continue by collective ministerial responsibility, then it is ministers who should decide on their advisers. If the Prime Minister feels a minister is insufficiently supportive of the government line, then they should consider that minister's position. Centralising the process might have upsides, or even be more effective, but it is a constitutional change in the method of governance.

Ministers should consider their own strengths, areas that can be improved, their priorities and the ways in which they can work more effectively with officials. Advisers need a good political antenna, to be able to work well with other people and to bring some wider political experience to the role. If ministers recruit advisers on this basis, the chances of success are likely to be much higher.

Special advisers help shield officials from political combat and in the long history of government, there are only a handful of examples of a civil servant (present or former) publicly firing a political bullet. More common are the difficult conversations that happen behind closed doors.

DIFFICULT CONVERSATIONS

Difficult conversations are part of life, and avoiding them can often be more damaging than having them. At the top of government, these are, usually, the occasions where a Permanent Secretary needs to deliver bad news or a challenge to the minister. At one extreme are the occasions where the Permanent Secretary needs to escalate an issue, which I asked Clare Moriarty about. She said:

> There are occasions when ministers are trying to do things which the Prime Minister has told them they shouldn't or the Ministerial Code says that they shouldn't. Those are tricky, but ultimately you use the mechanisms that exist. If a minister wants to do something, the Prime Minister's told them that they can't and

they don't want to listen to the answer, then you have to call in either the Prime Minister or somebody very close to the Prime Minister to have that conversation with the minister. There are certain things that can be heard from certain people. Aligning the message with the authority to give it is also important. Sometimes you might know the answer as the Permanent Secretary, but you're not necessarily the person who has the authority to give it. So you find the person who has got the authority and they decide whether or not they want to exercise their authority on that particular occasion.

Jonathan Slater was experienced in having difficult conversations during his time as Permanent Secretary:

> It is your job to identify the pros and cons objectively and to do so in a way which operates as effectively as possible within the style of communication that the incoming Secretary of State likes. Some people like stuff written down in a lot of detail. Some people like to do it in meetings. Different language works with different types of people. You've got to try to do it in a way that is most likely to be received well. Which is hard to do when you don't know somebody well, in which case you do your best and find out from people who do know that person really well and ask them, 'What is the thing that's most likely to be well received?' Find out who they like receiving advice from and who knows how best to get the message across, then find the way to communicate what the pros and cons are. If the Secretary of State thinks, rightly or wrongly, that you're trying to stop them doing something they want to do, that is bad. That is not your job.

I was interested in whether Jonathan had come across ministers who wanted advice filtered or only to hear advice which aligned with their established views, as Philip Rutnam had experienced at the Home Office. Jonathan said:

> It was vanishingly rare that I came across a situation in which a Secretary of State or a minister would say to me, 'I don't think you should have given that advice.' I wasn't interested in that, and they don't have to follow my advice anyway. We should produce evidence-based things objectively, laying out the pros and cons. The minister may then do as they wish, depending on which pros and cons they think are more important. What's the harm in that? Why would the minister not want that? If you [the civil servant] think something is going to happen if they do X and you don't help them, and then they do it and it happens, and you didn't tell them, then what are you doing? Why is that to their interest? Much better, from their point of view, to tell them what you think will happen so that they've got a plan if it does.

As established already, the ability for civil servants and ministers to have open conversations with each other is critical to working together successfully. Sometimes this is because of personality. But ministers are humans too, and confidence can play a major part. I returned to Clare:

> Insecure ministers are really hard work to deal with because they want to be in a position where the civil service is giving them the advice that they want. That's tough because that is when you start asking people to compromise what they do. Or even if you

don't ask them to compromise what they do, they end up doing it anyway, because they will pick up the signals.

Confident ministers who take responsibility for their own actions and are happy with what they're doing [are easier to work with]. Charlie Falconer, as Lord Chancellor, would have robust debates about things which were completely unthinkable, like abolishing Parliament. He was a barrister and therefore very happy with robust discussion. He didn't mind if people disagreed with him. What you can end up with is a fragility of not wanting people to disagree, but that then puts an awful burden on people who might want to disagree and feel that it's not a safe space to do that.

Sometimes the environment between the two is difficult or may even be hostile. This can make it complicated to establish intentions and clarity from the minister. I asked Philip Rutnam how he navigated this at the Home Office. He replied:

It is core to the job of the Permanent Secretary to provide support to senior civil servants (SCS). There are lots of other aspects of the job, including leadership, motivation and professionalism of staff as a whole, but part of the job is managing that relationship [with ministers] when things are difficult. I often had meetings in my office where I'd have senior civil servants trooping in and saying, 'This is all terrible, we don't know what to do. They [ministers and advisers] want to do this or that and there are value for money or propriety issues.' All kinds of problems. I'd listen to them and go through it trying to steadily identify what the heart of the issue really was, whether there was another way of approaching it and in which we could support and deliver what the minister wants, asking if we had thought about it creatively enough. We'd spend an hour wrestling with the problem, trying to turn it round into something where the conflict is de-escalated and getting to the heart of any difference. Was it a difference of fact or judgement, or is it about conduct? We would define the issue and then optimise the options. It's a professional task, decomposing things into their component parts to see if you can rearrange them in a way that reduces conflict, increases alignment, delivers what ministers want and gets to a good outcome. Many times it's possible; sometimes it's not. I think getting this type of support right is fundamentally down to the quality of the leadership at the top of the department. It's not just the Permanent Secretary; the director generals should be good at this. Good directors should be good at this. For those who are facing into and working for ministers closely, it should be a large part of their job.

DISAGREEMENT AND CONFLICT

'The occasion where I really clashed with the civil service and civil service advice was over the privatisation of Royal Mail,' Vince Cable told me.

Civil servants should be prepared to deliver difficult messages effectively, but there are also occasions where there is conflict, of some kind, with ministers. Many civil servants are taught the Thomas–Kilmann model of conflict styles: competing, collaborating, avoiding, accommodating and compromising (all mapped against assertiveness and cooperativeness). They are skilled at identifying how to resolve conflict and the approaches involved. But the causes of disagreements are often not as much personality- or style-related as they are a clash between institutional positioning and the individual will of the minister. Vince continued:

> It had been delegated to Michael Fallon, who got this particular plum of managing the [Royal Mail] privatisation and who insisted it was a [Prime Minister] Cameron priority. So I let him get on with it. And then it was clear about a week out that the price they had agreed for selling Royal Mail was going to lead to over excess demand for the shares. People thought it was too cheap. We know in retrospect it wasn't, but at the time, it seemed that it was too cheap and I, with the Permanent Secretary and the top officials, said, 'Look, we don't have to go through with this in this way. There are ways that we can maximise the returns for the taxpayer.' And I said, 'Look, I know you feel very comfortable with what you're doing and this is the way things are normally done in the City' – it was being guided by City advisers and the shareholder executive. 'But politically, this is not going to look good. So you need to change.' And there was a confrontation one day where we had to choose between pulling the whole thing or just going ahead with it.
>
> It quickly became very clear that pulling the whole thing would have serious repercussions. I wasn't willing to use [political] nuclear weapons in this situation, but I felt very unhappy with what I was being advised to do, and I knew I would be strenuously attacked for doing it. It turned out, ultimately, that we had done it more or less correctly, but I didn't feel comfortable with it. That was partly because of a Permanent Secretary who was very committed to following the advice of his advisers, who happened to be

people in the City and who may have had a vested interest in the way it was done. So that left a bad taste [with me]. What I insisted on doing was to get in an independent person, a Labour former Finance Minister, to review it and tell us whether we had actually done the right thing in the right way. The Permanent Secretary, in particular, was absolutely adamant that we shouldn't rake over the coals, but I insisted on it. The study took place, and he broadly exonerated me and the department from having seriously mis-sold it. But that whole episode felt like a classic *Yes Minister* type of situation.

My special adviser was very good in this instance. He said, 'Look, when it comes down to it, you've got to trust these guys, the specialists who are doing this IPO. You've got to trust them.' If he had told me to stick my neck out and do something differently, I'd have probably gone along with it, but I was on the edge, and he wanted me to go along with civil service advice.

Ministers and civil servants are not alone in their relationship. As the role and number of special advisers has grown over recent years, they have become an intrinsic part of governance. Several SpAds I have spoken to described themselves as a bridge between ministers under enormous pressure, who sometimes lose sight of what's going on, and overly cautious, unimaginative, institutionalised civil servants. This may not be a wholly fair characterisation, but it provides an insight into where many advisers feel their role is and also the important function they can perform: bridging a gap between ministers and civil servants. Fundamentally, SpAds can ensure civil servants are not caught in the political elements of a minister's activity. But good ones can also help de-escalate conflict and find resolution which neither civil servants nor ministers could carry alone. I asked David Gauke about his experience with conflict, as a minister. He said:

> [At the MOJ] there were one or two areas where I took a different approach to the issue of prisoners than the department, although I understood why the department took their particular position. They were, I think, scarred by suicide cases that had occurred amongst trans prisoners and, understandably, were worried about that. I completely understood and supported that. But then there was the issue of biologically male prisoners on a female estate and issues were emerging, so I wanted to be a bit more cautious. I didn't want to turn that into a big political issue; I just wanted to kind of quietly change the approach.

I asked how he managed that quiet change in approach, as institutional positions can be difficult to shift. He replied:

> It can, but in the end, ministers decide. It was an evolving story at the point that I left and I suppose there can be a certain persistence required. I remember my SpAds being very engaged with it and helpful in managing it. It was a smallish issue and I just wanted a different tone. I wasn't trying to be a culture warrior and it wasn't really a central policy for me, but I felt the department's instincts were heavily focused on health issues and suicide risk for trans prisoners and less focused on the safety of female prisoners in the female estate. I can remember my SpAds saying, 'We've had another piece of advice, and it's still orientated this way' and we're pushing back on it and [my response was] 'Great, keep at it.' It was

at that level. It wasn't fundamental and nor was I trying to turn it into a big issue to burnish my credentials.

This role for SpAds reflects a modern understanding of their purpose, in understanding the mind of the minister to the extent that they know exactly what they will think. This, by extension, allows civil servants to almost (but not quite) have preliminary conversations with (the mind of) a minister in advance of bringing them advice or a recommendation. But conflict still happens and there will always be clashes between the political urgency of the minister and the civil servants' realistic assessment of delivering the minister's ideas. I asked Clare Moriarty about bridging the gap, when a minister asks for something but civil servants don't think it can be done. She highlighted:

> You're always finding ways in which you can make things possible because the answer to those questions is 'OK, so you can't have it exactly the way that you want it, but is there a version of this that can be done?' In terms of conflict, the first stop would always be to understand whether it really is a conflict or whether it's a different way of expressing things that are important. The classic civil service thing is that the minister says, 'I want to do X,' and the civil service blanches and thinks, 'Well, you can't do X,' and seeks to have a conversation where they say to the minister, 'Actually, to do precisely what you've asked for would be pretty difficult, but if we can have a conversation about where it is you're trying to get to, we are absolutely in the market for finding a way that is practical that will get you to that point.' That should always be a good answer.

Sometimes ministers are less interested in the outcome and more interested in the precise thing that they want to do. In which case, I might flip the conversation over and say, 'OK, so it's not a question of you wanting this outcome and we can find a different way, you just really want this thing.' At that point, we want to find out more about the thing they want and try to understand the circumstances in which that thing would make sense. Is there something that the civil service is missing?

One of the things that I spent a lot of time saying to people is that you have to increase the margin of appreciation, particularly where the civil service's instinct may be to think something is a terrible idea or not possible. Actually, sometimes they *are* possible. I think one of the lessons of Brexit was that the minister said, 'We're going to do this.' And the civil service got very entrenched in some places in saying, 'Well, you can't, that's not possible.' Some of it turned out not to be possible. But in other cases, very unlikely things can actually happen. So you have to give quite a big margin of appreciation.

If the conflict is about whether or not something is possible or if something is more imaginary than real, it's important to recognise there may be a conflict. Sometimes when things felt challenging with some ministers, I would explicitly think, 'Well, is there a world in which this might make perfectly good sense, even if it's not the world that I'm used to inhabiting?' And if it was reasonable for a minister to say so, then I would do my best to make sure that it did happen, even if it went against some of the natural instincts of the civil service.

Sufficient self-reflection and the ability to step back and look for the minister's perspective provide good conditions for demonstrating empathy and building trust. It makes sense that if the minister believes civil servants are really looking for the world in which the policy idea can be delivered, they can trust that there is a commitment to support and ensure the minister's success. In the moments when the minister's and civil servant's perspective is aligned, this will not be such a problem. But that is not always the case.

In the process of building a relationship with the minister, senior civil servants (and particularly Permanent Secretaries) also face an issue of timing any difficult conversations or potential conflict. In a football match, convention dictates that a referee generally does not brandish a yellow card to players in the first few minutes, in order to let players settle and the game to generate some momentum. With regard to building a relationship with incoming ministers, I asked Philip Rutnam whether timing the first 'no' was something Permanent Secretaries needed to consider. He replied:

> It all depends on the issue, the context, the significance of it and also on the relationship. In the early days of any minister, particularly if he or she is relatively new to senior office, the most important thing for the Permanent Secretary and the top of the department is to create that relationship. It would need to be something really serious and clear cut for you to feel the need to go in to the new Secretary of State in the first twenty-four hours and say, 'I really don't think you can do this.' The kind of thing that could come up during the early days and that would need addressing is more likely a proprietary issue than a policy issue. I have to say, it never actually happened to me, but it's conceivable you might find a new minister who doesn't necessarily understand the rules around use of public resources or public money or cars or official travel or appointments, something like that. And

you may need to intervene quickly to protect the public purse but also to protect the minister's own interests. In my experience, that kind of thing usually happens inadvertently because they just don't know what the rules are. That's not absolutely always the case, but more often than not it is. In general, the priority in the first weeks and months – not just days – is to get that relationship going and show that the department really is there to serve. It exists to serve the public interest by serving ministers.

There were occasions where I had to tell ministers that what they wanted to do was a proprietary issue. First of all, I would advise, of course, and explain that 'it's not a good idea to be lobbying X or Y in relation to this business which happens to be in your constituency. Not a good idea.' If they didn't accept that advice, I might need to explain in more detail, perhaps get somebody else to add to my explanation as to why it might not be a good idea. At the end of the day, depending on who it is, they might need to be told. And for junior ministers, that's something which may be necessary. For a Secretary of State, it's still in the realm of advice, but it could be quite firm advice.

All kinds of practical issues can come up where [a minister] might want to do something different from the official advice, but it rarely actually became a conflict as such, because what you're trying to do is turn a disagreement into a calm, professional process of: here are the facts, here's the framework we're operating within, here are the reasons, therefore, why doing this or doing that is not a good idea in our view.

Permanent Secretaries are deconflicting things most of the time, rather than escalating things into conflict. There were occasional things where there were announcements towards the back end of a parliament and it was clear that what was being presented was very political and might raise serious questions about value for money or, in some cases, propriety. And you might need to be firmer then, because the scope for misalignment with the standards that we operated to was greater, but you're still trying to find ways through and to avoid conflict. Typically, the worst that might happen is you're asking for a ministerial direction, which is an appropriate mechanism to my mind for settling that, recognising the respective professional roles. With the Secretaries of State I worked with, I did ask for a number of directions. And they were always, after discussion, happy to give them, because they understood the difference in our roles.

The final point, about ministerial directions, is an important one. Civil servants are tasked with executing the decisions of ministers, regardless of their personal opinions on the matter. However, as each Permanent Secretary serves as the accounting officer for their department, they hold direct accountability to Parliament for public spending. Consequently, they are obligated to obtain ministerial approval for any financial decisions that fail to satisfy the four tests of regularity, propriety, value for money and feasibility. The accounting officer (Permanent Secretary) must ask for a written direction to continue from the Secretary of State. At this point, it becomes the minister who bears responsibility for the use of public money. One of the ministerial directions Philip Rutnam had requested related to the ill-fated London Garden Bridge project. This caused immense frustration at the centre of government,[5] but Rutnam's insistence on a direction was vindicated, as it was later revealed that the projections of return on investment were (to be generous) built on sand rather than rock.

Most ministerial directions relate to value for money. Amongst the ministerial directions that Jonathan Slater issued (as a Permanent Secretary) was the very first feasibility direction in 2018. This related to the introduction of T-levels (technical-based qualifications), which Education Minister Damian Hinds (and Prime Minister Theresa May) instructed to be rolled out by 2020. Slater had concerns about the speed of implementation. I wanted to understand more about his experience with ministerial directions but also to gain a better understanding of his views on saying 'no' to ministers, which is where we started. He said:

> I don't think it is the job of the civil service to say, 'I wouldn't do that if I were you.' It is the job of the civil service to understand what the Secretary of State's outcome or ambition is, to identify the four or five different options they might take towards accomplishing that and the pros and cons of each. For some of those options, there might be a lot more cons than pros. But that is their job. It is not their job to say, 'As a result of this, don't do A, do B.' The whole point of politics is that there isn't a right answer to the question: which do you do? It depends on what your objective is. If there was a right answer, we wouldn't need politicians.
>
> You may find that I'm unusual in this. For example, Andrew Lansley comes in, and he wants to reform the NHS. It's not your job to say no. It is definitely your job to say, 'If you do some big top-down reorganisation of the NHS, these are the downsides. And also these are the upsides.' The risk is that you don't do that because you fear that he's not going to want to know the downsides, that he's going to want you to just crack on. And it's a double risk in circumstances where the two of you don't know each other very well because you only just started. That's the risk.

As we have established, rather than saying no, there are points where a Permanent Secretary (as the accounting officer) does not believe a policy satisfies the tests of public spending and therefore requires the minister to make a political decision and take further responsibility. This is a perfectly reasonable aspect of the system. In 2010, minister John Denham said, 'There is no point having a democracy if ministers are unable to make a judgement that civil servants are wrong.'[6] It is a good point. But Slater's request for a ministerial direction on T-levels was the first relating to feasibility. He shared some of his experience:

> I didn't really get very much support at all. There's a Treasury officer of accounts in the Treasury, who oversees this process, and so it was my job to have a conversation with him in advance. It's good to have somebody like that who can explain the technicalities of it to you, what you've got to do and what you shouldn't do. But that's it. I was looking back for prior examples to learn from, and I couldn't find any in the context that I was operating, which was about feasibility rather than value for money. So that was problematic.
>
> The point I was making to the Secretary of State and the Prime Minister was that there was a significant risk if they implemented T-levels at the speed they wanted and that it wouldn't really work. But it seemed to me completely legitimate for politicians to decide that speed was more important. That's not bad. You create momentum even if there's a risk that it'll be slow, or if there's a risk not many people will take it up. That's a legitimate choice. Fast equals few; slow equals more. There's not a right or wrong answer. I said to my minister that there was a significant risk that

it won't really be able to get going at the speed he wanted to do it. That assessment came from the team doing the work, rather than me, but I looked into it in detail and I agreed with them. If the minister then decides to do it, then there is inevitably a ministerial direction coming. There isn't very much to think about. Either that's true or isn't right. If it's not true, don't say it. If it is true and they decide to do it anyway, issue a direction. It should be straightforward. It shouldn't be a big deal. It shouldn't be courageous. It should just be a system operating.

In my view, it wasn't my job to persuade Damian Hinds not to do it at the speed he wants to do it. It was my job to make sure that he knows that if he decides to do it at that speed, I think the adverse consequences for feasibility are X and Y. And then for him to decide. Not to think I was trying to stop him.

I felt that I was a bit of the exception here, but typically, Permanent Secretaries would think of ministerial directions as something to be threatened, in order to persuade the Secretary of State not to do it. And it's therefore a failure to issue the ministerial direction because that meant you didn't manage to persuade them. And the success is therefore that fewer mistakes were made by government because ministers listened in the end so avoided ministerial direction. In fact, once the Prime Minister had decided to stick with the timetable, despite my advice, I was asked, what's the point of direction? To which the answer is: that's the system. Parliament wants to know if ministers are deliberately choosing to take risks that civil servants would say are risky. That's the system working. It's not a tool designed to stop them doing things.

It would be typically seen by a Permanent Secretary as a sign of failure, in practice, that a [ministerial] direction had to be sought because you hadn't been able to use it to leverage what you wanted. I think that's the wrong way of thinking about it. It's completely fine to choose speed over feasibility but to do so openly. And if Parliament wants, as it does, the civil service to draw to the attention of the minister the risks, that's the check and balance in the system. You can go fast, even if the consequences are a risk to feasibility, but the check and balance in that system is that it will be publicly clear that that's what you've done. What's wrong with that system? It's a good system. But a system which says, 'You're allowed to take risks, but your Permanent Secretary has got to try to stop you as much as they possibly can,' is a different system. And I don't think that's a democratic one.

I had heard of many closed-door examples of a request for a ministerial direction being used as a deterrent. This framing suggests the threat of issuing the request might be strong enough to stop or reverse the decision of a minister, by making them accountable for the outcome. This returns to the adversarial structure sometimes encouraged in the workings of government, but it also undermines the interdependency between ministers and civil servants. Jonathan continued:

One never knows [about other examples of directions being used as a deterrent], of course, because one's never in the room. But that was the impression I got. My only direct experience of this was being asked, 'Why are you issuing? Why are you seeking direction if you've lost the argument?' To which I said, 'No, I've not lost the argument. I'm just doing the system.'

So, what is causing ministerial directions to be thought of as a deterrent rather than a proper functioning of the system? Jonathan replied:

> It's not credible. The system doesn't work when everything is secret for twenty years, other than a small number of things in the category we've described. When things are done in secret, that becomes the predominant culture of the organisation. That's what people learn to do. We shouldn't be surprised if an operation that works in secret finds it hard to come out into the blinking light of day, occasionally. We shouldn't be surprised if it thinks of that as a failure, because the system working is secret. It's all very well to say, 'It's a secret world. Except if they want to take risks and then it's a public world.' But that's not the way that people behave. To which my answer is: well, let's make it a public world, then.

This lack of transparency and leveraging of the system are not tools that build trust between people. It is understandable that Permanent Secretaries might feel cornered on an idea that does not appear to meet public spending criteria and that it is easier and quicker to encourage abandonment of the idea, rather than see through the process in place. There is also a reluctance to publicly display differences with the minister. That is more the fault of the system and its expectations than it is of those individuals. Jonathan continued:

> It was important for Damian to know that I wasn't just trying to block him or didn't care about what he was trying to achieve. Therefore, the way that I phrased my public request was important. That it's completely legitimate if you want to go fast, which I think I would have said. And then when I was asked about it, in select committees, that's what I said.

I only needed to do it once. And with one Secretary of State. It's possible to imagine it being different in certain different circumstances. I think that a Secretary of State will generally see it as advantageous if their senior civil servants are advising them without fear or favour, so long as they think they're doing that for the right reasons and without some sort of ulterior motive.

Coalition minister Francis Maude said, 'Any minister should be confident enough in the judgement he or she has made to be willing to justify it in public'.[7] There is truth in that. An adjustment in expectations to allow ministerial directions to function as they are designed to would allow more freedom for ministers, be more democratic and help increase transparency. That would strengthen the ability of civil servants and ministers to navigate disagreement.

DIFFERENCES

There are lots of differences between ministers and civil servants. Fundamentally, there is a difference in roles, whereby civil servants advise and ministers decide, but there are also different lenses and cultures through which both view the world. Of course, not all ministers are the same, nor are all civil servants, but there are some things which characterise Whitehall (in particular) that distinguishes officials from politicians. Andrew Lansley had been both a civil servant and a minister. I asked him about his experience of the major differences between them. He replied:

> From a Secretary of State's, and any minister's, point of view, the desire to introduce complexity is a fundamental difference between civil servants and every politician, who constantly wants

to simplify. That is one of the big cultural divides between [civil servants and ministers] that has to be managed. It's difficult to manage, because it's very hard for ministers to say, 'No, it'll be fine, we'll just state what we want and off we go.' And that's because of our legislative system. When we look at bills in the House of Lords, quite often the policy is in the first half-dozen clauses. The next seventy-eight clauses are all about what happens when everything goes wrong.

But who's responsible and who has to answer for it? And what are the penalties? And what if you don't do what you're told to do? It's not like French legislation or even Roman law. Once upon a time, common law and statute law were a lot simpler than coded Roman law, but it's now completely reversed. Roman law is much simpler because its purpose is to say: you're not allowed to do anything unless we tell you can do it, and you can do it for certain reasons to meet the purposes of our legal construct. Whereas we always create something that says: you can do whatever you like unless you're told not to. Which means we have to specify precisely what you're not allowed to do, which has resulted in our legislation becoming progressively more complicated.

Rory Stewart had also been a civil servant in his early career (as a diplomat), before later becoming an MP and then a minister. He had expressed a lot of frustration with the way civil servants operate and some of their resistance to engage with his suggestions and directions, if they competed with the status quo. I wondered whether Andrew's notion about simplicity, complexity and Westminster's legislative system had been a factor in some of Rory's frustrations. Rory told me:

At DfID, I was supposed to sign off on every business case over £10 million. Each one of these was 100 pages long. And some weeks, they would drop fourteen of them on my desk. Did they really think that I'm reading 1,400 pages, along with all the other stuff I'm doing in this department and as an MP and in Parliament? And if not, what kind of accountability are civil servants getting here? What is it they think is happening? Am I really making a decision? Are they really producing information for me to read and assess? If so, that is ridiculous.

Much more helpful, if it was a question of whether they genuinely wanted my view on whether the education programme in Lebanon, for example, was a good idea, would be for me to talk for twenty minutes to the person who designed the education programme in Lebanon and be reassured that they seem to sound like they knew what they're talking about. The other thing that we're not honest about is that ministers have very little information on which to make a decision. I'm not an expert on the details of what the Education Ministry is doing with refugees in Lebanon. I barely know whether Syrian refugees are allowed in classrooms or not. So pretending that I can make a decision on whether we should be putting £40 million through UNICEF with the Lebanese government, as opposed to putting it through Save the Children with the Lebanese government, is ridiculous. All I can do is try to talk to the programme manager and get a sense of whether they sound reasonable, sane and as though they know what they're talking about. And if they say to me, 'Listen, Rory, I understand it's a bit confusing. Save the Children is very good in Afghanistan, but they're not so good in Lebanon. The UNICEF office has been there since 1952, and nine of them speak Arabic fluently. They're very close to the ministry, and I think they'll be a great deliverer.' What else have I got to say except, 'Great, go for it.'

It struck me that this approach may play more to a minister's strengths and resources. Ministers have spent tens of thousands of hours talking to people as they have made their way up the political ladder. Face to face, most ministers are usually good with people (if sometimes inexperienced at managing them). But they are also extremely time-poor. I raised this with Rory and he replied:

> Yes, this would have played to the fact that the minister is time-poor; giving them lots of documents is nonsensical. But there is an ignorance point which is really central. Part of the problem is there's an illusion that ministers can master their briefs and that civil servants have mastered their briefs, whereas in fact, civil servants are moved around very quickly. Of the people briefing me on Afghanistan, 90 per cent of them had never been to Afghanistan. They were junior officials who have not been in the department for very long or they had been moved from some other desk. They were then given some proposal, which was probably cooked up by the ambassador in Kabul talking to his Japanese colleague, where he's going to give some money to the police. They then have to put that into a document and present it to me.
>
> But if the minister understood that backstory more clearly, and the civil servants were more open about that, you wouldn't get stuck in these very painful conversations. It's because they're presenting themselves to me as though they are deep experts on policing in Afghanistan that I get annoyed. If they said to me, 'Listen, Minister, this is a kind of fait accompli. I'm really sorry, but the ambassadors promised it to the Japanese ambassador, and

it's part of a more complicated relationship with the Afghan government. I'm sure you're right that the Afghan police is a waste of time, and this money will be largely wasted, but there's a bigger picture here. We're spending £100 million in Afghanistan, and this is a relatively small fraction of it.' You can totally imagine my signing off on it because I'm being treated as an adult. I'm being made complicit in this rather complicated political calculation. But if they present it to me technocratically, and try to convince me that the Afghan police is anything other than a complete, corrupt waste of time, then of course I'm going to dig my heels in.

Civil servants can find themselves in a difficult position, particularly when they are in a policy environment which encourages consideration of all eventualities. But Andrew Lansley raised another point to consider:

The Freedom of Information (FOI) Act operates, in theory, on the basis that the advice given to ministers by their senior civil servants is privileged. But it isn't. It's constantly being found out, and if it hasn't been found through the FOI, it's being exposed through inquiries and public inquiries. This is potentially very disruptive of trust because I think ministers now are, correctly, assuming that many civil servants are writing for the record rather than giving them their open and frank advice. Freedom of Information has made it very difficult to do things without anybody knowing, even if the public interest is not served by people knowing. Public interest doesn't require to know all the workings. It requires to know what your policies are and who's influenced them.

This may not have been exactly what was happening in Rory's case, but it's a consideration for ministers and a potential issue in encouraging more frankness, openness and authenticity from civil servants. Civil servants are certainly very aware of Freedom of Information requests and that everything produced will stand on record. While FOI helps bring transparency to some of the opaqueness of government, it can make it more difficult to address sensitive and complex topics which require open and frank conversations. Civil servants still manage to ensure these happen, but it is a challenge which frames how they need to operate.

Clare Moriarty worked with Rory Stewart at DEFRA. I asked her about some of the differences between civil servants and ministers. She highlighted:

> When Gus O'Donnell was the Cabinet Secretary, he had the four Ps of performance, pride, pace and passion. Passion is really interesting because civil servants are not invited to be passionate. When your job is to give the best advice that you can and then implement whatever you've been told to implement, whether or not it corresponds to the advice, passion tends to be something that gets in the way more than being a benefit.
>
> For a politician, for a minister, passion – really believing in what you are promoting – is something that is important and will help you. Whereas for a civil service leader, passion is something that you have to manage quite carefully. All of the signals tell you to be able to say one thing and do another, which is quite difficult. When I started saying to people that the Darwinian survival characteristic of the senior civil servant is the ability to say one thing and do another, there was generally a sharp intake of breath. But it was something that I said, because other people had said things that indicated this was the case but they didn't necessarily want

to say it out loud. It's an incredibly difficult position to maintain while also being an authentic leader and connecting with people and doing all the things that create followership.

I'm also very interested in conscience management. An academic, expert adviser or consultant has the luxury of saying what they think and walking away with their conscience untroubled. The civil servant, meanwhile, is engaged in a constant process of conscience management. How do you manage through a situation where you might feel, instinctively, unhappy about something? I had to constantly work out which things were worth asking about and which weren't.

These distinctions are important. Senior civil servants, in particular, are constantly having to manage themselves and adjust to navigate how they can help deliver for a minister. Ministers, meanwhile, can be driven by instincts and preferences. These are the unseen complexities of government and of the relationship between ministers and civil servants. And it is the unseen elements and pressures of the relationship that can have the most significant effects on its management by both ministers and civil servants.

WHAT YOU DON'T SEE

'The thing I had to get used to was the red box with ten to twenty [daily] briefs,' Vince Cable told me:

> Partly because of the nature of the subject, they were very, very complicated. And I'm not sure the civil servants appreciated that as a politician, you're dealing with Parliament, you're dealing with the media and you have to make decisions. So having big,

complicated, detailed descriptions of the policy analysis was difficult and didn't always help. I think that much more simplified, clear guidance on complicated policy would have been more helpful.

There are some things about civil servants that ministers don't see. And there are aspects of the life of a minister that civil servants are less aware of. Lots of ministers complain about the lengths and number of submissions and briefings in their red box. The civil service has taken steps to improve the brevity of submissions and briefings with sustained investment in training for officials. Indeed, in recent years, 'advising and briefing' training famously (in government learning circles) overtook 'preparing for retirement' as the most popular course across the civil service. But there is still work to do and ministers continue to note the challenge of the sheer number of briefings and submissions that they have to get through.

Ministers also wear several hats with commitments to Parliament, constituents and the party. Robert Halfon represented a classic bellwether marginal seat (Harlow), which Labour won in the 2024 election (Robert did not stand for re-election). I asked him whether the civil servants he worked with really grasped the level of constituency involvement that MPs continue to have, even if they become a minister. He said:

> I think that they gradually got to learn about it. I was a very active constituency MP. I love my constituency and it's going to be a wrench to give it all up. I would do stuff on Thursdays and Fridays, although I would usually encompass FE [further education] college visits then. I used to go all over the country, thousands

and thousands of miles getting up at five in the morning, getting to the north-west or whatever. I did 843 miles in five days at one time in National Apprenticeship Week. From Cumbria to Cornwall, I've been all over the country seeing FE colleges, universities, all of it. I think it's hard for [civil servants] to understand the constituency pressures on an MP, particularly in a marginal seat or at least not a traditionally safe one. You simply have to do stuff all day Friday and Saturday, even though you've got to give evidence at a select committee on Monday or Tuesday. It's hard for them to understand that at first, but as they get to know you and you explain it to them, things improve.

I think all civil servants should shadow an MP in their constituency on a few Fridays, so they see an MP do a surgery. Not to comment or get actively involved, but just to observe. To see the MP going to a school, a factory or a business would help them understand what's involved on that side of things. Even to see a local party HQ with leaflets being prepared and bundled or MPs canvassing on a Saturday morning. It's very hard, if you've never seen it, to understand that it's not just a job – it's a way of life. I would recommend that civil servants should shadow MPs to really understand what they have to do in their constituencies.

It's an important distinction that different MPs have different constituency pressures. Private offices and those working closely with a minister (when they are an MP) will appreciate the travel time required to get to and from a constituency that is far from London or lacking in direct routes, but many other civil servants may not realise the strain this can cause. The physical and electoral pressures on an MP in a safe seat in the south-east of England are very different to those on an MP in a marginal seat 200+ miles from Westminster. David Gauke held the former of these but highlighted that all MPs are still committed to their role in Parliament:

> One point I would make about the civil service is they can struggle with the parliamentary side and understanding that sometimes you do need to spend some time over in Parliament. Or that the diary today is not going to work because this or that is going to happen in Parliament. Or that I really do need time with my parliamentary team.

There are also many aspects and strengths of the civil service that ministers forget about or do not see. Una O'Brien pointed out one of these: 'In my experience, policy officials in the senior civil service work collaboratively within and across multidisciplinary teams very effectively. This is rarely visible to ministers, as they tend to conduct their interaction with a department through a series of roundtable or one-to-one meetings.'

Having limited engagement with officials outside of their immediate vicinity can restrict a minister's understanding of what really happens in a department. Sue Owen had worked in several government departments and we had talked about how difficult it can be for ministers to see the level of complexity in delivering big policy changes. She highlighted:

> People always forget that less than 10 per cent of the civil service is working in Whitehall, and less than 5 per cent is working on policy. Most civil servants are doing things like border control or call centres about pensions or job centres, that kind of thing. I think ministers don't see that side very much.

When I was in DWP, Iain Duncan Smith wanted to basically reform the whole welfare state, which was a really big thing and something that had always been in the 'too difficult' box. And the trouble was that he wanted to do it very quickly because he was worried that George Osborne would get fed up with him or that they wouldn't win the election. So we all said this is a ten- to twelve-year project, but he wanted it done in three to four years. Which inevitably meant thinking, right at the start, about how things were going to be delivered, not just what the policy was. A big thing is trying to get ministers to see the nuts and bolts of things and to understand that if you are going to change these things, you've got to change the computer systems, everything in the job centres and the processing centres and all that kind of thing. Helping them understand that complexity is a good idea because it helps them get some kind of handle on it. Encouraging them to go on visits to things is good because they can see it in action. But there's still this terrible tension between the maximum length of a parliament – five years – and some things that you can't do in that amount of time.

Jonathan Slater built on this idea of the tension between political urgency and the reality of delivery:

It's self-evident that changing anything complicated takes time and the process takes longer than the average life expectancy of a Cabinet minister – which they are aware of. I worked for intelligent Cabinet ministers, generally. Not always, but generally. They are perfectly aware, as I was, of the fact that they want to impress the Prime Minister, and quickly. Because it's going to be the PM that decides what their next move is, and achieving improvement in exam results in five years' time, for example, wasn't going to be the answer to that question.

There's no reason why you can't have an open conversation with your Secretary of State, and other ministers, about the tension between those two things. Doing things to keep up the popularity of the Secretary of State and the government, well, that's politics – that's democracy. But it would be weird for the civil service to say, 'Stop focusing on whether the government and you [the Secretary of State] are popular.' Equally, it would be very disappointing if the Secretary of State said, 'The only thing I'm interested in is my popularity today.' So you're trying to get a balance between the two and to be really clear when you're in one mode and when you're in the other mode, so that nobody is confused or disappointed.

I was struck by how little they saw of what most civil servants do. I tried to make sure, as the Permanent Secretary for the Department for Education, that whatever the subject matter the Secretary of State and I were discussing, they always had a Grade 7 – upper mid-level role – in the room who knew the most about it. And that turned out to be really quite a countercultural thing. Some ministers in some departments didn't want that; they just wanted the most senior people in the room. But the most senior people in the room are the people who know least about it. Part of my job was to get the junior person who knew most about the subject in the room. Sure, I would have some senior people around to help them navigate the politics, but I would then get the minister to see all that the civil service can offer.

It is true that there is some burden on a Permanent Secretary (and their senior civil service) to help a minister engage with the department and to find the right people to be in the room to enable good decision-making. Often the best way to help someone see what they cannot is to make it visible. The pressure on ministers is enormous. But there is also a great deal of pressure on civil servants, who are trying to balance many competing demands. I talked to Clare Moriarty about this, who offered some thoughtful reflections:

> There's a huge pressure on the civil service to be objective and being objective gets translated into being detached, analytical and intellectual. I think that's a historic culture. But there is also a difficulty of operating in an environment where civil servants are expected to adhere to the civil service values, including impartiality, while simultaneously operating all the time in a political environment. The most important thing to do in terms of building trust with ministers is to show them that you get it. That's not about showing that you're politically aligned, but it is about showing the empathy to understand what it is that they are trying to achieve.
>
> So some things which might appear capricious to the civil service actually make complete sense when you see them in the context of the different pressures that exist on ministers. But it's hard, then, for civil servants who are constantly being asked to hold to different sets of values. You're walking a line whereby however definitive you feel that the advice points in one particular direction, if a minister decides to do the opposite, then it is your responsibility, under the Civil Service Code, to get on and implement whatever they've decided. So you can't afford to invest yourself too much in what you're doing because you could create a situation where it becomes almost impossible get on and do the implementation properly. There are lots of things pushing on

people to hold back, which then fight against being authentic. Everything about being in the system pushes you towards not being authentic. And then we turn around and say to people – quite rightly – 'Be authentic.' They're both truths, but they coexist with a certain amount of discomfort.

Governing is complex, and people are complex. Those complexities are magnified and pressurised in a political environment. Finding ways to connect and triangulate authenticity and empathy with logic will not eliminate these complexities, but it will help build trust and see that civil servants and ministers are not frustrating opponents but people. People with hopes, families and who want better outcomes for the country.

WE ARE PEOPLE

'I kept a regular weekly advice surgery, and a very good case worker followed stuff up. I always took Friday afternoon off because I had a dancing lesson, which I combined with the surgery,' Vince Cable told me.

He had been a popular MP in Twickenham. The life of a minister has an unending waitlist of demands, which could consume several lifetimes, and lots (particularly Secretaries of State) do not continue with their weekly constituency surgery on a Friday – the time traditionally set aside for seeing local constituents. With all of the other hats a minister wears, they are also a person with all the basic needs of any human. Vince continued:

> I had a family and I'm very lucky. I had a wife with whom I had a very good relationship; my children were close, got on well and

were always very supportive. And one or two friends, including Lord Oakeshott. But the problem is the friendships got frayed because of all the frictions within the coalition years, so I didn't have many friends outside of my family. But I had two political colleagues, notably the parliamentary [private secretary] Tessa Munt, who was MP for Wells in Somerset. She was absolutely brilliant, and she managed a lot of the tricky relationships in Parliament, which the civil service didn't want to deal with. I was constantly bombarded with MPs saying, 'Why aren't you providing money for a factory in my constituency?', blah blah blah, that kind of stuff all the time. She managed that and set up regular surgeries for me to talk to MPs. So I had a very good support network organised by her and one or two other sympathetic MPs who were trying to be helpful. My private office were also very supportive. Then I had the same Permanent Secretary for three years and I got on well with him. And then I had my team in Twickenham, who were really excellent. I had them for nearly twenty years and they were very loyal, very competent and very nice. And they'd been through very bad experiences because people were targeting me locally. So they were also a key part of my support network.

Support networks are critical for ministers to stay grounded and look after their mental health. That is the case for a minister's political life as well as their personal life (as Vince confirmed). Not all ministers (or MPs) are equal, in that they don't all have equal circumstances. I asked David Gauke about his own support network. He replied:

I'm conscious, since I left politics, how much more time I now spend with my family, and how I appreciate that. I'm conscious that on one level, I couldn't be fully there for them, as much as I might have been. But having said that, I was fortunate. I had a constituency that was just outside London and I spent every night in the family home; I was fortunate I could make it work. If I had a constituency the other side of the country, that would have been another matter. I do not envy MPs who have to make a choice on where the kids go to school, for example. Do the kids have to go to school in the constituency? That means you don't see them Monday to Thursday. Personally, I think MPs should be strong enough to say no and that the family is going to live with them. That they will come up to the constituency at the weekends and maybe the family will come up but no moving school. You have to be quite gutsy to do it, but I think I would advise any MP to, if they are facing that decision.

Pretty well every Sunday morning, I was still able to be there watching the kids play sport. I might have been on the mobile phone talking to colleagues at the same time and during some practice sessions disappeared off to the car and gone through a few ministerial papers, but I was still able to run that part of my life. I also could actually do the constituency work. My parliamentary office was very effective and it was a sort of safe seat, so I wasn't under too much risk. It was an incredibly busy and frantic period, but I felt I was just about able to keep everything going. Looking back, in truth, it was a very exciting time. Some moments were very dispiriting and others very stressful, but it was just about doable.

Vince and David had talked about their families being part of their support network, but every minister must also make decisions about where to spend their time. This can cause major strain on relationships and I know of several examples where marriages have broken down because a minister has committed to the role at the expense of their spouse. Ministers have to be intentional about connecting and being with their family as well as the job, because the appetite of the job is insatiable and will never stop consuming a minister's time.

Beyond acknowledging the human pressures which ministers face, there is also the evolution throughout their time in office. Over the lifespan of a ministerial role, the person occupying it will inevitably change. Particularly with first-time ministers or Secretaries of State, civil servants have to keep getting to know the changing minister over the different stages of their time in office (which is reflected in the structure of this book). Lots of Permanent Secretaries reflect on ministers who 'settle' into a role and who become more competent and perhaps more decisive. I asked David about his own experience of changing over time. He highlighted:

> On reflection, I probably became more open as a person, but also over time you develop more confidence. Before 2010, I had barely even stepped inside a government department and didn't really know civil servants at all. By the time I finished in July 2019, I had been in for nine years. Not that many people alive today have been ministers for nine years or more. By the end, I was a pretty experienced minister and with that comes a degree of confidence. The role of Secretary of State is a bit different to being a junior minister, in that you are more big picture and strategic. I tried to be reasonably strategic as a junior minister, but you're dealing consistently with more senior officials as the Secretary of State.
>
> Something that helped my confidence increase was the quality of officials I worked with early on. I was always impressed by how

good the junior officials were at the Treasury. I should add that the senior officials were excellent, but the depth that you'd have was impressive. For example, a 25-year-old in charge of gambling tax and completely on top of it. Everyone was pretty impressive. I think I always had quite a relaxed approach towards civil servants. I was never into throwing mobile phones or shouting and screaming. That is something that didn't change over time.

Vince Cable spent five years leading the same department. I asked him how he changed over that time. He reflected:

The first year felt like lurching from one nightmare to another, just trying to understand what was going on, trying to make decisions under pressure, trying to learn how to do things when all these difficult decisions were having to be made. The last year was totally different because I'd been there years. I actually knew more about most of these issues than any of the civil servants and was able to correct them when they failed to remember what was supposed to be going on. In terms of departmental management, I was totally in control of BIS at that point. But politically, it was very uncomfortable because we were heading for very bad results, and I wasn't able to do a great deal. I grew much thicker-skinned over that later period.

Being on top of the brief is (hopefully) to be expected over time. But attitude and relationships are vital to ministerial success.

'By the time I became a Minister of State at DWP, I had learned a lot, but you're still quite lonely about things,' Caroline Flint told me:

Along the way, you build up some support on the back benches, which is helpful. People are interested in your policy area and you develop relationships with them. Building up your support amongst the backbenchers on your side is a really important element, as they will then put in questions.

If civil servants think you're really interested and you're not just biding time for the next ministerial job, thinking, 'God, I wish they hadn't given me this; I'd rather be somewhere else,' that counts for something. We all get job satisfaction from knowing that the people we work for actually care. I think they felt, she [Caroline] cares about this, she thinks this is a priority, she's passionate about this. Where that worked well is that they got to understand that I didn't like just sitting in Whitehall. I like to go out and see things for myself. I like to meet different people.

Caroline had raised an important point. MPs are almost always MPs because they want to make things better. Politicians disagree on how that should happen, or what should be prioritised, or whether making things better should be achieved through radical transformation or slow, careful improvements. But, on the whole, they are there because they care about their country. Civil servants also care about their country, about making things better and about public service. It is a distinctive, and human, point of connection. But serving can also be tiring. Robert Halfon talked me through the size of the ministerial workload:

I really love the subject, but the workload is beyond enormous. No one outside it understands, because each stakeholder only sees you engage with them. You have to do three things:
You have to be a minister in Parliament and at any time you could have a UQ, a statement, questions, Westminster Hall

debates. You could also be told to go and cover [for someone else doing those]. There might be a general Education question about schools, which was nothing to do with me, but there's no other minister available. So you're told to go and do it.

You have got your ministerial work. You've got to deal with policy every single day and big decisions about whether you are going to give this grant to an FE college or whatever it may be. Every single day, big stuff comes through. There's very rarely one day when you're not doing that. Then you have to do the hundreds and hundreds of questions. Civil servants draft them, but you often need to change them. They come through all the time, every day. After they've been drafted, I would have to write stuff on the side of the letter. Then I would get submissions. Let's say six submissions in a day, on top of about twenty or thirty letters and maybe anything from ten to twenty written questions every single day.

Then there's cross-government meetings and committees. Michael Gove, for example, ran really impressive levelling-up meetings across government. That might include the Education Minister, the Culture Minister, the Transport Minister or whatever the task force was at that point. Gove's ones were an enormous amount of work because you have to be on top form with him. He was a master craftsman at work, like somebody building a great violin or something. It's unbelievable how he chairs it and sums up everything at the end. Some of the other government ones were just talking shops.

I'm not complaining, but the workload of a minister and the workload of a Secretary of State is ginormous. And it's relentless. You don't have any free time to read anything else or do anything else. It's all-consuming. I don't think ministerial roles in their current format are sustainable. I know it's gone on for years and it's always been like that, and it's unlikely to change. But I think you would get better decision-making if ministers weren't so burdened. There are so many things to do and that could change if we would get better ministers. It burns people out. Most ministers seem to last a maximum of two years, and that's a long one.

Although I'm sad to leave, the one nice thing is that you get a bit of quality of life back. I see my wife, for example, who is a wonderful and kind person. And we can wake up on a Saturday and go to Costa or something. Although not this Saturday, because I'll actually be doing local election campaigning.

I suspect that under an electron microscope, you might see the word 'campaign' written within Robert's DNA.

Alongside all the other relationships a minister considers is that with the Permanent Secretary. This book is focused, heavily, on that particular relationship, but there are human considerations that ministers may overlook. I found Clare Moriarty's reflections thoughtful and helpful:

It is a deeply imbalanced relationship. Andrew Kakabadse famously talked about the unrequited love affair between Permanent Secretaries and Secretaries of State. It was an interesting choice of language, but it is true that it's a relationship in which the Permanent Secretary does pretty much all of the heavy lifting. It's partly to do with the structural nature of being a minister. You've got five or six ministers in a department that could have 3,000, 5,000 or 80,000 civil servants. Ministers are not told they need to build a relationship with their Permanent Secretary, but Permanent Secretaries absolutely are told they need to build a relationship with their minister. Hence the penny in the jar saying. Ministers are not thinking about how they put pennies in the jar or the relationship with officials on the whole, because they've got lots of other things that they're trying to do.

So the emotional labour of building relationships very much sits on the civil service side. That Secretary of State–Permanent Secretary relationship is really critical, and I've seen when it doesn't work. Far more things go wrong than you think would hang on just one single relationship. There's quite a lot of burden of empathy on the Permanent Secretary. Being a politician is a job that is very much about emotions and responding to people and so managing that crossover point is challenging.

Ministers are people. And so are civil servants.

TRUTH, IMPARTIALITY AND AUTHENTICITY

'The one period where I felt the ability to set quite fundamental evidence and advice in front of ministers was really being impaired was after the referendum. Not in the initial period after the referendum but 2019 onwards,' Philip Rutnam opened.

Much of the beginning stages of a minister coming into post is about establishing preferences, priorities and pace for the department, understanding what it does and determining what it should do. After that, the middle phase is dominated by behaviours, working together and political reality. But the basis of successful working between civil servants and ministers in this period rests, absolutely, on trust and the ability of civil servants to present truth, facts and evidence to ministers. Rutnam continued:

There were occasions when I and the top of the department [Home Office] were told very firmly by the Secretary of State's office, 'No, we should not put advice to the Home Secretary because it was not going to be welcome.' It didn't happen very often, but it did happen. It was just about the first time in my career, and certainly the first time on any major issue, that I had a clear warning sound in my head because it put the civil servant in conflict, between the Civil Service Code, the standards to which we had to work and the message being presented. It wasn't quite a written instruction, but it was the message that we were being given from those acting immediately for the Home Secretary, in her office.

It hadn't always been this way in the Home Office. The famed 'hostile environment' policy, introduced by Theresa May in 2012, had probably seeped into the deeper culture of the organisation, but it has always been a defensive department as it deals, primarily, with the idea of 'protecting' the public. When Caroline Flint was a Home Office minister, she had always wanted transparency, to be given all the evidence and to hear any bad news as soon as possible (before there was a surprise on the front page of a newspaper) – Secretary of State David Blunkett took the same approach.

If civil servants are unable to communicate fundamental evidence to ministers, or are told to filter messaging, it is not only the minister who is being put in a compromised position; civil service impartiality is also questioned. The ability to speak without fear or favour behind closed doors is fundamental to the impartiality of civil servants and is part of the foundation on which the relationship with ministers is built. What can civil servants do if this is compromised? Philip Rutnam continued:

> I don't think it is in the country's interest to create a culture amongst civil servants in which it is believed we need to throw ourselves over the ramparts or out of the trenches and into some machine-gun fire coming from politicians. It's about professional tasks, trying to align with ministers' objectives and trying to decompose problems. You get to the core of the problem and by decomposing things, you stand a much better chance of finding solutions which align ministers' objectives with what is doable, what is affordable and what is legal. However, I think we also need to be conscious of the human position that civil servants are in. When I resigned, it was a difficult phase, but, in a sense, I had not that much to lose.

I asked him whether this really was the case, as his resignation statement had included the words 'I know that resigning in this way will have serious implications for me personally'. I asked if that was the case or if we were talking in semantics. He smiled and shrugged:

> I was already a Permanent Secretary. There were some costs to me, but fundamentally, in weighing up, you have to make a choice: do you stand by your principles or do you compromise in some way because there could be benefits? That needs to be recognised. That's a human calculation people will make. I was in one set of circumstances, but it's important to recognise that for somebody who was not so senior, somebody who still wanted to progress further in their career, somebody who had less financial security, they might make a calculation differently.
>
> I do worry about more junior people who are senior civil servants, but perhaps in their late thirties or early forties, are not actually paid that much relative to the level of responsibility; they've

got kids, they've got a mortgage and the pressures on them to conform can feel intense. As Permanent Secretary, I would have meetings in my office in which I was effectively counselling people, trying to calm them, reassure them that even though the SpAd had said they must be [metaphorically] sent to Siberia, they were going to be OK. I would say that we were not, I was not, the organisation was not going to be vindictive, that we were there to support them, political lifespans are shorter and that they still had a career.

In any complex organisation, where there's a career structure and people are encouraged to be ambitious, they've invested personal time and energy in building that career. But over time, their options tend to diminish and they're going to be making calculations about their actions based on the context. If there's a strong message, whether it's coming from the Cabinet Secretary or the Prime Minister, that conduct or action of a certain type is expected, that is likely to have an effect.

I worked for several Cabinet Secretaries. Being a Cabinet Secretary is a very difficult job. They're not perfect, but I would defend them in terms of the standards of conduct that they expected from the [civil servants] in the system. That's very important. However, Cabinet Secretaries can't necessarily protect civil servants that much. If you're a senior civil servant and you are out of favour with the Secretary of State or with the special advisers in your department, you can, depending on the character of the small number of individuals involved, find your career turns to Siberia.

The right way of dealing with this, to my mind, is to try to make sure that we have expectations that are at the right level to support good decision-making, including giving good advice.

That we have systems and processes and a culture that support all of those, rather than to suppose that the answer is heroic action. We should not run any system on the basis that it relies on heroes. We need to move the average standard of conduct, the average quality of advice, just up a few percentage points, then we'll get better results.

The word 'unprecedented' has entered common parlance, particularly since the Covid pandemic. But the use of the word by Lord Kerslake to describe Rutnam's resignation was a self-referential linguistic moment. A Permanent Secretary had not resigned in such a public way before, and certainly not with direct criticism of the behaviour of their Secretary of State or with the promise to take the government to court. Sir Philip Rutnam's reputation was as an experienced, measured leader who, if anything, was possibly too good at sticking to his lines as a civil servant. The person I met was reflective and astute. I asked him about the 'unprecedented' nature of his resignation. He replied:

Yes, it was unprecedented. But it was an unprecedented context. Unprecedented that No. 10, for example, should be briefing the media that they had a 'shit list' of top civil servants that they were planning to get rid of, essentially the Permanent Secretaries in each of the main departments – the Treasury, the Foreign Office, the Home Office – and each of whom left in the end. That was unprecedented. Dominic Cummings's role, as chief of staff, was also unprecedented. To my mind, that raises a series of issues about how much power should be in the hands of somebody who is not accountable to either Parliament or to the Cabinet Secretary. I think [the resignation] was unprecedented, but the context was unprecedented. Is there anything I'd do differently? I actually got on perfectly well with Priti Patel, most of the time. Obviously, we had some differences on particular issues, and I did need to talk to her a number of times about her conduct, but on the whole, we got on perfectly well.

Three weeks before I resigned, we were having very friendly conversations and then the media briefing started. The thing that I remember, in this difficult period of 2019 when No. 10 had suddenly become much more aggressive, was that I felt it was my public duty to stay. Even though I knew other colleagues were leaving or thinking of leaving, I felt it was my public duty to stay because the Home Office is a very difficult and complicated department, and I thought it wouldn't be good for the department for me to leave. Perhaps there's some egotism in that. You always think you're more important than you really are. Everybody's dispensable. Was it the wise decision? Maybe not. I might have chosen to do things differently. But we make our choices and then face the situation that results.

After Philip Rutnam's resignation, Prime Minister Boris Johnson tasked his ethics adviser, Sir Alex Allan, with investigating Priti Patel's behaviour. Several months later, Allan's report concluded that the Home Secretary's actions 'amounted to bullying', citing examples of 'shouting and swearing'. The report also noted that Patel had breached the Ministerial Code, 'even if unintentionally'. In response to Allan's report, Patel said, 'I am sorry that my behaviour in the past has upset people. It has never been my intention to cause upset to anyone.'

Many people will recognise this as a classic 'non-apology' apology. Not 'I'm sorry for my behaviour', but 'I'm sorry you got upset'.

Despite cloaking the evasion of the actual issue (bullying) in what appears to be superficial regret, there was another important issue which Patel raised: intentions. Anyone can say that their intentions are good, even if the impact of their actions is negative. Expressing regret for someone else being upset fails to acknowledge the cause of that upset, and claiming the intention behind the behaviour was good undermines the impact of it – more so when the charge is bullying. Are good intentions enough? They aren't accurately measurable by ourselves or by others and they do not provide a sufficiently reliable pathway to respectful or positive behaviour. Good intentions, alone, are not good enough to build genuine trust. I asked Philip about his thoughts on this and also whether he had reflected on his own response to Priti Patel's behaviour. He replied:

> I think that it's relatively easy to say that we don't intend to do something. But the truth is, we're all grown-ups. We're judged as grown-ups, and we need to be responsible for our actions. Part of that responsibility is being thoughtful about the likely effect. Everybody gets things wrong and nobody should be held to an unduly harsh standard of getting things wrong. My general observation on any of these systems or processes is it's about trying to help people do better. It's not about justice in the sense of exacting [an eye for an eye].
>
> The context of government from July 2019 onwards, the context of the Home Office in that period, the behaviour that I had to address was what it was. There are lots of things I would tell my younger self to do differently, but I wouldn't tell my younger self to prepare to behave differently in that set of circumstances. It's worth remembering this [behaviour of Priti Patel] wasn't the first

time; in fact, Alex Allan's report also looked at [Patel's] behaviour in the DfID. Being a senior minister is a very difficult job, but it's not like this was the only instance. What I think has happened is we have now surfaced directly, in public, an issue which had been kept concealed before. It's not an attractive issue, but hopefully we will find better ways of helping people in very stressful situations to deal with that stress in future and, personally, I think that's a good thing. I have no doubt lots of people would wish this weren't so, but it is and we need to recognise that the risk is real. Ministers can behave in inappropriate ways. It could be bullying or it could be other types of behaviour. They are extremely powerful people, rightly so, but with power comes the risk of abuse of power. Therefore, one needs to think about ways in which to curb the risk of abuse and preferably eliminate it.

There needs to be a culture whereby if there are concerns, they're well-founded concerns, they can get aired quickly, they can be addressed in a non-confrontational manner, and some change in behaviour results. That requires the right tone from the very top and then the right systems and processes. I don't believe it has to lead to ministers resigning – the idea of having a graduated series of sanctions is perfectly sensible. We should be trying to approach things in a calm, professional way, promptly break them down to understand what the source of the problem is and see if we can fix it rather than pursuing individuals with massive media coverage.

Recognising what is real is important. Philip had noted how powerful a minister can be and it is also true that the relationship between a civil servant and a minister is not one of equals. Clare Moriarty helpfully expanded on this point:

One of the things that is fundamental to the nature of the relationship between ministers and civil servants is that the servant bit isn't for nothing. It is not a relationship of equals. I remember in some of the discussions that have happened in the last few years about ministers shouting at officials, it was not so much a debate about whether it was OK for ministers to challenge officials; it was sort of accepted that [shouting] might happen. But the very idea of an official shouting at a minister is simply inconceivable because the relationship is not such that that would ever happen. It is a very unequal power relationship. So when you're managing conflict from the perspective of the person with less power but a lot of accountability, you really have to think carefully about what you can do on your own authority, what you need to question, whether you really need to go into battle and whether something definitely needs to be addressed. It is unnecessarily damaging to the relationship to try to do something when you don't have the authority to do it.

Clare is right about these questions, which should be considered. The relationship, even between a Permanent Secretary and a Secretary of State, is an imbalanced one. Nearly all the ministers that I have spoken to have said that they want to be told the truth.

'That's what every human being says,' Simon McDonald told me:

Some mean it and some you can do it with. Even if they don't like it, the relationship survives, but some people don't have the character. I think character is very important and I think Prime Ministers, when they are choosing their Cabinet, should think about character as much as experience and intelligence and political allegiance.

Simon had several instances where he made a decision to confront the behaviour of a minister or speak the truth about something that would be unpopular. One occasion, for the latter, involved him revealing how he had voted in the 2016 EU referendum, which raised questions around his own impartiality. But it also highlights a potential conflict in values: can truthfulness compromise impartiality? I asked him about this first example. He said:

> I knew it was unusual behaviour and I thought long and hard about it, although I had to be quick because I revealed this at an all-staff meeting on 24 June, on the morrow of the referendum. The reason I did it was that I knew that the people in front of me and the people around the world were mostly grieving, shocked, disbelieving of what had happened because most of them had been part of the consensus that, on balance, UK membership of the EU was a good thing for the UK. All these people had seen the imperfections of the EU, but all had some professional experience that, on balance, [membership] was better. I also knew that this wasn't the absolute united view of the [FCO]. I knew I had to talk to those who were not pro-EU. The third thing I knew was that of the ministers who were going to come into office – and we knew there would be a new set because Cameron had already announced his resignation – absolutely every one of them would look at me and think, 'You're a Remainer. You may pretend, but I know what you are underneath.' And I thought, 'I'm going to embrace it.' So the two things I really wanted to do were to connect with my colleagues in the Foreign Office but also tell them and signal to ministers that our personal views were not the bloody point. Our task could not have been more different from what we expected, but it could not be clearer, and we had a professional

duty to throw ourselves enthusiastically into this new task. And I was with them in this. This new task would guide me, and I expected it to guide them. So I was trying to be a leader and trying to signal to a new ministerial team: 'Yes, your assumptions [about my views] are correct. But I know my job and I'm going to do my job.'

I wondered whether Simon's authenticity, in this instance, had in fact reinforced his impartiality. In being more open and transparent, he was able to address the elephant in the room and confirm his commitment to the government of the day's primary policy focus. He confirmed:

> That's exactly what I was trying to do. Impartiality is not about not having opinions. It's about not being directed or governed by those opinions. That was the key thing I was trying to convey, both to the people in the room and to a ministerial team that was about to come into office. And what really interests me about this as much as anything else is that the meeting took place in June 2016. The person who leaked it afterwards was *ME*. Nobody at the time went out saying, 'Oh my God, guess what the [Permanent Under-Secretary] has just done?' Because I think they understood the spirit of it and it wasn't a news story. It was the civil service boss in the Foreign Office telling the team, in no uncertain terms, that his task and theirs was now totally different.

Where trust sits on a basis of logic, authenticity and empathy, the authenticity of speaking truth to reinforce impartiality makes sense. For some people, that alone might be enough, but some of the subsequent uproar might suggest that other trust elements were missing from his relationship with ministers.

Andrew Lansley had been a civil servant before entering politics, with a few years in industry between them. The issue of impartiality is one that has been questioned, particularly following the 2016 referendum, with some criticism from ministers and political commentators that civil servants drag their feet or silent protest on policies they disagree with. Andrew decided to leave the civil service when he felt he was no longer impartial:

> When I finished working for Norman [Tebbit], I had been his private secretary for three and a half years. I had reached the point, as a matter of professional pride, where I could draft letters for him and he didn't need to change them. A few months after I left his office, I left the civil service because I had realised during the 1987 election that if Labour had won, I couldn't have worked for them. I couldn't have done it because I wasn't impartial any more. So I concluded that I shouldn't be a civil servant any more and I stopped. But I ended up leaving the civil service and thinking, 'I don't know what I think. I know what Norman's view would be of that, but I don't know what *I* think.' After a while, I realised that Norman's prejudices and my prejudices were quite different, and I had to develop my own. It took a while, but eventually I did.

I'm not sure most ministers have any idea about that element of civil service professionalism. They assume that because the civil servants are supportive of them, they would find it difficult to be supportive of opposition ministers. I don't think that's true. Unless a minister had been a senior civil servant – not many have – and they've seen it happen, they wouldn't realise how straightforwardly professional you can be. That's why civil servants should be very worried about Sue Gray because [leaving the civil service to work for the Labour Party] was a transparent breach of the principles of impartiality. She was a civil servant. Her brain shouldn't even have encompassed the possibility of doing what she did.

It is possible that Sue Gray was also able to be straightforwardly professional until the moment she exited the civil service, or that she decided to leave at the moment she felt close to the line of impartiality. Only Sue Gray knows the answers to those questions. But another point is that recognising one's own prejudices might be seen as a mark of authenticity. This needs variation between a politician and a civil servant, naturally, but it allows a greater degree of openness that can reinforce the possibility of empathy and the conditions for understanding another person's logic.

I returned to Sir Simon McDonald who, beyond telling the truth to reinforce impartiality, faced several other instances where he had to call out unacceptable behaviour from ministers. Not simply on the basis of his own judgement – but in accordance with the Civil Service Code, the Ministerial Code and employment law. One of these related to former Foreign Secretary Dominic Raab, who, in 2023, resigned as Justice Secretary after an independent investigation upheld bullying claims against him. In his resignation letter to Prime Minister Rishi Sunak, Raab said he was 'genuinely sorry for any unintended stress or offence that any officials felt' – an apology that other people were upset and confirmation that it was unintentional. You would be forgiven, reader, for feeling a sense of déjà vu.

Simon McDonald had addressed Raab's behaviour in the FCO on several occasions, directly:

THE MIDDLE

That was very difficult. But the fact that every week I had a bilateral with him meant that at least there was a framework within which I could have difficult conversations. If that regular meeting hadn't existed, it would have been impossible to have the conversations because there wouldn't have been a moment. No doubt he would have suspected my asking for a particular moment and ducked, but because we met regularly, I had the opportunity to do the difficult stuff as well as the standard business. I rehearsed the lines in the mirror. I said the words I thought he needed to hear. And it was to my astonishment that they just didn't land.

Was he receptive?
Simon replied:

No, not at all, but that's a human characteristic. None of us likes being criticised. Small children don't like being told off. Grown-up men *really* don't like being told off. Denial and deflection were the immediate reactions, so then I had another go. But another human trait is that when something is repeated, you refine your reactions, and it didn't land any time I tried. But, if I may say, we all saw the results of his inability to process that message.

I asked whether Simon would have advised his younger self to have done anything differently. He told me:

This is something I think about, especially because in retirement one of my interventions led to the investigation that led to [Raab's] downfall. So you think: why was it right to do that? Why did I do that? And I'm internally conflicted about it. There's part of me that thinks civil servants' loyalty to their ministerial bosses continues until death. That it's something that is expected long after you've stopped working for a minister. But in this case, I thought the minister's behaviour was atrocious and was continuing to blight not only a ministry I cared for and colleagues I cared for but the conduct of government business, because his personality was an obstacle in the sensible discussion and implementation of policy. Part of my problem with Raab was that many people were complaining about his behaviour, but when they came to me, nearly all of them, if not all, said: 'You mustn't use the information I'm giving you to confront him, because if you do, he will know I'm the one that has complained, and then my professional relationship will be destroyed. I don't want that. It's very important for me that you know about this because you are the professional boss. One day something may go wrong upstairs and I need you to know the background and, frankly, to look after me professionally on the other side. But you're not allowed to use the information.'

Because I wasn't using names and specific examples, it was easier for [Raab] to deny and deflect and it was very frustrating. But in the end, you can anonymise things and there can be a body of evidence that you can make the points with. So that's what I did. I was retired [when sharing the information] and it was an honest and fair point I was making. I still would have said it to his face, so I said it into a microphone.

It should be noted that not all claims of bullying against Raab were upheld by the investigation, but it is clear that despite repeated warnings from the most senior civil servant in the department, the minister was unwilling to change his behaviour. Behaviour which Adam Tolley KC subsequently described as 'an abuse or misuse of power' in a way that undermined and humiliated civil servants. There is no organisation in the world that would recommend leaders act this way to maximise results from their teams. But it is also not how humans should treat other humans.

The other major intervention which Simon McDonald made, in speaking uncomfortable truth, was the political firestorm involving former FCO minister Chris Pincher. On 30 June 2022, Pincher, then Deputy Chief Whip, resigned following allegations of groping two men at the Carlton Club, a private members' establishment. As the scandal progressed, it emerged that Pincher had a history of similar accusations. Initially, Prime Minister Boris Johnson claimed he was unaware of specific allegations against Pincher prior to his appointment. However, this narrative soon disintegrated, revealing a more complex and troubling reality. The pivotal moment arrived on 5 July 2022, when Simon McDonald wrote a letter to the Parliamentary Commissioner for Standards, disclosing that Johnson had been briefed in 2019 about a formal complaint regarding Pincher's inappropriate behaviour, contradicting earlier statements from Downing Street.

The letter precipitated a wave of resignations within the Conservative Party, most notably those of Chancellor Rishi Sunak and Health Secretary Sajid Javid, both of whom expressed a loss of confidence in Johnson's leadership. The ensuing public and political backlash underscored a government grappling with serious questions about its integrity and commitment to accountability. On 7 July 2022, Johnson announced his resignation as party leader, marking the end of his tenure as Prime Minister. I asked Simon about his intervention. He replied:

I never, ever thought that within forty-eight hours, the Prime

Minister would have announced his resignation. I discussed this at length with my wife in advance, and there were two things that really troubled me before talking in public. One was personal, the sour grapes narrative of: 'Well, we all know the history between Johnson and McDonald, and he's just getting him back. It's personal and unreliable, a bit spiteful. Ignore it.' And the other was systemic because by the summer of 2020, it was absolutely clear that a large part of Johnson's government had the civil service in its sights and thought the civil service was part of the problem. My analysis is that because the traditional bogeyman of Brussels had been booted out, someone else had to be to blame. It couldn't be Brussels any more and it wouldn't be the ministerial team, so it's the civil service. I thought there was a risk that if I intervened in a distinctive way, that would be evidence for these critics that the civil service was fundamentally unreliable. I intervened because I thought what was at stake was more important than that, and I did it in public, in my own name. It wasn't a briefing. It wasn't what we see in politics all the time, where you just phone up a mate and give them a steer and things magically appear, then people scratch their head and wonder where it's come from. I thought I would do this myself, because it's important. Because the truth is important.

The No. 10 operation was lying and changing its story and continuing to lie. It didn't start on that Tuesday morning – 5 July. It started at the weekend with the *Sunday Morning* politics show on the BBC, when my wife [Olivia] and I watched Thérèse Coffey looking as uncomfortable as someone can with a line they are required to take by the boss, which she clearly knew was not complete. I looked at Olivia and said, 'We both know why she's looking so uncomfortable.' So that Sunday, I got in touch with my successor, with the Cabinet Office, and contacted No. 10 to say, 'Look, this has been running now since Thursday morning, and you're still not getting it right. You can look at the papers. You need to clean up the lines to take. They need to be truthful. I know the truth; and I'm now retired.' So there was, I guess, an implied threat that if they didn't clean up their act, then someone could do it for them. All three [Permanent Under-Secretaries at the Foreign, Commonwealth and Development Office, the Cabinet Office and No. 10] were differently active, and on the Monday afternoon, new lines appeared, which clearly pleased the Cabinet Office and No. 10, but they were just as bad and even more contorted than the previous lines. I was on the train coming home from Westminster to Winchester and I thought, this is not right. So I wrote my letter and I sent it the next morning, and the rest is history.

But there are three points I would make. Why was it so impactful? All I did was stick to the facts, but I was a believable spouter of those facts. The first point was that there had been formal complaints. No. 10 said there was nothing formal, that whatever had happened was resolved and there was 'nothing to see here'. Well, I, as Permanent Under-Secretary in the Foreign Office, had personally received the formal complaint.

No. 10 said, 'There was no investigation, it was much more general and informal than that.' Well, I, as [the Permanent Under-Secretary] in the Foreign Office, instigated the investigation and received the report and discussed the report with [Chris] Pincher.

They said, 'Oh, the Prime Minister didn't know anything at all.' But I was dealing with someone in the Cabinet Office whom I've never named, and that person briefed the Prime Minister every step of the way and informed me the same day as those conversations with the Prime Minister. So that was one step removed, but I still think I was a credible conveyor of that fact.

Those three clear contradictions of No. 10 turned out to be very powerful. I know that after the letter and after the interview on 5 July, No. 10 tried to find any weaknesses to try to unpick it. But they couldn't because it was all accurate. So at 5 p.m. that afternoon, the Prime Minister calls in Chris Mason at the BBC and gives one of the most abject interviews I've ever heard a Prime Minister give in which he [essentially] said, 'Yeah, I did know, but I'm a very busy man.' This was a horrible allegation [against Chris Pincher] and it is not an adequate excuse to say, 'I was so busy, it slipped my mind that I had a sex pest on the team.' And so within half an hour of that interview, [Johnson] lost two senior Cabinet ministers, and the end was nigh.

Failing to operate within the truth was a major factor in the downfall of Boris Johnson, but beyond being the straw that broke the camel's back, McDonald's intervention also highlighted the void of integrity in Johnson's government. Civil servants are, rightly, expected to act with integrity in their actions and roles, both by the Civil Service Code and by the ministers to whom they are accountable. The public, to whom politicians are accountable, expect the same from ministers. If ministers are unwilling for civil servants to speak truthfully and impartially (particularly if it is something they don't want to hear) and unable to develop sufficient awareness of the impact of their own actions, the relationship is likely to break down at some point. Conversely, open and authentic communication strengthens the relationship between civil servants and ministers and increases the likelihood of a successful tenure and legacy.

But what if civil servants are unwilling to speak openly and honestly? It is for good reason that not absolutely every aspect of government is in the public domain, but ministers should expect that they will be told the truth, particularly if they have asked for it. Rory Stewart shared some of his frustrations with opacity and evasion within the system:

> Quite early on in my first DfID job, I discovered we were giving £120 million a year to Yemen. I knew Yemen reasonably well, and I knew that [the civil servants] hadn't bothered to tell me that we had no staff on the ground there. I knew we had no staffing arrangements, no embassy and no DfID staff on the ground. So I asked, 'How do we know what's happening?' And they said, 'We can do Zoom and Skype calls with Yemenis.' I asked for an example of this, just a recording of a three-minute Zoom or Skype call with a Yemeni so I could see what these conversations were like before I signed off on this money. They all sort of turned white, and then four weeks later, more senior people came back and said, 'Minister, why is it you want to see these Zoom calls? With the Yemenis?' And I said, 'Look, I can provide lots of pompous reasons for why I think, if we're spending £100 million a year, it would be a good idea to talk to someone. But there's a more basic point, which is that I asked you to do it.' And they almost didn't seem to care. I was thinking, 'Go and fake it up and just do it, for goodness' sake, this is ridiculous.' So they all said, 'Well, of course, Minister. So sorry, so sorry,' and then went away. Then another four weeks passed, and of course my poor private office is then getting it in the neck because I'm asking, 'What's happened to this thing? I asked for it eight weeks ago. If they're genuinely doing these calls with the Yemenis, why haven't I seen one yet?' Finally,

I go to see the Permanent Secretary to tell him that I'm getting a bit annoyed about this. He says, 'Absolutely, Minister, I'm so sorry. I don't know how that had happened. I hadn't heard about this, but we'll get straight on to it.' And sure enough, two months later, nothing's happened and I'm reshuffled. And that, I think, is a problem.

I tried to tell this to [former head of the civil service] Gus O'Donnell recently, who said it was almost certainly to do with secrecy and classified documents that I probably wasn't authorised to see. But that's not true. I think what happened is that the unfortunate junior official panicked and lied to me. I think they probably didn't do Zoom calls for the Yemenis, and they didn't have the confidence to come back and say, 'I'm really sorry, I panicked in the meeting' or 'I was wrong. We don't do these calls,' which could have stopped the whole thing immediately rather than my chasing for weeks.

It works best, certainly for someone like me, if instead of falling back on bureaucracy and procedure, they come in and are open about what is happening. For example, I refused to sign off on a particular programme in Kenya, which seemed ridiculous to me when I looked at it. What resolved it was a very senior DfID person coming in to see me, who said, 'Hi, Minister, listen, this Kenya programme, I know that you are suspicious about it, but I've been working in the department for twenty-five years and I promise you it's one of the best programmes I've seen.' Of course, I then say, 'Oh, OK, fine. Do it.' Because that's much more convincing than a 300-page document.

In the case of a junior official reporting to a minister, there is clearly a significant power imbalance, and people make mistakes. But civil servants also need to build trust by finding ways to be open and authentic with ministers. The minister's perspective is important and if civil servants are unwilling or unable to put one foot in the minister's shoe, the relationship is likely to struggle.

There is also another point, particularly around the ability to admit mistakes. Helen MacNamara made this point particularly well in her Covid Inquiry witness statement:

> It's problematic for the civil service overall if there is a culture of not acknowledging mistakes, even internally. It puts tremendous strain on individuals and is antithetical to core civil service values. I saw this more in my latter days in the civil service, not just in the Cabinet Office but in other departments where senior leadership would re-draw a boundary to try to make something acceptable in retrospect, not least because they could see the alternative might be to be blamed and fired. They were not wrong to think that. Trust goes both ways and ministers also suffer the consequences of this kind of culture, in terms of the quality of the service that they get and in benefiting from the kind of trusting relationships where they can rely on their civil servants to keep their confidences and be loyal.[8]

This is absolutely right. But sometimes the same mistakes are made repeatedly and perhaps are not even seen to be mistakes. This suggests they might be a feature rather than a bug. Or a blind spot in the system. These exist and it's important to try to identify them.

BLIND SPOTS AND WEAKNESSES

The UK civil service remains very good, by international standards;

it was ranked top, globally, in the 2019 International Civil Service Effectiveness (InCiSE) Index.⁹ It is right that quality and standards should be consistently pushed to improve and there are many other governments whose administrative functions the UK can learn from. But the standard of the civil service is far better than it is often given (mainstream) public credit for. That said, there are blind spots and weaknesses in the system. And people make mistakes; that is simply a feature of working with humans. There are two important elements for this, in the context of how civil servants and ministers can work better together: the first is identifying blind spots and weaknesses, then finding solutions to remedy them; the second is acknowledging that people will sometimes make mistakes, which raises the questions of whether the impact of those can be de-risked in advance and how the leadership will respond when that does happen. I asked several ministers about problems and blind spots they had encountered, starting with Robert Halfon. He highlighted:

> What was terrible was the months and months I had without a diary manager. You may think, 'Who cares about that?' But it was a nightmare. There would be a temporary person week by week and it was only when I was leaving that they finally found someone permanent. And that was frustrating because you can't run an office without that type of support; it's a Minister of State's private office. And then there wasn't a correspondence person, to do letters, for quite a while too. Having said that, the head of the private office was incredible and she did end up appointing very good people. I was sad to go when I did because the private office was just becoming a Rolls-Royce machine. But it had taken a very long while to get to that point because [the head of the private office] and the other permanent staff were doing the work

of twice as many people. It should have been properly staffed and that was really frustrating.

I can think of a time when an MP was expecting me in Cumbria and I just couldn't do it because of my diary. He was very upset with me. I had actually spent three days doing a Cumbria tour previously, so I said, 'Oh, what do you mean, I was there just a few months ago, visiting every part of Cumbria, every FE college.' But somehow it had been in the diary from a previous person and then got missed. So that MP was very upset, understandably, and I had to write to him [to apologise]. Every minister should have a fully staffed office, not people missing or temporary staff, and the places need to be filled quickly. I should add that the way [the Department for Education] was run when I was there most recently [2022–24] was very different from the [department] of five years ago. I thought it was really impressive this time around. My private office were lovely to me, and the temporary people were very nice, but that was an issue that needs to be solved because it does make things difficult.

This type of staffing issue is not, to my knowledge, endemic within the civil service, but it is the type of problem that can hinder a minister's effectiveness and cause frustration. Plainly, this does not fill a minister with confidence or build trust. But sometimes issues are at a bigger scale, with longer-term consequences. Caroline Flint described how she felt she needed to keep questioning officials, particularly around an emergent policy area:

Sometimes a policy is presented and the minister asks whether there is anything wrong with it and the reply is 'No, there's been no new evidence, there's nothing new on this.' But that's not necessarily always the case because things and contexts change. I don't necessarily think it's a malign action, but you need civil servants who question the orthodoxy and can ask, 'Is that quite right? Have we got any new evidence to challenge our original advice?' That's key to helping the minister because you're not going to know everything. It's an important element of the trust between ministers and civil servants, for the minister to be able to ask, 'Is this the best information they could give me? Is it evidence-based? Is there any new evidence? Is there anything we're missing here? Because we're hearing all these voices from campaign groups and others. Are they wrong?' We see that with various public inquiries, which show politicians don't always get it right. And sometimes civil servants don't either.

There have been several recent public inquiries which have highlighted ministers receiving poor or insufficient advice from civil servants, including the Infected Blood Inquiry and the Post Office Horizon IT Inquiry. Vince Cable shared some of his own experience with the latter:

> I was there when key decisions were made about the Post Office, and I've been reviewing the minutes. I was being given terrible advice by the officials but didn't realise it at the time. Just to give an example, I've discovered one little minute which basically refers to my first encounter with Mr Bates, in 2015, I think. [The minute] referred to something like 'Mr Bates and his thirty to forty troublemakers'. That was, unfortunately, how the minister and I were being advised. Terrible decisions were being made and the department, I'm afraid, did not do well.

There is a spectrum of impact and acceptability when it comes to mistakes and at this level, the impact is enormous and the mistakes are unacceptable. But errors at this level are not frequent occurrences (although, arguably, for them to happen at all is too frequent). More common are low-level mistakes, narrow vision or blind spots that are seen in lots of organisations. For these, it is important that civil servants and ministers can find space to acknowledge and minimise the risk of mistakes happening. I returned to Caroline, who said:

> I would say [to officials]: put yourself in my shoes. What would you be like? What would you want? When I was Housing Minister, I was going to a meeting at No. 10, around the time of the financial crash [2008], so lots of people were coming in to see Gordon Brown. Within that context, I was looking at housing and particularly at repossessions. So I went to the meeting at Downing Street and there were some tough things I had to lay out, on the housing front: that things were much worse than we thought [that the housing market was going to drop 5 to 10 per cent]. Afterwards, I went back out, got in my car, got back to the office and someone from the comms team was waiting for me. They looked straight at me and said, 'It's got out. It's on the news that you went into the meeting and said it's worse than we thought.' I went, 'Oh my God, how has that happened? How has this been leaked?' Except it hadn't been leaked. My folder had a clear plastic front and the photographers had snapped it. So it was totally my fault, mea culpa, and I had to really apologise. Obviously, from then on, I never used a clear plastic folder again. I wasn't the first minister this happened to, and I certainly wasn't the last. Sometimes these things happen.

But sometimes there are operational mistakes, where it's not really to do with you as the minister. You didn't direct it, but, whether you like it or not, you're the one who's got to get up and say sorry to Parliament. And then you go back and ask, why did this happen? How are we going to make sure it doesn't happen again? Things like bags of correspondence falling off the back of a mail van. There is an unwritten rule that you don't blame the civil servants – and I get that – but sometimes the management, the supervision or something mucks up, a ball gets dropped. Sometimes an individual civil servant might have done something wrong. It could be there is just too much to do or not enough resources, but something goes wrong, and that happens in all organisations. But it is quite a weird situation because I'm sure a lot of that goes on and it never meets the public gaze. When it does, you, the minister, are up there in front of Parliament or the select committee to answer for it.

These situations sit on the line that links empathy and authenticity. It is the minister who is publicly accountable and it is they who have to answer for a mistake. Therefore, civil servants must find ways to put one foot in the minister's shoe: what do they need to know? What will the impact be like for them? But both ministers and civil servants need to be authentic and honest in acknowledging genuine mistakes and apologising. Partly this is cultural, but it is something that Rory Stewart had raised several times in our conversation:

There is a problem in not being authentic when you screwed up. For example, [the civil servants] claiming that they're doing these Zoom calls with Yemenis and then spending months covering up. Their inability to tell me who's made the decision to fund in Syria and let me talk to them. Their inability to be normal and straightforward. Part of the uncomfortable conversation is that civil servants, of course, are not daft. They understand that what you're asking them is perfectly reasonable, but they're just not going to do it. But they also can't explain why they won't do it, partly because they can't acknowledge it to themselves.

In recent times, there have been examples of private conversations between senior civil servants and ministers being leaked to the media, embarrassing both sides. There are two fundamental issues with the impact of this behaviour: the first being that civil servants simply do not have a right of reply in public; and the second that both sides need to be able to trust that private conversations are not made public for immediate political advantage. But the flaring of this type of behaviour is a more recent phenomenon and, frankly, the absence of it should be a baseline expectation.

Sometimes ministers need to step in to understand where a bottleneck is and why something is not happening. I returned to Caroline Flint again:

> I didn't have any reason to mistrust civil servants, but often some of the civil servant teams I dealt with had very limited staff and resources, which had an impact on how much they could do and then had an impact on what I would receive as a minister. One of the things which is weird is that as ministers, we're not operational and we've got the Permanent Secretaries who are responsible for running the departments. But sometimes I felt that I couldn't really influence some of those things around staff capacity. I did try to have some input into it when I was

Housing Minister: Eco Towns was one of the policies. You get all these induction briefings for your policy area when you first start, and so when I asked about Eco Towns, it turned out there was only one person working on it. Well, the mission was to build or create ten Eco Towns. Ten. With one person working on it. So we had some discussions about how important it was to make this work and more resource was provided. But I had to make it clear that I wanted the senior staff to take more interest in it, understand it and recognise if we needed more resource. Having one person working on it was something that had been decided before I'd arrived, but I just thought, 'This isn't going to work.' Was that overstepping the boundaries as a minister? I don't know. It wasn't fair on this particular individual and I wasn't sure how on earth we'd been making any progress. By the time I was Housing and Planning Minister, it was my fourth department, so I felt much more emboldened to have those conversations than I did when I first became a minister in 2003.

Blind spots like these probably require an additional perspective to see the wood from the tress. A minister (Caroline Flint) was able to immediately see that the policy could not be managed by a single person. But sometimes the issue is not about numbers of people but about perspective and institutional thinking, particularly if it relates to seeing a trend emerging. I asked Caroline Flint about this and she said:

Whitehall is not as good as it should be at spotting trends emerging. It might be something that seems really small at that point, but if we're not careful, it can quickly get a lot bigger. The danger for politicians is that we constantly see blips of things happening, and everything feels like it could explode so we need to solve it before that happens. You always want to react and have an answer. In my experience, the civil service were sometimes the other end of the scale to that and not always attuned to the early stages of a developing problem. When I was at the Home Office, one of the areas in my brief was organised crime, which also included sexual exploitation. At that time, the grooming of young girls was coming to our attention. Not in Rotherham and Rochdale, which came later, but some other instances. There was another minister who also had responsibility in this area, too, and [Secretary of State] David [Blunkett] was also engaged because it was really worrying and awful, hearing from parents whose daughters had ended up in prostitution. They didn't feel empowered to get people to listen to what was happening to their daughters or empowered as a parent to do something about it.

Roll on, long after I've left the department, and this vulnerability of young women, young girls, started getting wider attention. Part of the reason it took so long was that some of the different agencies involved thought these young girls, who were children, were part of their own problem. That they were consenting and just a bit off the rails or from a bad family. And that was simply not the case. They were groomed. Their vulnerability was being exploited. But they weren't being treated as children. Since then, there has been big exposure on this subject, involving the police and local authorities, and it's got some of the attention it requires. But it took that to actually change the culture of some of the agencies and their attitudes to these girls. I'm not saying we didn't look at it, but there's an issue where something might be happening with a relatively small part of the population and there needs to be a mindset exploring whether this could be happening elsewhere by different protagonists. We should be asking questions: what should that tell us about safeguarding our kids? If it's happening in one place, could it be happening elsewhere? Could it take a different form? Is there something we need to do? What if this is happening in one police force where they're not taking the voice of kids seriously? Where is this happening elsewhere?

As an MP, over twenty-two years, I had thousands and thousands of cases, on all different topics, come in. And MPs have a – rather archaic – system of trigger words, which indicate if something is cropping up a lot. If someone came to me about something, I'd speak with my [parliamentary office] staff and we'd agree to keep an eye on it and see if it was something emerging as more systemic. Sometimes we would spot something growing, but we didn't necessarily have the sophisticated means to spot trends every time. We all have to be thinking about where the next challenge is going to come from. I think Whitehall is still not as good as it should be on that and it should be better at helping ministers do it.

Some of this problem can be recognised in the loss of institutional memory. Some civil service departments have made improvements in this regard, but it can be a struggle to identify and link similar problems when high-performing civil servants move around so much. Caroline continued:

> A good example is the huge amount of really positive work that's been done on reducing smoking. But the government hasn't been ahead of the game on vapes. Vapes were obviously an alternative to help people stop smoking cigarettes. But they weren't ahead of the curve on the emergence of flavoured vapes to attract

children. They should have known that. When I was a [Health] Minister, we had alcopops coming through. There was a moment when they were suddenly everywhere and children were drinking them. Where's the collective memory across Whitehall that learned from that? Trends and fashions reoccur just in a slightly different form. We've been here before. What were the warning signs and signals?

Part of the purpose of this book is to explore the middle ground between ministers and civil servants and identify ways that trust can be built and the relationship improved. That is not simply in response to a particularly bad period in relations but also so some underlying factors can be addressed to enable each side to understand the other better. I have deliberately included a range of views because ministers vary in their personality, preferences and approach and because civil servants, also, are not uniform in nature. Relationships involve navigating the connections and differences between people. Rory Stewart's reflections on being in government include a lot of frustration and difficulty. Candid views, such as his, should be considered and taken seriously, amongst the positive experiences that other ministers have had. He shared about some of the challenges of mindset within the civil service:

> I had a recent conversation with Gus O'Donnell [former head of the civil service] where I said, 'Civil servants sometimes have a pretty poor view of ministers.' He said, 'Absolutely not. We write the boring speeches, but you have to go and deliver them.' And I thought that was very revealing. Here's this guy that was the head of the civil service who, in the first example that comes to mind when he's trying to think about what the relationship

should be between a civil servant and a minister, is that they write the speeches and the minister delivers the speeches. And that the reason they respect the minister is that the minister is more of an extrovert and can read a speech. It's a very odd idea. You can't imagine in any normal organisation that if you said there's a problem between the bosses and the staff, they're saying, 'Absolutely not. We write the speeches and the boss delivers the speeches,' as being the example of why it's a good relationship.

To be blunt, part of my problem is that I was a civil servant. And that I did know something about these subjects, and I was relatively ambitious to get things done. If you preside in a charming, dignified fashion, read their speeches, are polite to them and, broadly speaking, follow their line, the civil servants like you and they are wonderful. But if you think there's something wrong and you're trying to change it, you're in real trouble. There is, of course, the Liz Truss problem – another sort of problem – which is a Secretary of State who is reckless, totally uninterested in the facts and just doing silly things to get headlines. I think that's terrifying and it's very unfortunate that our democratic system throws up these people. A lot of [the civil service's] behaviour is to do with the fact it has received a series of very poor-quality ministers who are reshuffled very frequently. So it's not very surprising that they don't take ministers seriously. But the truth of the matter is: they don't take ministers seriously and they can't recognise it or see it. It's so embedded in their DNA, this belief that they're there to serve and that they serve well.

My experience of Simon McDonald, for example, was somebody who was unbelievably patronising and grand. Sort of astonishingly so. He was in the room when I went in to talk about which part of the world I should get. And this first meeting was very revealing. Simon was sitting there and I'm looking to him for support and saying, 'Listen, Boris, I've spent the last fifteen years of my life working on the Middle East and Asia. I've just been the DfID Middle East Asia Minister, so at least I should, I think, get the Middle East or Asia.' And he and Simon just delighted in the idea of giving me Africa. I don't know why. I tried to say to Simon, 'Listen, you make this big deal about how you believe in expertise. Why have you just done this?' And he just laughed. I had been a Foreign Office diplomat, and I did know a little bit about what I was talking about. I have never been treated with such patronising grand condescension. Almost any idea I came up with, he sort of brushed aside as though I was a kind of child.

Then he made comments to people, quite openly, when I tried to do stuff in Zimbabwe and stop his ambassador, who was basically endorsing this war criminal, Emmerson Mnangagwa, as Mugabe's successor. He said to people, 'I think Rory is very naïve.' It was incredibly patronising.

Some people don't click with each other, but there is a broader point to be made around ministers feeling (and being) respected. This book has explored several of the many examples of ministers behaving unacceptably towards civil servants; in fact, Simon McDonald was instrumental in some of these instances coming to light, by speaking out. Ministers should seek to build trust with civil servants, but civil servants must also make effort for ministers to be respected and feel understood. There are other occasions where civil servants have bent too far backwards, and this can create a different sort of blind spot or weakness. I spoke with Jonathan Slater about the separation between ministers and civil servants focusing on policy and on messaging. He said:

The Secretary of State is the one who is focused on what's going to make them look good today and tomorrow. And they've got a team of special advisers around them whose job is to help him or her do that. I didn't see it as my primary role to come up with wizard ways to make Justine Greening look popular. When she would want to give a speech or announce an initiative, it would be my job to make sure the department was trying to facilitate that. Rather than saying no, I would try to help make that happen in a way that would reinforce the changes that she was trying to drive over the medium term.

The civil service is used to coming up with wizard wheezes that can get announced. These even have a name: announceables. No. 10 might want to fill up its grid over Christmas or something, but we all know that [an announcement] is nothing to do with improving children's lives over the medium term. It's the cut and thrust of politics – there's nothing immoral about it. Civil servants work up things for ministers to announce, but you just need to be clear that that's what you're doing and that you're in mode A rather than in mode B. We should be able to walk and chew gum and do both things, but we should be clear [about which is which].

There is a risk that announcing something is not going to make any difference to children but might make a difference to the popularity of the Secretary of State. Fine. We'll do that then. We're trying to change children's lives and do something else. And you just need to be able to do both those things, rather than run the risk of thinking we are achieving change when we're actually just in the world of special advisers.

With the passage of time, this may be viewed as a quirk of a communications-focused Cabinet (rather than a policy-focused one), but it also may reflect the politics of the latter stage of a political or electoral cycle, where there is less time and political capital to enact meaningful change. Jonathan also suggested there is a risk that it could cause civil servants not to provide frank advice:

> I think civil servants self-censor too much. They think that a comment is not going to be received very well so they don't make it. That is hopeless. I've generally not been in rooms or seen examples where ministers said, 'It's not your job to tell me that.' Even when I got to the extreme level of a ministerial direction, I got no grief at all; and that's when it was put in the public domain. Normally it wasn't, because normally it's not something that needs to be. The trouble with operating behind closed doors is that you focus almost exclusively on what you think the person you're advising wants to hear. But you'd be amazed at how much civil servants get that wrong. That they think the minister doesn't want to hear their evidence, their advice. They're really wrong.

An approach that provides advice based on what someone might think the minister wants to hear can set a minister up for failure, creating blind spots and false confidence. In theory and conversation, very few civil servants would defend this approach and it is not in line with the professional values which officials commit to. But it quickly becomes a problem when it does happen.

Much of the civil service prides itself on providing evidence-based advice, rooted in clear logic and consistent methodology. This can be a helpful component in building trust, but it is not always matched (as we have seen) with empathetic and authentic engagement. This has been true of ministers also, but ministers are individuals who come and go, whereas civil servants exist within institutional structures. I asked Sue Owen about some of the weaknesses and blind spots that this has created. She replied:

> A long time ago, when I was still in the Treasury around 2005, Gus O'Donnell was Permanent Secretary at the Treasury and was trying to think more about leadership rather than management. And we had a day, about twenty-five of us as the top team, where we all did a Myers–Briggs test of your personality type. And it turned out that about 85 per cent of the Treasury were the same, quite unusual, personality type: an INTJ, where the characteristics are to be polite and professional and courteous and have a secret plan to kill everyone in the room.

INTJ is a personality type with the introverted, intuitive, thinking and judging traits. Also known as the mastermind, it is the third least common personality type. About 2.1 per cent of the population are INTJs.

Sue continued:

> I turned out to be one beginning with E [indicating extraversion], a very common type. And it showed there was a lack of diversity there. You need a whole variety of ways of thinking in a top team. You need a variety of types and you need some people where it begins with E, not I.

The civil service has worked tirelessly, in recent years, to improve diversity across departments. Very substantial improvements have been made and it has an enormous amount to be proud of. But my own experience is that within the senior civil service, there is still even a mixed understanding of what emotional intelligence is; one person even described it as 'instinct not grounded in fact'. For absolute clarity, that is incorrect. I asked Clare Moriarty about this. She said:

> I think the civil service is too obsessed by intellectual analysis and much too unfocused on emotional intelligence and people. I probably spent the last fifteen years of my career going around shouting into the wilderness that we need to understand the language and we need to be thinking about people and relationships and how we work with other people. It's very interesting in the civil service context and also very interesting in the civil service to ministerial context. All of the training and culture has been tending towards emotion being an unstable thing, and so we shouldn't bring it into the way we think about things. That analysis is much safer, with a whole 'leave your personality at the door' piece. And then as leadership and management started to get a bit more 'discovered' by the civil service, people started to use the language. But civil servants are very good with language. So things like values and behaviours and emotional intelligence got taken into an analytical place where they felt safe. The thing that used to trouble me is that people used to use the language – you could hear the language all around you. But it wasn't connected to a real understanding. I spent so much of my time talking about empathy – I still do – because this is the thing that makes the world go round.

Change has been taking place in the civil service, but civil servants can also be masterful at adopting language without really changing behaviour. Some of this is understandable; fads come and go. But being able to empathise with ministers is a critical component in building trust and a better relationship. It must be valued higher.

CONTROL

'The departmental line to take is generally about control,' Andrew Lansley began.

The *Yes Minister* portrayal of a Sir Humphrey Appleby-style Permanent Secretary puppeteering a hapless minister is far from reality, but government departments do retain biases of their own which influence their lines to take. Andrew took me back to his experiences as a civil servant:

> The old Trade and Industry Department wasn't about whether we were intervening in industries or whether we should be privatising or not. It was about how many of us there were and how much we were spending. Because those were the terms of reference for the group that I was secretary to. It was designing schemes that employed more or less the same number of civil servants and spent more or less the same amount of money.

My experience is that this had long ceased to be the case, but I asked him whether he thought it was still an issue. Andrew replied:

> Overall, I haven't seen evidence that it isn't. The driving consideration for most civil servants, particularly those in charge of an area of activity, is control. If they can change the policy and retain control, they'll be perfectly happy. But if change in the policy means losing control, they will be very unhappy and will try to

resist it. It's nothing to do with the prejudices and policies of the government of the day; it's just about maintaining control. That might be harsh, but it's true.

There is an apocryphal story about the Permanent Secretaries Christmas party, where they have games. One of these is a bicycle race, which, considering it is taking place in the combination room of an Oxbridge college, is surprising, as there isn't sufficient space for it. And they say, oh, it's not a problem at all, because the object of this race is to demonstrate that you can retain complete control of the machine while making absolutely no progress whatsoever. It's all about control.

I'm not alone in thinking this, which is why people, including politicians, believe in devolution. Devolution wrests control away from central government departments. But boy do they fight against it. Ministers should be aware of this, and many probably are not aware of it. Too many politicians think either that civil servants are slavishly committed to the policy of the government of the day or they are temperamentally opposed to the policy of the government of the day and do it because that's their job. Whereas, in fact, they are professionally committed to supporting the government of the day, but they have a departmental interest which will steer them wherever they possibly can to secure the government's objectives while retaining control. How much legislation have we seen, which is basically designed to allow ministers to do anything they want? But, of course, it isn't that minister – they come and go – and the minister probably didn't even want it, but the civil servants want the ability to write statutory instruments as and when it suits them. If you could measure it, I suspect the ability of the civil service to write statutory instruments dictating what people should do, all over the country and in all sorts of circumstances, has grown enormously. It grew during Covid and I suspect it will never quite roll back either.

There is another important point to be made here, which is especially true for the Department of Health and the Ministry of Defence. Within the department, there are a substantial number of people who are occupying civil service posts but who are not civil servants. Their loyalty lies elsewhere and they are not necessarily understanding of the professional obligation to put the government of the day's objectives first. This was the case all through my department up to and including David Nicholson, who was effectively head of the NHS inside the Department [of Health], which is an absurdity. He had whole cadres of people outside – in the NHS – and inside the department who were working for him. They weren't working for me, as Secretary of State; they were working for him. It wasn't quite the enemy within, but it wasn't far off. Some of the things I regret, that would have made a big difference in the subsequent implementation of the clinical commissioning groups (CCGs), were blocked by David Nicholson. For example, I wanted to expose to competition the commissioning support units and he wouldn't let it happen. We negotiated that they would be free from competition for, I think, five years. Everything, subsequently, I've discovered, tells me that they didn't use that time.

The NHS managers didn't like the plan for CCGs and subverted the whole process. Because in the NHS, who's in charge? The issue is one of control. The managers wanted to be in control and my reforms would have meant clinicians being in control, and they didn't want that, so they stopped it. I was moved on and they then had nobody to stop them. In my view, people who want to be

NHS managers should be out managing the NHS. People who want to be policy-makers in the civil service should be inside the Department of Health doing that. People should not be pretending to be one or the other in the same organisation.

There are some experiences which are common to most ministers, and others which are very specific to the departments they have been leading. Not all of the civil service is the same, nor are all departments and nor are all civil servants. But this topic of control is an interesting one where I experienced a range of views. The majority of, but clearly not all, former ministers (and nearly all civil servants) I have spoken with have said they had not experienced civil servants focusing on control. But that does not invalidate the idea or the experiences of those who have encountered it. It simply shows us that not everything is everywhere all the time. Not all things are binary, linear or simply one side of a line or the other. Rory Stewart had been clear that he liked and had good relationships with the civil servants he had worked with but highlighted, in more examples than I have included, his experiences of civil servants having their own agenda:

> One example, in DfID, was that I would say, 'We've got a £1.2 billion budget totally unrestricted for research. I would like us, please, to do a research project on what we have achieved in Malawi over the last forty years.' And [the civil servants] would come back three weeks later with four options, of which option one was do nothing, option two was do research on the whole of Africa, option three was do a randomised control study and option four was do what I'd asked them to do. And I'd say, 'What is this? I just asked you to do this. Why have you produced four options?' The

truth, of course, is they didn't want to do a research project into what we've done in Malawi because they knew perfectly well we hadn't achieved anything in Malawi in forty years, having spent billions, and they didn't want to look at that or think about it. And they thought it was too dangerous. It's understandable. They were worried that if they bothered to study it, the *Daily Mail* would see it and they'd get in trouble. But it doesn't get around the fact that I can see that too. We should be talking about that risk openly, not just refusing to do it.

The culture is so much about managing politicians that they never fully attempt to understand them or respect [ministers]. Nor do they really harness them to their benefit; they don't really know how to use them. The only time I ever got compliments from civil servants is when I performed well to a select committee. But they never thought really that my analytical skills or my knowledge or decision-making was remotely interesting to them.

You would have thought [the civil servants in the FCO] might see someone who has been in the Foreign Office, speaks three Asian languages, has written three books about the region, has thought about it a great deal and very much wants reform, and that it might be quite exciting to understand him and talk to him about what his vision is and see what we could do to change the world. That's not at all what they think. They just have a programme that they're pushing ahead with. That's part of the problem. It's never clear who's programme the civil servants are pursuing.

When I ever tried to answer the question of who's idea something was, it was almost impossible to get to the answer. I tried to stop a project of funding jihadi groups in Syria and could never work out who wanted to do this. It was clear it was happening, and it was clear they weren't going to let me stop it. I had heard it was this director and then this small group, and then maybe it was the Americans, and then maybe it was the security service. I'd go round crazily trying to track all these people down and sit at a table with them thinking, at that stage, that my big mistake as a minister was believing that I could have reasonable debates and convince people to change their minds. I would approach these conversations like a seminar, where we all sit around a table, committee-style. I thought I could hear from everybody around the table, come to a conclusion and then finalise what we're going to do. Sometimes they thought I could get there by compromising. I would say at the end of the meeting, 'Listen, I realise you don't seem, from your body language, very comfortable with what I'm saying. What is it you're uncomfortable with? Maybe I can compromise. Maybe we can do this in a different way.' But they would freeze because they didn't want to get into that conversation. I was trying to behave like a senior civil servant and they simply didn't view me really as a decision-maker in that sense. A fundamental problem is that civil servants view a minister as a sort of non-executive director on a board, not as the chief executive.

I think one thing is that civil servants are not awfully good at trusting and delegating down to local communities. So if I take the example of what I was trying to do with trees [at DEFRA], the only way we were going to get all those trees in would have been by trusting the farmers to plant the trees. I was trying to say, 'Listen, in exchange for your single farm payment, you will plant sixteen trees for every acre of land you have. They should be native trees, but you can put them where you want and you can choose whatever tree you want.' But, of course, that was absolute anathema to the system. The system wanted to control exactly which tree and exactly where it was being planted. Which, of course, made the whole thing completely unaffordable. You can say to a farmer, in exchange for a £65 European Union grant over a five-year period, 'You plant sixteen trees that cost a quid each and you can put them where you want.' They just slam them in and it takes them three minutes to plant the tree. And some of them will die and some of them won't be exactly the trees you want, but you would end up with a couple of hundred million more trees in your landscape.

That is not a model that the civil service like because they feel, all the time, that they are there to control risk and to deal with attacks in the *Daily Mail* and whatnot. Therefore, the only way they can really imagine trying to deal with every eventuality is to try to specify, at incredible cost. The most extreme example was DfID, where I discovered we were spending £40,000 per school project, which was delivering £2,000 of output. Literally delivering five red plastic buckets and two small brick latrines. The other £38,000 was control. It was programme design, strategic plans, logical frameworks, monitoring and evaluation mechanisms etc. If I said, 'Listen, we could do twenty times as many schools, if we just gave £2,000 to each head teacher,' [the civil servants] just turned white. Randomised controlled trials demonstrate that you have far better impact by giving cash to people. I don't want to be too unfair because the DfID did support some cash programming in certain areas, but they tended to be small-scale humanitarian efforts, and that certainly didn't involve doing it with things like school programming. So I think that's one element of control. Fundamentally, all their briefing, all their culture, was predicated on the idea that they were telling me what to do, not that I was telling them what to do.

Whatever the motivations or drivers behind behaviour which leaves a minister feeling frustrated, it is that feeling which is important in the context of how ministers and civil servants work together. Control can come in many forms (behavioural, process, systems etc.), but when its presence feels overwhelming, it can undermine trust and discourage authenticity. Clare Moriarty had worked with Rory Stewart at DEFRA and I asked her about this idea of civil servants wanting to be in control. She replied:

> I haven't heard an accusation about civil servants wanting to be in control, but what I would recognise is the feeling that [as a civil servant], you're constantly out of control. It's quite common to have situations where everybody thinks that somebody else has got the power. The civil service certainly doesn't feel that it has the power. They spend so much time making things right for ministers and chasing after their ideas, that they feel like they don't have much control. I can see how that could be perceived as being in a constant search for control.
>
> When Rory Stewart was a junior minister in DEFRA, he came and talked to us and we were trying to get the senior team to 'get it' better. There was this idea that it felt as though civil servants were constantly not doing what he asked them to do, not prioritising what he thought was important and dragging their feet. I'm sure that fits with a broader narrative of 'they're trying to own the agenda and be in control'. Collectively, we had a bit of a lightbulb moment where we said, 'Honestly, as far as we're concerned, you are definitely making the decisions. But as a junior minister, the Secretary of State's word is going to trump yours.'
>
> Some of this is because there is not enough honest dialogue between ministers and civil servants about what it feels like for

the minister. Ministers feel they're tiny in number, isolated and in a position where you don't talk in front of the civil servants. So those open conversations don't happen. Which means everybody proceeds on the assumption that they're making it about what somebody else thinks. Civil servants make assumptions about what politicians do based on what civil servants would do and vice versa. And that usually leads to gaps of misunderstanding and misattribution opening up. That's the type of conversation which could help to make things better.

I wanted to get a further minister's perspective and so asked David Gauke about this question of control. He said:

What civil servants will have is a fear of a minister being out of control, which is different from them wanting to retain control. There is a nervousness about ministers who are off on a frolic of their own in terms of their policy development and pursuing things that aren't going to happen or are obviously ill thought out. Civil servants will occasionally fear that a lot of civil service and ministerial time is going to be wasted on things that the Treasury or No. 10 are very obviously going to block. So in that sense, there might be some restraining out-of-control ministers. There's also the concern of ministers who might shoot their mouth off or say things that are contrary to the government line. So, in that quite narrow sense, I think there's some truth to it.

But one thing that ministers need to know about officials is that they like a decisive minister. They like a minister with an agenda. They like a minister who's got a purpose, knows what they want to do with their time as a minister and where they want to go.

If it's a junior minister who's trying to pursue something that their Secretary of State is going to veto, that's where the civil service will use all the tricks to try to control somebody. But they don't dislike ministers who've got an agenda and are trying to get stuff done. Quite the contrary. And that's an important lesson. Any minister who was finding the civil service really being very obstructive probably ought to have a long, hard look at themselves just to make sure that this isn't as a consequence of them, the minister, pursuing things that are clearly a waste of time.

I should be very clear that Gauke was not referring to Rory Stewart in the last of these comments. Rory's experiences were real and any civil servant prepared to brush his concerns away, rather than take them seriously, would, in fact, be confirming them. There is a wider, perhaps difficult, conversation for ministers to have with civil servants about this topic, in an open manner. Government departments are large organisations and their direction can be slow to change. When there is a high turnover of ministers (every few months), it is understandable that there may be caution in channelling all resources into ideas which will take longer than that. Equally, civil servants are there to serve the minister and must be supportive of implementing ideas in a way which that idea will see its best outcome.

PART FOUR

THE END

DISTRACTION

'How did you handle ministers becoming distracted by something external?' I asked Sue Owen. I wanted to understand more about when a minister's mind was elsewhere, distracted by other things vying for their attention. We were speaking via video call and at that moment Sue's husband walked in the room.

'Hi,' he said. 'I need a password.'

'I'm doing an interview, on the record,' she told him.

'What's the password for the *FT* account?'

'Sorry,' Sue said to me. 'My husband needs a password.'

'No problem at all,' I replied.

'Yes. OK. Distraction,' she said. 'What was the question?'

Every ministerial tenure comes to an end at some point. Having made it through the intense beginning and navigated the accountability and difficulties of governance, every minister is aware that their star is either rising or falling, trending towards promotion or demotion. The gradient of that trajectory can be steeper or gentler, but nobody is flatlining and a reshuffle can come at any moment.

Crises (political or otherwise) can also come at any moment and external distractions can consume a minister's attention. Some suspect, but many do not know, the moment the end will come and that means they must be ready to work with ministerial colleagues to defend the government (or themselves), when necessary, perhaps at the expense of their attention to the department. I asked Simon McDonald about his observations of ministers entering the end point, consciously or not, and the role of distraction. He said:

> I think with most people, the longer they're in a job, the more comfortable they are with that job, and so the more capacity they think they have to do other things. That absolutely happens, but the best ministers I worked for never let that take over. You never let the distraction be the principal focus; I don't think you would do the job very well if that happened. Most ministers I worked for wanted to do a really good job. I think [the end] must be on their minds. The end in politics is generally brutal. And final. And unfair; or, at least, sometimes hard to understand the full picture of the person being sacked. I think that on day one, you're able to push that thought completely to the side. But by year two, year three, that must be coming closer and closer to the centre of your thinking.

There is a natural temptation to want to be as helpful as possible to a Prime Minister, and No. 10, where there is the prospect of a more important and exciting role in government. This is equally the case if a minister's position is more tenuous. But sometimes a minister is under pressure for (and distracted by) other, perhaps personal, reasons. I returned to Sue Owen to see how she handled this happening. She highlighted:

Well, you have to talk to them about it. And they can react in different ways. Maria Miller was being hounded about her expenses. I was a relatively new Permanent Secretary then, and I did ask several times, whether we should talk about how it was going to be handled. But she was so upset by the whole thing that she didn't want to talk about it at all. She just said the Prime Minister would back her, which he did to start with but then ultimately didn't. So that was quite difficult.

When John Whittingdale had some unpleasant publicity coming, which was all completely unfair and ridiculous, my strategy was to be really helpful because it was in our interest to get him back focused on the work of the department as soon as possible, which we managed. If it's the threat of a reshuffle, it's best just to chat to them about it, really. The relationship with the junior ministers can be quite important. A good Secretary of State will see the junior ministers as a team and will have a weekly meeting and one-to-ones and that kind of thing. Then they can delegate to junior ministers if there are things that have to be done.

Brexit was quite a big distraction in the sense that there were a lot of additional meetings to go to. And then you would just have to have discussions about what the top priority was for the rest of the work, how they wanted to handle things, whether they wanted to just not do some things or delegate or let officials do them. Sometimes what happens with distractions is that other things just go on the back burner. Like appointments [to boards of arm's-length bodies], for example. And then that just builds up over time, and you end up having to handle a lot of very frustrated other stakeholders like the arm's-length bodies etc.

Brexit was an enormous distraction from everyday governance.

Those types of seismic changes don't happen very often, but the period provides an extreme picture of ministers being constantly sucked in by demands external to the department. David Gauke was a Secretary of State for a significant portion of the time when Brexit was the predominant (and, at points, only) narrative:

> Particularly those last nine months, I reckon maybe a year as a minister, so much of the focus was on Brexit and that really was the one that caused us to break down into our little teams really. And so I had my political allies who I was speaking to all the time. Although, you remained objective, just like the other Secretaries of State. But that felt really very much a strong team game.

As Permanent Secretary at DExEU, Philip Rycroft was in the department whose sole focus was Brexit. He saw several Secretaries of State move on, both there and in previous roles:

> They don't see what's coming up. Mike Moore, for example, was completely shocked when he left. David Jones, I think, probably wasn't that surprised. With David Davis, he came out of that Chequers meeting apparently on board. It was only over the weekend that he resigned. He was probably on resignation watch, as was [Dominic] Raab. But that was part of the turmoil of that moment. My experience of it was that they were all, to a greater or lesser degree, very conscious of the political context and very conscious of their place in that firmament. Politicians at that level, almost by definition, are really ambitious, so lots of them default to 'I've still got road ahead of me'.
>
> But others, as you got to know them better, would be tempered by a realism about what their job prospects really were. It's quite

personal, of course, but I think many of them recognised when they had got about as far as they were going to get and then focused on doing their job, in their own way and using their influence as best they could in this very complex ecosystem: jostling with party colleagues, Cabinet, keeping onside of the Prime Minister, as well as their own constituency etc. It's a very complicated world that they inhabit.

There is always a point where a minister is distracted by something external to a department. From the civil servants' perspective, Una O'Brien highlighted to me (as had Sue Owen) the importance of being a sympathetic leader, also adding: 'On a practical level, you need to make adjustments to the working week; re-allocate the load of visits and visitors etc. If things look particularly shaky, keeping the Cabinet Secretary informed is a wise move.'

But it is ministers who are the ones managing the demands on their time. Major distractions come and go, but a constant of government is that ministers are part of a team. More experienced ministers (and sometimes less) are expected to play their part by promoting and defending the government in public, itself a further job on top of the long list of ministerial responsibilities. I asked Robert Halfon about this, who said:

> Then, of course, you have to do the media rounds. Suddenly, Downing Street will say, 'Right, we want you on the morning rounds.' I was on a tour in Exeter, once. I'd been at Exeter University doing a whole load of speeches and was due to visit Exeter College the next day. It was 7 p.m. and I was being hosted at a dinner when I got a call telling me I had to do the morning round. It wasn't even about skills, it was about childcare policy, because Claire Coutinho

wasn't available for some reason. But I couldn't leave the dinner because I was being hosted. So I got back to my Premier Inn at 11 p.m. and crammed for two hours, learning everything I needed to know about childcare policy. Then at 5 a.m., I'm up doing two hours of morning-round interviews, from my Premier Inn room with bad Wi-Fi, hardly knowing anything about the policy. And I had basically turned into Alan Partridge. That stuff happens all the time. And then you go back to do your constituency work.

We didn't discuss the pedestrianisation of Norwich city centre – Robert only had eyes for his constituency of Harlow. But his anecdote helped summarise distraction as a significant theme of the later stages of a ministerial lifespan. The minister does not know when the end is coming, nor do they plan the distractions which consume their attention. But it is an inevitable part of the latter stages of a ministerial lifespan (whatever length that takes) and both ministers and civil servants have to find ways to adjust to it.

THE END

The end, for a minister, is often described as swift and brutal. There are many manners by which a minister's tenure can finish, but there are only three decision-makers who can pull the trigger: the Prime Minister, the electorate or the minister themselves. When it happens, it happens quickly and the department immediately begins preparations for the arrival of the next minister. The process is clinical and unforgiving.

Some ministers know the end is coming, for good or ill. One end, of course, is to another more senior ministerial position (at the behest of the Prime Minister); a loyal, reliable or politically savvy minister may be confident a promotion is coming. That may well be at the expense of another minister who has made high-profile mistakes or not shown enough commitment to the party line. Those ministers often know the end is coming, and it can be a distressing experience. Vince Cable encountered his end via the electorate:

> There were some awkward issues at the late stage of the coalition. There was a very bitter dispute over arms to Saudi Arabia, which I was trying to stop through the arms export licensing system, but the Ministry of Defence adamantly insisted that the arms go ahead. To give him credit, I was 100 per cent supported by my Permanent Secretary and the department. But basically, government discipline was breaking down at the point we saw an election coming; most of our attention had switched to the general election and defending our seats. And psychologically, that's where we were. I had got some quite encouraging data that turned out to be rather misleading. I was reasonably confident that I would be re-elected as an MP, although certainly not as a minister; we had assumed the coalition had come to an end.

Vince also lost his seat as an MP (although returned to Parliament in the 2017 general election). Loss of government discipline causes volatility and can dilute the potency of a Prime Minister's threat of a reshuffle. Strangely, a reshuffle can then become more likely because a Prime Minister feels they need to reassert control. The coalition government created a strange political environment where the Conservatives and Liberal Democrats were partners in government while being competitors outside of it. Vince Cable saw the sharp end of this in the 2015 general election. But both parties competed throughout their time of joint government.

Andrew Lansley was effectively demoted in a Cabinet reshuffle in 2012, from Secretary of State for Health to Leader of the House of Commons (although remaining in Cabinet). He recounted his experience:

> David [Cameron] and I had a conversation. To be fair to David, there was nothing brutal about it. Coalition is a funny beast because even though we were in government with the Liberal Democrats, in the run-up to any local elections, they had to be against something. In 2011, they were against what Michael Gove was doing; in 2012, they were against what I was doing. Unfortunately, Michael Gove survived, and I didn't. David didn't give them the scalp, but he said to me, 'Look, if we're going to reset this with the Liberal Democrats after they've been having a go at us, we're going to have to move people around a bit.' And so that was the change in 2012.
>
> I think he genuinely wanted to keep me on as part of his core advisory team of senior ministers who you can rely upon, but I said to him in late 2014 that I didn't want to go and learn how to do my job in a different department. I didn't feel like I was John Reid, moving around. In order to do my job in my way, I would have had to thoroughly understand a whole new department and I didn't really want to do that. I was lucky because that meant I left in 2015 and David was kind enough to send me to the Lords. I was perfectly happy with that because I wasn't in the Commons for the Brexit nightmares that followed.

In most cases, a minister is told, by the Prime Minister, that their time has finished in their current role and they have been selected for another one. If a minister resigns having made a grave error, it is often because they have been guided to do so. But occasionally, there are other reasons ministers decide not to continue in their role. Robert Halfon had two very different experiences leaving his role as Skills and Apprenticeships Minister:

> The first time, Theresa May decided to move me on, but I was very lucky. I was very close to George Osborne and I'd been in Cabinet for a year under him and that was amazing. Attending Cabinet is something I won't forget in a hurry, because that was the referendum year. [May] had put me in there and then decided to move me on. That was her decision to make, but I was very sad about it. I then immediately stood for Education Select Committee chair, and there were five other people standing against me. The election of a select committee chair is a weird PR system, which I still don't understand to this day. God knows how it works, but somehow, I won it and that was a great five years of my life.
>
> I actually wouldn't have given it up for any other job in government. Give up an amazing select committee chair post? No way. You say what you want, you do what you want and, as a select committee chair, you're a campaigner. Interestingly, you sort of get a private office as a select committee chair, but in the form of two or three clerks, and they were brilliant. It's run like a private office in a way, and they're very impressive, the Commons clerks. But because [the ministerial post] was skills, apprenticeships and [higher education (HE)] and I was asked to go back to do it, it was a huge compliment. Having the HE brief was huge because normally you have a separate HE minister. Thank God, student finance was Baroness Barran and freedom of speech was Claire Coutinho and then David Johnston, so I was able to concentrate on things I care about, which is skills and universities and things

like that. It was a mammoth job to do because Labour had two shadow spokesmen. So when I was doing bill committee, I had two shadow spokesmen to answer to, which was really tough. One would get up, then the other one, and the same in the House. Nevertheless, it was a great decision because it meant that we had the same agenda for HE as for skills in general.

Robert resigned from his role as a minister in 2024 and decided not to seek re-election for Parliament. I asked him when he knew it was time to go. He replied:

> I loved it. I had been in the system since my twenties, basically like an inmate with Stockholm syndrome. I always come back, and fighting a seat like Harlow is incredible. But it's a seven-days-a-week job and it's tough. And residents want you to work hard in a constituency like Harlow. I've done six elections, ten years as a candidate, fourteen years as an MP working. It's time to do something different. But it was very sad stepping down as a minister.
>
> I was sad to go. Because the last six months were the best of my political life. I did eighteen months in [the final ministerial role]. In the first six months, I was bringing a bill through called the Lifelong Learning Entitlement and had to appear before five committees, which was an enormous amount of work, and I was just submerged in that. But by the end, we were delivering well and they really understood what I wanted to do. The private office, particularly in the last six months, became amazing. I was very sad to go, but it's often better to go when things are going well rather than when things are going badly.

And so the lifespan of a minister ends. Often suddenly, almost always definitively. And then a new minister arrives and the process starts again. This is the life of a minister. Civil servants, meanwhile, remain and seek to build good relationships with a new incumbent, discovering what time they like to start work, their preferred lunch and the font size that all documents must now be written in (a true and frequent consideration). But 2020 saw a different experience for some of the most senior civil servants in the country: a purge. Civil servants are not politically appointed, but, in quick succession, several Permanent Secretaries departed in a manner more consistent with a ministerial exit than a mandarin. Clare Moriarty was one of the departures and recounted her experience:

> I was leading edge, as it were, for the 2020 departures. I was made redundant, which is very unusual for a Permanent Secretary, but my department closed down and my job disappeared; I met the technical definition of redundancy. In reality, I was ready to do something different at that point, but it felt very painful because I had been a civil servant for thirty-five years. I had given a huge amount of my time and energy to it. However it happens, being made redundant is a deeply difficult, emotional thing. It probably felt to me as if there was a bit of a political flavour, because that's not what had happened in the past. Then from the outside, I think it felt to me as if the departures became increasingly political as the year went on. There was certainly a sense of decisions being made in a much more political way than had been the case in the past.
>
> I didn't feel anything like as directly targeted [as the others]. I wasn't briefed against in the same way that that others were. I had to think through whether I wanted to push hard and say, 'I really want to go and do another Permanent Secretary job.' But you have

to commit and really immerse yourself for the next five years. I felt like I was ready to do something different. So I wasn't particularly wanting to stay on, but I would have liked to be treated a bit better. It felt very sudden when they said, 'We think the answer is to make you redundant,' particularly as it turned out to be the beginning of the pandemic, and it might have been handy for them to have another experienced Permanent Secretary around. It felt like a very deep rejection.

PROBLEMS: WHAT'S GONE WRONG

For most ministers, the end of their tenure, like the end of any job, evokes emotional response and reflection. There are some baseline behavioural expectations (particularly from ministers) that can facilitate good and better working between civil servants and ministers, which in turn will deliver better outcomes and governance. But there are also cultural quirks, particularly within the civil service, which ministers have found difficult and which civil servants themselves recognise as being unhelpful in building trust. Andrew Lansley offered his thoughts on the civil service's focus on outcomes:

> In my view, policy as a policy-maker should be all about outcomes. I don't think any civil servant has ever devoted anything like sufficient attention to the achievement of outcomes. We created an NHS outcomes framework and whenever I go anywhere in the NHS nowadays, I ask people, 'Do you know where you stand in relation to the NHS outcomes framework and international comparisons for those?' They almost never know. They know everything about the waiting list targets, four-hour waiting, eighteen-week target etc., and that's been true for two decades.

Jeremy [Hunt], credit to him, tried to move the A&E targets on, but the four-hour target is still what everybody talks about. We should really be focused on how long it is before somebody attending an A&E department sees a qualified clinical person who can identify the relative severity of their condition. Over his and my periods, we brought that down from something like seventy-eight minutes on average to about thirty-three minutes. That made a big difference to outcomes, but it also meant there was a significant body of people who were seen quite quickly and then put to the back of the queue – which they didn't like. They're just upset that they've been waiting over four hours. Four hours is not that important, really. If a child has come into an accident and emergency department having possibly swallowed something under the sink, most of the time you would put them under observation, they sit in A&E for a few hours and you find out if they're OK or not. But if that time goes over four hours, you've failed, which is absurd.

Each minister has their own experience and I suspect there is a cogent argument that ministers could do more to establish clarity in outcome targets (and there will be plenty of people ready to defend the importance of the four-hour A&E target). But speed, clarity and expertise from the civil service side is vital for successful policy outcomes. Philip Rutnam validated this point:

I have definitely seen cases where people are too focused on process and not enough on results. I also think we need to build expertise. I worked in some fantastic organisations and with some fantastic people, but there were also areas where I thought, 'We really need to know more about this.' It's not a universal point about expertise, but the civil service has a core reason for being there: to provide expert advice quickly to ministers.

Ministers are not in post for long and join a department (and therefore structure and culture) which is already well established. In which case, civil servants should ask themselves whether their existing culture is set up to develop policy which produces clear outcomes and measurably improves people's lives. This is easy to say, difficult to do but important to get right.

Andrew Lansley had also mentioned the frequency by which Permanent Secretaries move between posts and across different specialisms. Caroline Flint echoed something similar:

> Another frustration for a minister is that there's quite a lot of movement of people within the civil service. I remember someone who was a leading specialist on a policy area, and they ended up moving to a communications role, but they didn't have any experience at communications. So I was thinking, 'How are they going to do that?' And then someone else came in and took on that person's policy area. They had done policy before but didn't really know much about the policy area. There were then points in the conversation where I knew more about that policy area than the person who was leading it. There are lots of experts in there, but often there's quite a lot of movement of civil servants, which means they are also getting up to speed with what they're doing. Getting the balance on that right is important to a politician, because you want the person giving you policy to really know it, not to just take it from someone else and then feed in to you. There just ends up being so many degrees of separation between the person who really knows their stuff and the policy advice arriving in my inbox.

A frequent criticism of the civil service is that there are too many generalists and a lack of specialists. It is an oversimplified criticism, as there are a lot of specialist civil servants, some doing roles which could only be done in government, but they are predominantly mid-level in the hierarchy (and therefore pay). For many years, the structure of the civil service has rewarded generalist managers with promotion and so the senior civil service has (perhaps) been over-populated with very intelligent, very capable non-specialists. There is certainly an argument that frequent shuffling and movement of generalists doesn't allow them to settle into expertise. This provides a problem for ministers, who rely on civil servants to advise, should they stay in their own role long enough to become an expert. Jonathan Slater provided some insight into a further consideration within this criticism:

> I would always think that a downside of the civil service system was that we [civil servants] spend too much of our time in Whitehall, and it's not good enough. We should know more than Damian Hinds [former Education Minister] about every aspect of education. The fact that he goes to talk to some people in a surgery in Hampshire on a Friday is not an excuse. But quite often, a minister knows more about X or Y because of that. The civil service should be able to do better than that.

The idea that civil servants are insufficiently outwards focused or exposed to the public is an interesting one (and could easily form the basis of a thesis). However, it could provoke a response which would allow officials to keep up with the rapid acceleration of knowledge acquisition any minister must enact upon gaining office, particularly once the minister is on top of their brief. Understanding the lens through which a minister sees policy and politics (i.e. via constituents' experiences and public attitudes) may also enable a greater degree of empathy towards a minister's perspective and a better translation of evidence-based options and recommendations. Where civil servants understand the drivers of a minister, they are more likely to be successful in presenting advice which satisfies the need for a base of evidence and the reality of delivery with the vision and motivations of the minister. Unfortunately, the latter of these is not necessarily confined to whatever the existing machinery of government (structure of government departments) is in that moment. I returned to Caroline Flint, who said, 'My other my big frustration was how siloed working was in Whitehall but also how siloed ministers were both within departments – as a team – and also across departments. I think that's still a cultural problem that exists.'

The accusation of siloed departments (and ministerial teams) is widely recognised but also complicated. The civil service is not a single organisation in the traditional sense. It is a collective of organisations which adhere to the same principles and rules and are coordinated centrally; but each organisation has its own structure, leadership and significant autonomy. Each department also answers to its own ministerial team and Secretary of State (or the Chancellor). In recent years, the civil service has introduced the concept of 'professions', which links civil servants in a specific professional area across all departments. This deserves credit but is still evolving and, ultimately, it is the department that still employs (and holds to account) those individuals. Perversely, the frequent movement of civil servants between departments is (in practice) one of the counteractive forces combatting siloed thinking, as individuals build networks and contacts across the civil service.

Rory Stewart highlighted a different concern:

Fundamentally, the system involves the civil service deciding what it's doing, presenting it to ministers to be signed off and occasionally allowing very big manifesto commitments or very clear steers from a Secretary of State to shift it a bit. But they're totally uninterested in my sitting down and saying, 'Can we look at our programmes in Bangladesh and can we agree that this programme is good and this is less good?' [At DEFRA] they were completely uninterested in my suggesting that the Lake District National Park is putting too much emphasis on rewilding. As soon as you get into anything which is remotely about the 'how', there is a problem. And in Britain, 90 per cent of the problems are the how. The system assumes that we have this incredibly efficient civil service that delivers everything brilliantly. So all the minister has to do is provide a little bit of strategic policy direction, and then they'll work out all the details and implement it flawlessly.

The truth is that again and again I saw incredibly poor implementation. If I went back and said, 'Listen, you've just taken me to see a clinic in Nigeria and we turned up and there was human excrement on the floor, there was a fan but no electricity. There were no patients in the clinic and there were no medicines on the shelves.' They don't know what to do with that. When I ran an NGO, or anything else I've been involved with, if the boss says a piece of implementation is a disgrace, everybody jumps to it and tries to work it out and fix it and learn a lesson from it. What you would expect in a healthy organisation is they come back and they'd say, 'Oh my God, Minister, that's terrifying. I'm so sorry. I'm putting my best person on to reviewing it. The Nigerian clinic programmes will be back to you in two weeks.' And then they should come back in two weeks and say, 'You're absolutely right, Minister. That particular clinic is a disgrace. But we've reviewed the others and actually 70 per cent of them are fine. But obviously, the implementing partner is no good, so we won't be renewing with them. And in the meantime, these are the fixes we're putting in place to improve things.' But I never ever had anyone do that with me.

Whether or not civil servants believe this really happens, it is a problem that a minister thinks or feels that it does. How can a minister trust those working around them if they feel like they are being manipulated? The logic may be consistent, but if a minister believes there is an absence of authenticity from the 'civil servants advise and ministers decide' process, why would they believe it is true? And what of democracy? If a minister does not believe the process of decision-making is reflective of the democratic system in which they were elected (because they feel they are simply rubber-stamping decisions of civil servants), that undermines the system itself and creates divide between politicians and officials. For better or worse, we do not live in a technocracy and it is important ministers feel understood and have faith in the democratic system of governance. Feelings are not the only thing that matter (far from it), but they do matter: they are essentially the basis on which politicians are elected in the first place.

All ministers are different and so this is not a call to throw the baby out with the bath water but for civil servants to tune in to those differences and pay attention to how trust can be established through logic, authenticity and empathy and the strands that connect them. There are plenty of examples where civil servants have been very effective at this, but clearly, given the plethora of examples over the past few years, there is more to do. Rory Stewart had been very open about his feelings that civil servants were not good enough at asking questions of themselves. I asked him what he would suggest to de-escalate frustrating interactions where both sides could ask more frank questions of each other. He replied:

> You could have a little phrase for a particular moment where you can both acknowledge what's happening, get out of the standoff, step back and talk about what's really going on. It's like a relationship where you're arguing about who's taking the bins out, but there's all this stuff hidden in the background. In relationships, you need to be able to say, 'OK, can we just stop for a second and try to get back to what's really going on here?' If you could have a code phrase where your private office or the minister can push the reality button, that might help. Where a civil servant could say, 'Minister, don't waste your time on this Yemeni thing. I have no idea why they said that, but you're never going to guess it and you're going to drive yourself mad trying to get it,' rather than believing there's a procedural answer to everything. At least it gives me a chance – as minister – to ask myself how much this really matters to me. Is this just an example of completely bizarre civil service crap that I'm never going to understand? And I'll just forget it? Some things are like that. Some things you can handle like that if you've got a decent relationship. But people have to be able to put that authenticity in.

The final thing I'd add to the trust triangle is the idea of moral purpose. Again and again what I would be trying to say to them was: would you do this if it was your own money? Would you spend £38,000 out of £40,000 monitoring something and delivering £2,000 of benefit? Would you allow air quality to be where it is? Would you do this and forget all the weird stuff that's going on with your bosses and your views on the *Daily Mail*? Does this make sense? Is this the kind of people we want to be? Is this how we want to change the world? Is this the kind of country we want to create?

This final point is complicated territory for the civil servant, because of collective understandings of impartiality. A civil servant's response to this might suggest there is a political element in these distinctions, that their own opinion is not relevant and that it is the minister who decides. Civil servants must serve the government of the day, which, as recent history has shown, can change direction and composition frequently. Civil servants injecting their personal views and moral guidance into their roles is not straightforward and often inadvisable. But there is a broader point in the frustrations this can cause ministers. Politicians need to be able to communicate plainly and if something looks and feels obviously 'wrong', that presents a problem and it undermines trust in the relationship. I'm not convinced there is a quick or easy solution for this, but it is one which needs working through between individual ministers and the inner team of officials who work with them.

Philip Rutnam presented another problem which has undermined the interdependent nature of the civil servant–minister relationship:

> Civil servants used to be anonymous. But over the thirty-odd years of my career, they've progressively become less anonymous and there is a significant risk that the attractiveness of a career in the civil service drops as a result. Not necessarily at entry point, but more so people questioning whether it's worth progressing up the ranks. Because if the risks increase and you just happen to find

yourself in the wrong place at the wrong time, the consequences can be huge. Somehow that worry I've just expressed has got to be reconciled with the equally understandable desire for sharper accountability, good performance management, a culture of improvement, all those good things. But that does not mean that the answer is that when somebody finds themselves getting blamed by a powerful politician, laid out in a tabloid with no opportunity to answer back, that that is appropriate or fair. Over time, it will damage our capabilities as a country if we go down that route.

I asked Philip why he thought civil servants had become less anonymous over time. He replied:

> I think the media cycle is a major factor. One of the structural factors affecting the entirety of the political system, including the relationship between ministers and civil servants, is the greater intensity of the media cycle, the proliferation of outlets, the role of very rapid comment on social media and the volume and intrusiveness of news, which has increased. There are lots of good sides to that, particularly for greater transparency. But then you've got to design a system that is resilient and can cope with that. I'm not sure we've got it in the right place at the moment.

Briefing and counter-briefing the media has undoubtedly further damaged relationships between ministers and civil servants. It breaches trust, destabilises openness and counters the conditions which support authenticity and empathy. Simon McDonald built on this point:

> Senior civil servants now talk to too many other people. In the

jobs that I did, I talked to other civil servants, but I never had a conversation with a journalist that wasn't explicitly authorised. I never briefed them. My feeling is that an awful lot of that now goes on and it gets back to the boss. Even if the briefing is meant to be sympathetic, why the bloody hell is it happening? Civil servants shouldn't talk to journalists, full stop. Of course, this has changed and it has changed in my retirement. But my personal rule is to talk on the record. I don't like background briefings. Someone who wants to be on background always has a reason that they want to be on background, and it's probably a reason that their ministerial boss won't like.

Part of the reset for me is recapturing the background quality of the civil service. There are very few civil servants that should engage with the media. They are in very clear jobs and they have very clear ministerial instructions. Everybody else should be silent unless very specifically authorised by their minister.

That part of the relationship needs to reset. It's not only civil servants [who need a reset]; the military needs to be part of this too. It started with the military and it spread. The relations between senior officers and the *Daily Telegraph* are just jaw-dropping: the stuff they leak and the opinions they share that then appear with no consequences for the senior officers doing it. Across public service, your job is to work diligently for the government of the day within the law, and ministers should commit to respecting officials, not using them as a scapegoat or a whipping boy. Civil servants don't leak to the media. This is the way it used to be and the way I think it should be again. But if you [a civil servant] decide that you're going quietly to ignore this rule and the minister finds out, there will be proper consequences – and there should be proper consequences because this is very important.

Journalists are going to be really upset by this because they love having all these sources. I'm a big admirer of Tim Shipman, but if the consequence of what I'm saying is that Tim Shipman has a pretty thin column on a Sunday, then that's just tough.

PROBLEMS: BORIS JOHNSON AND DOMINIC CUMMINGS

'There was a moment in time when Dominic Cummings was Boris Johnson's chief of staff and he was removing Permanent Secretaries,' Jonathan Slater shared.

The premiership of Boris Johnson accounted for an enormous amount of damage to the relationship between ministers and civil servants, breaking carefully constructed constitutional norms and setting precedent for unrestricted and unaccountable ministerial behaviour. Given the unwritten nature of our constitution, those precedents cannot now be undone. Jonathan continued:

> That was obviously not a good time for a relationship between Secretaries of State and Permanent Secretaries. I think the Secretaries of State were observers in that and it was Dominic Cummings who was doing the work. I say this because he was clear that's what he was doing, and it stopped happening when he left. With one exception of Liz Truss and Tom Scholar; but that was very weird.

Tom Scholar had been Permanent Secretary of the Treasury and survived Johnson and Cummings's purges of 2020. Scholar's exit was politically motivated and, to a degree, enabled by the precedent set by Johnson and Cummings. Johnson was reportedly committed to adversarial organisational conflict in order to drive performance.

THE MIND OF THE MINISTER

Helen MacNamara (former Deputy Permanent Secretary in the Cabinet Office) shared her experience of this in her evidence to the Covid Inquiry:

> Mr Johnson had said explicitly on a number of occasions that he thought that organisational conflict was a pre-requisite to get the best from people and keep them sharp. He wanted the people who worked for him to be jostling for position – he often said that the competitiveness would make them better (he also said – with reference to the removal of Permanent Secretaries – that teams performed better once you sacked the head. I disputed this at the time).[1]

Johnson discovered the weakness (or consistency) of this logic when he himself was removed from office in July 2022. It's a little unclear exactly who was steering the ship when it came to removing Permanent Secretaries, but adviser Cummings appeared to have as much say in breaking constitutional norms as Prime Minister Johnson did. Simon McDonald added:

> It was a weird episode because Boris Johnson made Dom Cummings the second most powerful person in the country without actually knowing Dom Cummings. They hadn't been muckers through the referendum campaign. The basis for that appointment was not clear. It felt as though a new Prime Minister was reaching for a comfort blanket or a sort of magic friend. He wasn't reaching for someone he knew well and trusted and he knew to be worthy of his trust.

It is possible that Johnson didn't really value trust very highly. If this was the case, he successfully transferred that view to several of his ministers and some of the subsequent behaviour undermined it with civil servants. Notoriously, Cummings had drawn up a hit list (termed the 'shit list') of the Permanent Secretaries he wanted to get rid of. Simon McDonald suggested the approach may have had an element of control in it:

> Everybody in the system is more or less insecure, but over time, you get a bit more confident. And I think the one thing that the hit lists had in common were they were senior civil servants who were relatively more self-assured and so less likely to do the bidding of Cummings and Lee Cain. There's something interesting around that. But I worked out that the lessons of childhood are valid when you're doing very senior work, that you tell the truth, that you don't allow things that you know to be wrong to happen just because it is personally convenient. And I think a lot of trouble comes from people not doing the right thing.

I turned to David Gauke for his thoughts. He said:

> I think there has been a certain amount of scorched earth as a consequence of the Johnson and Cummings period. I think that contributed to some of the problems over Covid, by the way. Most importantly in terms of the performance of the centre of government and the sense that any big figures were getting demolished with lots of anonymous briefings. I think that also played into the whole Partygate stuff. It created an atmosphere where no one wanted to be the one to say, 'No, hold on, we can't be doing this.'
>
> Dominic Cummings was trying to bring the civil service down to size, to show who's boss. But I think that comes with very

significant downsides, as we saw in the aftermath. A recognition of the importance of institutions is really important and that was absent for a number of years.

One of the major strengths of an institution is that it provides stability and confidence in difficult or tumultuous times. Part of that stability is underpinned by collective experience and institutional knowledge. Those two elements were substantially undermined by the removal of so many senior civil servants in 2020. But it also set precedent for the future. I had an extended conversation with Philip Rycroft on this topic, who summarised an important permanent change:

> Was Cummings right in his diagnosis of some of the weaknesses of the civil service? Yes. He was. I've no doubt about that at all. I didn't agree with lots of his prescription because it was partly his own personality-driven thing. He wanted to be Bismarck, at the centre, but I don't think he understood the complexity of the policy ecosystem he was dealing with.
>
> I don't think the Conservative Party thought about the wider constitutional space when it was doing some of these things. If you knock down all of the barriers that are, effectively, constraints on executive power, when somebody else comes into power, all their constraints are gone because you've destroyed them. You've made the executive even more powerful in a system where the executive is too powerful anyway. One of those constraints was an historical reticence to take political decisions about who should be in the top jobs. Once you've breached that, you can't undo the fact it has been done.
>
> Whether or not an incoming government says they will [return to a] status quo ante, it asks a much bigger question about

accountability and also whether the relationship between civil service and ministers is, in generic terms, fit for purpose in the way the world is now. Should it now be a more transactional one, where the accountability lines are clearer? One option there could involve a *cabinet*-style system, where you have a Secretary of State who has quite a big office of civil servants and special advisers, but it is essentially a political office. I worked in a *cabinet* in the [European] Commission. The deep discussions about policy direction would happen there, followed by a more formal transmission of instructions to the department who would be tasked to develop it. But the quid pro quo is then that the advice that comes out of that is more public, so that the civil servants are then held accountable publicly for the quality of the advice and ministers are held accountable for the decisions they took on the back of that advice.

The notion that we have to keep the existing model ad infinitum is not right. It needs to be stress-tested all the way along. Perhaps the shedding of senior civil servants [during Cummings's era] is a warning signal the old relationships can't carry that stress or that strain in a way that allows for transparent, robust, accountable decision-making. Because that was not transparent, robust or accountable decision-making. It was arbitrary decision-making.

At a minimum, it is worth thinking about whether the current model can sustain the pressures that are now on it. People may say, 'The problem's over, we're back into business as usual.' No, we're not. You can never set the clock back to where it was. Labour will come under pressure in the next five years at various points and they will be tempted. There will be a falling-out and there'll be tension. Someone will ask the question: 'Well, the other lot did it, so why can't we?'

A wise government would be putting in train some work to think about that deeper relationship.

MAKING IMPROVEMENTS

All ministers receive an induction when they first arrive at their new department and this process has been honed and improved consistently over the past few years, with, admittedly, a lot of opportunity to practise. But when the ministers (and civil servants) I interviewed reflected on what could help set the relationship with civil servants on firmer footing in the early stages, it was the first acquisition of knowledge that emerged as a strong theme. Several others made similar points, but Andrew Lansley opened proceedings:

> Civil servants assume that because they have put something into the large-scale briefing that ministers receive when they arrive, ministers then know it; but almost all of them don't. There is this assumption that ministers just have to sit and tell you what their view is about things. Well, that's not how it works at all. They need more help understanding how government works.

Caroline Flint reflected on her own start in government:

> When I first came into the Home Office, as well as meeting the different teams and being briefed on the state of policy, I probably would have liked something more practical about how they work, to understand the hierarchy and then more on things like the funding arrangements in departments. How they went about looking at the different policy demands and where you put funding in and what, as a minister, could I do to influence that. You

learned it on the job, but it felt like there was a presumption that you knew all that or you didn't need to be told any of that.

There was this huge presumption that you know all of this and for lots of ministers, that's just not the case. What's the hierarchy? How does it work? Where are the staff based for each policy area? It would give more texture to how they operate and would have helped me understand what actually happens. Some more practical stuff would have helped, too. Some dos and don'ts. When I got submissions, I used to scribble notes all over the place, things like 'WHY?' and 'Do we really mean this?' It was probably mentioned, but I don't remember being explicitly told that this could all end up in an archive. MPs use Post-it notes that could probably be taken off and binned somewhere. Maybe they will make a good read in the next few decades, who knows.

Sue Owen noted the challenge of the role itself, of which civil servants are aware but new ministers may not (immediately) be:

Very often, when ministers arrive, they have no concept of what is involved to run the ship, the day-to-day stuff. There's all manner of other things that take up a minister's time: meeting people, going to events, answering parliamentary questions, letters, letter signing, going to Cabinet, going to interdepartmental committees, question time, departmental question time. There are huge amounts of that kind of thing that have to be done and it's quite difficult to anticipate the volume before you arrive as a minister.

This begs the question as to whether more could be done in advance. There have long been suggestions that ministers should complete some form of training, to help get them up to speed on the department, policy area and industry, either once they have started or during an interim period between being asked to take on the position and starting. David Gauke also mentioned this:

> I do wonder whether you can put together some sort of learning which is outside of the department, in addition to the introductory submissions, the sit-down with your Permanent Secretary and the conversation with your principal private secretary.
>
> But, ultimately, an enquiring minister with some intellectual curiosity is able to fill the gaps quite quickly by contacting their predecessors, reading some books related to the subject matter and talking to outside bodies. They will have lots of meetings as a minister and start to get a sense of how they want to do it. The most important thing is having the ministers with the intellectual curiosity in the first place, having the right people in there who are prepared to do all of that hard work. They need to have the skills to absorb the information and understand the arguments, rather than the knowledge, necessarily.

As ever, Gauke's suggestion seems sensible and reasonable. Political mentorship is not a new idea, but perhaps part of the answer is also for ministers to have access to ongoing support (akin to an executive business coach). This would likely help a new minister to feel additionally supported in moments where the relationship with officials is more tested and strained or where they are under increased pressure.

Another suggestion for change that I encountered was to the nature of the relationship itself. The relationship between civil servants and ministers continues to be based on convention, precedent and understanding. For a considerable time, this has worked well (more often than not). But the world has changed a great deal in the past forty years (let alone 150), as Philip Rutnam pointed out:

> We still have a really good civil service by global standards, but I think the model has become frayed, and not just because of the political stresses of the last seven or eight years [2016–24]. There are some deeper structural things which mean there's more scope for tension. The intensity of the media cycle, in particular, means that the level of pressure and scrutiny ministers are under has increased. Some of that space has been filled by special advisers, and good special advisers have a really important, constructive and creative role to fill. But personally, I don't think our constitutional arrangements or the set-up of the civil service have been properly adapted to reflect that.
>
> In principle, the civil service and the Permanent Secretary still cover everything that they were expected to cover in, say, 1980, when special advisers barely existed. And at the same time, a whole load of additional processes have been added into public administration: impact assessments, judicial review, lots more economic appraisal and so on. So I think it's time to consider whether we actually need to be tighter in defining what the key role of the civil service is. And that implies a bit more distance between the top of the civil service and ministers, making sure that relationship is properly defined on both sides and businesslike.

Philip Rycroft agreed with this direction of travel:

> I would be tempted to think about stepping into that broader space where you rely less on unwritten conventions about these relationships, that have rather murky accountability. I do wonder

whether that model is now no longer fit for purpose and whether you need to move to a more transactional relationship. Other civil services have moved more into that space, for example New Zealand and Australia. You would still need a trusted relationship, but the parameters of that relationship are then more transparent and more publicly accountable on both fronts. It wouldn't stop ministers sometimes doing crass things, but it would put the price for doing so a lot higher.

Rory Stewart went a step further, calling for reform:

I think we should formalise, and I think, ultimately, the British system is broken. I do think it depended on a good-chap model, and it depended on ministers who were serious and civil servants who were well informed. It depended on a much more grown-up serious world which has vanished. We need to specify and formalise. I look enviously at Sweden, for example. There, the head of the prison service is completely independent of the government and can't be told what to do by a minister. The head of public health, as we saw during Covid, could reject lockdowns and there was nothing the politicians could do about it. It's a strange system and it would take a little time to adjust to, but if the DfID staff in India or Bangladesh were set up like an independent foundation, were able to set their own strategies and hire their own staff, they would be much more efficient. And you would then be explaining to ministers that these are arm's-length bodies, and your relationship to them is not what you imagine. That's an uncomfortable conversation, but I think it's necessary.

Calls to formalise the relationship are understandable, and there is no doubt that the current set-up has not kept up with the evolution and expectations of politics and government in the past decades. However, it would be a brave and confident politician that constrained themselves and diluted their own power and flexibility in decision-making. There is also the risk, as perhaps is seen with the NHS, of devolving decision-making while retaining the risk of being held responsible by the public if things go wrong. Formalising the relationship in this way would probably bring greater clarity, transparency and accountability, but it seems unlikely. A request to future governments: prove me wrong.

Until such changes happen, both civil servants and ministers should focus on how they can work better together and set better precedents and constitutional norms for the future. Clare Moriarty suggested this could involve some rebalancing of the emotional labour involved in the relationship:

> One of Andrew Kakabadse's shooting-for-the-moon ideas was ministers and Permanent Secretaries going through a formalised process of building a relationship, which would make it a bit more equal effort from both sides. I think he had an idea of something like a six-month process of formal relationship building. I don't know whether it's realistic for the ultimate power balance to shift, or if it would be the right thing because it's really important that democratically elected and appointed ministers are in charge. But I think if the balance could shift a little and the emotional labour could be made a bit more equal, that would be a really interesting development.

If there is no revolutionary constitutional amendment, then there must be evolutionary change through behaviours and approaches. The former is up to a government of the day to decide, but the latter is in the gift of the individuals involved. Civil servants can choose steps and approaches that make ministers' lives easier, that demonstrate commitment to see things from the minister's perspective and that display authentic openness to help build trust. Ministers must remember that civil servants are people, are committed to public service and will do everything they can to serve the government. Ministers should also remember that they, themselves, are people. A minister is under intense pressure and will change over their time in office. Self-awareness of one's weaknesses and mistakes, combined with a commitment to authenticity with officials, will make a better and more successful minister. Help and support is always available; it must simply be sought.

HOW TO BE A BETTER MINISTER

Upon leaving office, ministers have an opportunity to reflect on the lessons they've learned (sometimes the hard way) and what they might have done differently. Every minister is different, so there isn't a template for getting it right. But there is wisdom from former ministers who can offer insights for new, incoming and future ministers to consider. I asked former ministers what advice they might give to their younger self or an incoming minister. I've also drawn on some extracts from the Institute for Government's excellent 'Ministers Reflect' archive of interviews with former ministers.[2]

Here is a summary of their advice:

- Think ahead
- Prioritise and prepare
- Keep asking and learning
- Speak to your predecessor and speak up

- Don't forget Parliament or your constituency
- Be strategic
- Understand civil servants
- Control your diary
- It's a privilege – and it's temporary
- Develop open and honest relationships with civil servants
- Be brave

THINK AHEAD

Vince Cable

I think there needs to be more of an induction. I, and my colleagues, should really have thought much more about what we would actually do in government. We did have some scenario planning about finding ourselves in a coalition with the Tories, but it was at a very shallow level, and I think we should have spent more time thinking about what we, as individuals, would do beyond campaigning.

I think you also need to line up your team quickly, and if you're an opposition party, that means your special advisers. They need to be recruited early and understand the technicalities of the department you're going to. We didn't do that.

I think I started off as more of a narrative minister, wanting to get the correct positions and so on. But as time went on, I realised that actually delivering good policy and good outcomes was probably a more useful way of spending time.

Jeremy Hunt

I think the most important thing you can do is work out what it is you would like people to say about your time in office after you've gone. And the best thing to do is to choose one big thing to change and really focus on that relentlessly, because you're going to have to decide all sorts of issues that crop up left, right and centre. There's going to be all sorts of firefighting, all sorts of controversies, media slip-ups, but all that will be forgotten five years hence. But how many ministers can point to one big thing they changed that they're really proud of? The answer is surprisingly few, and I think my advice would be make sure that you're one of the few that can.³

PRIORITISE AND PREPARE
Robert Halfon
Be absolutely clear with the priorities. Be clear about how you want your box done, be ruthless about accepting meetings and act quickly when there's a problem. There are so many problems that crop up. I wasn't as good at this the first time, but I learned from it – I looked back at things I could have done better.

The other thing is you have to prepare. The first time [as Minister for Apprenticeships and Skills], if I had a select committee, I might just do it the weekend before. This time, I did three weekends of learning sessions. I'd relax in the evening, but I would prepare all day Saturday and Sunday and I'd have the whole day before blocked off just to prepare for committee. The first time, I would allow all my days to be full of meetings, but when you appear before a select committee, you've got the stakeholders watching from outside. They're the only people who really care about what happens there, along with the civil service and your bosses. If you do a crap performance, they're going to lose confidence in you – they all want to have confidence in the minister. So it's essential that you do a good job.

Margot James
The most important thing is to establish your priorities and to make a plan that enables you to focus two thirds of your time on those

priorities but that gives you enough vision across the rest of your portfolio to make sure that the things that are important to the stakeholders in those areas are properly delivered and that you are sited so that you don't get too many unwelcome surprises. But you have to be quite ruthless, I'm afraid, in assigning a large amount of the policy areas for which you're responsible to that category of 'park it over there, make sure I know what I need to know, make sure the stakeholders have a system by which their reasonable demands are met and make sure I don't get too many unwelcome surprises'. Because it is physically impossible to give all the time to your responsibilities that to do a good job you need to give, really. Surround yourself with some good people from outside your department, so make sure that you have the access to independent experts – get them in. One of the wonders of the role is that you can get to see pretty much anyone at a moment's notice, so make full use of that. Set up really good-quality, high-calibre advisory boards, manage your time, stay in touch with the outside world. I found continuing to read the media to be an important part of that. If you're a DCMS minister, do read the newspapers. I won't tell you more about that, but I do think that's wise advice. Because you are responsible for the media and for publishing and for the press. So it's no point exposing yourself to unfortunate questions that you can't answer because you don't make time for what they write and what they air.[4]

Nicky Morgan
Take time to understand the brief. Really think about what your priorities are and don't have too many of them, up to three. Particularly if you're a junior minister, two or three priorities is more than enough. Ask: what can I make my own? What is it that needs to be tackled? So, for example, when I was in the Treasury as Economic Secretary, Air

Passenger Duty was a big thing and we did actually get some movement on that; George [Osborne] understood that. I think the other thing is regard the officials as your... I was going to say your allies, but they're not the enemy; they are there to help you. But also be prepared to push back, don't accept the first piece of advice and always treat them as professionals, and I think they will be on your side because mostly they want to help you deliver your policy priorities. Don't be afraid to push back when you get the No. 10 'no, no you can't do that', but choose your battles and push back within reason.[5]

David Gauke
Make sure you've got your priorities and work out what relationships are going to be important to you politically. If you're a junior minister, work out what you're trying to do and your relationship with your Secretary of State. You need to fundamentally recognise that the civil service is there to help, particularly your private office. It's there to help. Next, you need to try to provide a sense of direction and some vision, which relates to your priorities. That makes it easier for your private office to convey to the rest of the department what the minister cares about. And then you need to keep following that up and underlining it. It's no good having three priorities one month and then three different priorities a month later. You've got to stick at it and persevere. Finally, there are the delivery elements. It's very little about the initial press release or the publication of a document. It's more about how you follow up and how you convey a sense that the minister is interested in stuff happening.

KEEP ASKING AND LEARNING
Caroline Flint
I would say you're not going to know everything straight away. If

you're not sure, find someone you trust to ask. I'm not saying I didn't have that, but it was also quite lonely. It's quite lonely being a minister. Speak up if you need a bit of help with something or when you need a bit of development and training on something. I would ask myself: can I do this in a way that I'm not going to be embarrassed? If you need support, ask for it. Be more confident about doing that.

Even if you move from one department to another, there is learning you will take from the experiences you have, which will prove helpful down the road. Nothing is unhelpful in all of this, whether it's things when they work or things when they don't work. I would also say, if you're in the room with civil servants and you don't understand something, be brave and ask the question. It might be that they think, 'Why on earth doesn't she know the answer to this?' But sometimes you put a question forward and they haven't got the answer. So don't be afraid of asking the question.

Chloe Smith
You need to provide political, democratic, lay leadership. You are performing this feat of bringing together your understanding of what needs to be done with what people need from you, with the environment as it stands, and jumping into a set of technical subject matters that may well be brand new to you. So to achieve all of that, you do need to have an awareness of what you don't know. And you need to know where to go to ask for advice or wisdom or information.

I recall that, when I first went to the Treasury, I felt that I had very little time to address that need, so I basically went around armed with a copy of Gerald Kaufman's book [*How to Be a Minister*, published in 1980], which is a very good book and is very helpful but is not the same as taking advantage of where you can find the wisdom and the insight that you will need as you absorb all the information from your officials, and as you try to meld that to your objectives. I think you then also need to carry on that listening task as you go through your work. This is not just about the beginning of being a minister; you have to do that throughout. You have to be a listener. You have to be able to listen to citizens or customers or call it what you wish. But you have to be able to find a way to understand what millions of people require from your organisation and to be able to listen to new ideas and to be able to listen to wisdom as it continues to come.[6]

Robert Buckland
The first thing to do is learn how to be a minister. Spend the first few weeks just getting into the rhythm and learning about what makes a private office work, what you can do, what you can't do, what you shouldn't do. And then once you've established that, if you're a junior minister, work out one or two things you really want to do and can do within a year and get them done. If you're a Cabinet minister, it is a step change from being a junior minister; there's no doubt about it, it's a different planet. You then have to be very, very ruthless about your priorities. Be ambitious; don't be timid. You've got the privilege of sitting in charge of a great department of state, especially if you've got a majority in Parliament. I used to say there's no limit of what we can do if we've got the ambition and the will and the energy to do it. I still believe that. Yes, you've got to be realistic, but you apply your realism in choosing your priorities and, once you've done that, go for it. You'll find the civil service will help you if you've got a very clear mind. If you don't know your own mind, don't blame the civil service, because they will try to interpret what you're saying and no doubt they'll get it wrong because you haven't

thought it through. So be clear and be consistent. And be kind as well, because I think you can get the job done with a high degree of kindness, which is what we did in the department.[7]

SPEAK TO YOUR PREDECESSOR AND SPEAK UP
Amber Rudd

I would always suggest to ministers, and Secretaries of State, new to a job, to try to have a good chat with the exiting one. Of course, that's going to be more difficult in a different party, but not necessarily. So that they know what the key issues are. I think that if you're being promoted within the department, you're very lucky, because it's just so helpful knowing where to go. No sudden, early decisions, if possible. Because you look back after six months with amazement at how little you knew when you started. You've got to really just try to buy yourself some time while you get to know what's going on. Try to make sure you've got a good private secretary in the office. To women, particularly, I think that networking – everyone talks about networking as though it's something of the past – is so important. It's so important. It's like your earlier question about having got to know George Osborne. There is a kind of boys' club-type behaviour in Parliament because it is still more like a public school or a university club than anywhere else you'll ever go.

So, to women, I would say, always put yourself forward, always volunteer. It's like my mother used to say to me at school. As a backbencher, I was an absolute creep in the House, getting in there, making questions, taking speeches, the whole thing. It's also good practice. Someone like Stella Creasy [Labour MP], I think, is a very good example of someone who got herself established very quickly as a voice on women. I did a campaign early on as a backbencher on teenage pregnancies and how to limit them. It was a good way to work cross-party; it was my first showing on *Newsnight*. Women journalists particularly noticed, and I started getting mentioned.[8]

George Young
Talk to your predecessor to find out where the bodies are buried; talk to the junior ministers who have already been there; and then you need a serious conversation obviously with your Permanent Secretary as well. What I found was I needed to know what the priorities were for that department. And in the case of transport, which is the only place where I was Secretary of State, it was sorting out the public expenditure, sorting out the railways and bringing to a conclusion this integrated transport strategy. And OK, we have got two years before the next election and those are the three things I really want to focus on. So within that folder you get for incoming ministers, you need to distil that into some things that are really, really important, particularly if they are politically important like privatising the railways. So talk around and then after, perhaps a few weeks, work out what you want to do [and] where you want to be at the end of your time.[9]

DON'T FORGET PARLIAMENT
Margot James
Listen to Parliament, make time for Parliament. Politically, it's very important. Treat the whips with respect, because you have got a career to manage as well as your job to do, so you do need to take the whips seriously. If they want you on the front bench, get there. Get there and quick. In the end, you're a member of the government, it's a team and you've got to play your part for the wider team as well as for your own priorities and your own department etc. And make

sure you make time for getting colleagues' views and cross-party, as well, I think. That's very important too. Don't lose touch with your MP colleagues. So many ministers do that. I used to call it the black hole of the department. So many ministers disappear down the black hole of the department. You have to accept that you could do your work 365 days a year, sixteen hours a day, and you still wouldn't get it all done. You need to learn how to say 'no' and you need to make time for things that aren't necessarily urgent.[10]

Desmond Swayne
You've got to be good in the House of Commons, that's the first thing. You've got to work on that. If you can't perform at the dispatch box, you're not going to perform. The other tip I would say is make sure you're absolutely comfortable with your private office. In particular, the most important thing in your private office is making sure that the relationship between your diary manager and other diary managers elsewhere works well. The diary manager is the most important thing. Because there is nothing more frustrating if that doesn't work. I was very fortunate, I never had a problem, but I could see that was the critical area.[11]

Hazel Blears
You can't forget your constituency because those are the people who vote for you and rely on you for help. But that's the bit that the civil service never sees – that it takes your time to go on a Saturday morning, to knock on doors, to see your constituents. And it's a message for the civil service, really: you don't own us, our constituents own us because they've given us the honour and privilege of representing them. And that's as important to British democracy as any kind of ministerial system, in my view.[12]

BE STRATEGIC
Justine Greening
I would say policy on its own is not enough. If it doesn't have a strategy, doesn't have an implementation plan, if you don't know how you're going to transition from where you've been to where you're going to, if you don't know how you're going to track that day to day and if you don't have the wherewithal to know that you've got the capacity in your team to deliver on all of those things I've just mentioned, then don't be surprised when it doesn't go well.[13]

UNDERSTAND CIVIL SERVANTS
Greg Clark
First of all, you have the privilege of access to the best advice, from anywhere – obviously [from] your officials, in any department that you acquire. You will have people who share the same motivations as you and want to make a difference, want to make the country and the world better, and they are great to have on your side. But if you're a minister, you can talk to anyone, anyone would be thrilled to sit down with you and give you the benefit of their experience. So I really enjoyed getting out talking to businesses, trade unions, council leaders, scientists, and to really pick their brains. I'm not ashamed to say that most of the ideas that I've had, I've purloined from other people, but I've tried to bring them together and enact them.[14]

David Lidington
Understand your private office. Trust your private secretary, or if you can't, you don't think they are up to the job, talk to the Permanent Secretary about getting somebody else in. You will see more of your private secretary than you will of your wife or husband. You

can't do everything on your own; they are your gatekeepers. The right relationship will pay you dividends because they will also find out what's happening elsewhere in the department and in other departments with which you are dealing. They will talk to their counterparts in other ministers' offices. So, have the right relationship with your private office.[15]

CONTROL YOUR DIARY
David Lidington

Control your diary. Your diary secretary needs to be right – if you don't want to look at official papers normally on a Sunday, say so. If you are going to try to ringfence Fridays, or every other Friday, for your constituency, say so. If you go to the gym at 8 a.m. every day, say so. Remind your diary secretary you need to eat, because they do sometimes forget this! Have a structure to your diary and protect things that are important to your life, as you would office appointments in the diary – don't regard them as things to be squeezed in after anything to do with the department has been done.

My advice, when you start as a minister, is to have more meetings rather than have fewer, just to help you get to know the officials, put faces to names and so on. As time goes on, you'll learn, obviously, to trust more what's on paper, to take a decision on that. But if you have any doubts, call them in and quiz them and interrogate them. And remind them that ultimately, it's you who has to stand at the dispatch box [in Parliament].[16]

IT'S A PRIVILEGE – AND IT'S TEMPORARY
Damian Hinds

Make the most of it. You don't know how long it will last, but you have with you a private office [and] a private secretary who are there to help you to get your priorities done. In my experience, civil servants are an amazing group of people, in particular your private office is the key resource to work with. Also, just in that first period, there's so much happening all at once it's really important to try to retain clarity on what are the top, top things that you want to prioritise. It's very difficult, because there are always more things that you could and should be doing, but that prioritisation is very important.[17]

Eric Pickles
Just remember it's a summer lease. You're here today; you're gone tomorrow. Use every day and don't look back and think, 'Oh God, I wish I'd done that, I wish I had not been silent.' Speak your mind, do your best and try to make a change. Because all the effort that you put in is to make changes to public life and to enhance public life and, if you're just a passenger, you'll miss that opportunity.[18]

Matt Warman
Imagine that you are going to be moved on at the next reshuffle, whatever happens, because it will give you the impetus to go as fast as you reasonably can. It will make moving on feel like you haven't got unfinished business, and it will make firing feel much more bearable. Because I didn't. When I left DCMS the first time, I didn't feel, 'Actually, if only I'd stuck around, I could have finished the meat of it.' What I did feel was, 'God, I really hope, once we've done Cumbria, it works out in Norfolk and Essex, and blah, blah, blah.' But it was the implementation phase rather than anything else. And had I not had that little bit of a head start by knowing a bit about it and being able to crack on as quickly as possible, then I think I would have felt much more regret on top of the huge regret I've already got.[19]

Chloe Smith
One thing I would advise ministers to think about is to do the things you can when you can. One of them, for me, when I was Minister for Disabled People, Work and Health, was to say yes to the proposition of the British Sign Language Act [passed in 2022, it legally recognised BSL as a language for England, Wales and Scotland], rather than to say no to it. Famously, ministers mainly say no to private members' bills. But this was, I thought, a vital idea. I just didn't think there was any case to be made for refusing it. So I said yes. I said, 'Right, we're going to do it.' And it became a surprising piece of work, in some cases, to officials. I had to crack the whip a bit to make it happen. I had to marshal senior support as well to make it happen. And the end result was iconic for a section of the community. So do the things you can, when you can.[20]

DEVELOP OPEN AND HONEST RELATIONSHIPS WITH CIVIL SERVANTS

Hilary Benn
One bit of advice I was given, which I am sure is given to all ministers, is: you need to focus on a small number of things, because they will take a lot of effort to get them through. The one other bit of advice I would give is: two stories. When I became the Home Office Minister, I found myself dealing with the Sexual Offences Bill [which became the Sexual Offences Act 2003] in draft, updating of the law on sexual offences. One of the policies I inherited said that if you worked in a care home and had sex with someone who was living in the care home, you would be committing a criminal offence. Now, I am not talking about people who are vulnerable or have learning difficulties; you might fall in love with the person you are caring for! So I had a meeting of the officials, and I said, 'I don't really agree

with this, because I think there's a distinction.' I said, 'What do you think?' And there was this sort of look: 'What do you mean what do we think? Minister, this is the policy.' I said, 'No, what do you think?' And we went round the table, and it turned out that all of the five or six civil servants agreed with me that this was not a very sensible policy, so it went. Having a relationship with civil servants in which they can honestly express what they think is really important, and it's most important when you disagree with them.

And that's the second story. I had to deal with badger culling: the pass-the-parcel that was on my desk when I arrived at DEFRA. I came to the conclusion that we were not going to give permission for the culling of badgers. I knew that most of the civil servants in the team fundamentally disagreed with me. But I said to them, 'It's really important that you put all the arguments to me as to why I'm wrong because, when I go out there, I am going to get them in spade loads from people.' Establishing that kind of relationship [is vital], because if civil servants think, 'I am only going to say to the minister what I think the minister wants to hear,' they're not doing right by you and you're not doing right by yourself. That's an important lesson. It does mean you have to have confidence, that you feel you can say, 'I hear what you say, but I disagree.' In the end, you are the one responsible. You have to work it out in your own mind. When I got up in the House of Commons to announce that I was not approving badger culling, I think it was the only time in my ministerial career I was barracked, because there were a lot of MPs who thought I was completely wrong. But there you are.[21]

David Davis
The first thing is to encourage debate: make sure your officials know they can disagree with you. Secondly, stop them overwhelming you.

For example, the first day you get into office, call your predecessor and read them the contents of the first folder you're given to clear that night – your first box – because officials will bring you all the things that your predecessor turned down. I used to do this when I moved the other way around. I used to call the person who succeeded me and say, 'Just read me your box.' I'd say, 'Yes, no, no, no' and so on. Two reasons: it stops Whitehall pulling a fast one, but it also teaches Whitehall a lesson when the new minister says, 'No, you can't do that.' Number three, clear your diary. They'll fill it with things that they want to do, not what you want to do. When I went into the Cabinet Office, my diary was full of all that. Basically, in those days, they used to have lots and lots of foreign visitors and they used to use the Cabinet Office Minister to meet them all. I said, 'No, I don't want to meet them!' The last thing was in many ways the most important thing, although you can't always manage it: do your box in the office. Require the box at 5 p.m. and then do it. Now, your first night, you'll be there for four hours. But by the time you've done it a few times, you'll be there for two hours.[22]

BE BRAVE
Estelle Morris
I'd say it's about being brave, because essentially the things I complain didn't happen, I should have done more about. So be brave, build your links. And the other bit of advice would be never ever assume that anyone else is coping much better than you. They're probably struggling just as much as you but don't actually tell you about it. And I think that, when we all talk retrospectively now, everyone struggles a bit in politics. No one talks about it, and I think, for women, they're far more likely to want to talk about it.[23]

CONCLUSION

The central thesis of this book is that trust is the foundation upon which the relationship between civil servants and ministers rests, that those foundations have been damaged and that both sides must consistently and deliberately seek to build and rebuild trust with the other. It's important for the smooth functioning of government, more effective crisis management and better policy outcomes. But it's also important for maintaining public confidence in democratic institutions and government itself.

It is tempting to think that a period of calm and the de-escalation of conflict is sufficient to see past the events of 2016–24. But the trajectory of change has taken place over a much longer period than that and the nature of British constitutional norms means that when something 'unprecedented' happens, it creates a new precedent that allows it to happen again. By definition, those things cannot be undone and so ministers and civil servants must now decide the future direction of the relationship.

Precedent can raise the ceiling of expectations but also lower the floor of acceptability. The public nature of the poor treatment and scapegoating of senior civil servants achieved new lows that we have not seen before in this country. Many of the unacceptable (according to the Ministerial Code) behaviours from ministers have probably happened before but never so publicly and brutally. A turnover of government can bring energy, positivity and the feeling of a reset between civil servants and the new cadre of ministers. But the floor has been lowered for what a minister can get away with, and the more time politics has to play out through an electoral cycle, the more desperate a government and its ministers can become to reassert themselves, clasp for control or cling to power. It is in these moments that strong (rather than dysfunctional) relationships can navigate crises, uphold public trust and help avoid the erosion of democratic norms. And, whatever the performance of government at the time you are reading this book, those moments will come again.

I often find books and papers about improving government to be very good at diagnosing problems but disappointing in the conclusion and recommendations. Not because commentators and writers cannot think of solutions to prescribe; grand ideas of system overhaul are endemic in research papers and commentary. But anyone who has spent time amidst the workings of government knows (as the history of ministers and civil servants shows) that revolutionary change occurs very infrequently. And so suggestions of system overhaul remain, indefinitely, as suggestions. That is not to say that significant change cannot happen, but there is a great deal more evolution than revolution within British government. And until one of these suggested overhauls or revolutions takes place, the best way to make things better is to work on understanding and improving what is there already, ideally through mechanisms and processes which people already know how to use. That is not a sexy or exciting view. But in government, sexy and exciting things can quickly become fads and are forgotten.

It is much easier to diagnose and prescribe changes from the outside looking in than it is while you are in the thick of daily business; this is the basis for the management consultancy industry. Which is why it's important to deliberately determine an approach to maximising working together in advance. The approach to building trust in the relationship must be deliberate and strategic and it should also acknowledge Frei and Morriss's idea that trust has three drivers: authenticity, logic and empathy.

Good communication and competence from civil servants establish credibility and build confidence in ministers. This credibility enables the logic aspect of the trust triangle but also provides a platform for questioning and challenge, which encourages authenticity (experiencing a real truthful engagement with the other person).

Respect and openness are also critical components in establishing strong relationships. Civil servants are, rightly, expected to act with integrity in their actions and roles, both by the Civil Service Code and by the ministers to whom they are accountable. The public, to whom politicians are accountable, expect the same from ministers. If ministers are unwilling to allow civil servants to speak truthfully and impartially (particularly if it is something they don't want to hear) and unable to develop sufficient awareness of the impact of their own actions, the relationship is likely to break down at some point. Conversely, open and authentic communication strengthens the relationship between civil servants and ministers and increases the likelihood of a successful tenure and legacy. Ministers can take the lead in encouraging this by showing openness and transparency, which itself would encourage civil servants to reciprocate.

These principles should extend to colleagues in the departmental ministerial team.

For civil servants, self-reflection and the ability to step back and look for the minister's perspective, provide good conditions for demonstrating empathy and building trust. It makes sense that if the minister believes civil servants are really looking for the world in which the policy idea can be delivered, they can trust that there is a commitment to support and ensure the minister's success. It also means that if a policy truly is undeliverable, the minister is able to believe that really is the case.

A minister evolves over their time in office and civil servants must seek to understand that changing person again and again over the minister's tenure. No minister is the same person on the day they leave as the day they arrived, but their mandate remains and so the onus is on civil servants to keep trying to understand the minister, attuning to different personalities and preferences.

The permanent nature of the civil service makes it a natural home for institutional memory and establishing consistent cultures (although this is by no means guaranteed). Ministers, by contrast, are in post for an undefined period. They are not as bound and shaped by existing culture and those with the nous and drive have the ability to circumvent rules and frameworks. Ministers must make a decision to build trusting relationships with civil servants which prioritise logic, authenticity and empathy. To do so will yield better policy outcomes, better government and (more likely) a successful legacy.

Ministers, also, should be better supported while in post. Headline-generating fatuous generalisations of ministers as greedy and/or incompetent have undermined the truth that it is a relentless and ferociously difficult job occupied by fallible people who, in any other industry, would not be qualified for the role. I say this not to elicit sympathy for ministers but to suggest that, until the system changes (and many others have suggested good ways in which this could happen), they simply need more access to support. One frequent piece of advice that former ministers suggest for incoming ones is to contact their predecessors. I would suggest a step further, in which cadres of former ministers are equipped with coaching skills to act as executive coach equivalents for ministers in post. The process should be owned by the Cabinet Office or the political party in government and provide support for ministers beyond that which can be elicited from colleagues (who, it should be noted, can also be competition).

Two further changes need to take place. The first is that disagreements between civil servants and ministers need to take place in private – and as adults. The recent public nature of disagreements between the two has created an environment where it is not safe to acknowledge when a mistake has been made – for either ministers or civil servants. This failure to recognise what is real is unhelpful for good decision-making and bad for relationship building. Ministers should not blame civil servants for errors in public and civil servants should not leak or counter-brief to the media, as a mechanism of response. The emergence of this type of behaviour has been a damaging trend and served no useful purpose beyond generating headlines and feeding columnists. For clarity, there is a difference between whistleblowing (and journalistic scrutiny) and tit-for-tat attacks. It is the latter that needs to stop.

The second is that public discourse needs to rehumanise the language around ministers and civil servants. Adversarial, antagonistic and aggressive politics (particularly in the period 2016–24) has lowered the bar of acceptability when it comes to talking about those who occupy high-profile public roles. At best, this makes the job much harder and probably delivers worse results. At worst, dehumanising language puts politicians' (in particular) lives at risk (history shows this to be the case). The language must change and this must start at the top.

It is a fallacy that time, alone, heals all wounds. Patience, behaviour change and consistency play much greater roles, as does acknowledging the history of past mistakes so we are not inevitably doomed to repeat them. In the end, it will be up to the individuals who fulfil those public roles to improve how they work together. If relations are bad, it is not enough for civil servants to hold their breath and wait or hope for someone they get along with better; an amiable, favourable minister could be replaced at any moment. And it is not enough for ministers to simply decide that force of will is enough to bend and change the delivery machine of government. That approach forgets that the machine is, in fact, constructed of people.

It is that fact which provides hope. Humans have extraordinary capacity to make the decision to change. The changes required to keep improving relations between civil servants and ministers will take effort, but they are embarrassingly achievable. Of course, some people are already good at those things, but learning is a continuous process and the dividends of investing in strong relationships between ministers and civil servants are a better performing government which will deliver better outcomes for citizens. This book is full of reflections, experience and differing views: some of the base ingredients needed to improve something. And, I hope, it will be of use to both ministers and civil servants as they work together.

'Ministers decide.' It is newly arriving ministers who have the prerogative of the first move in their relationship with civil servants.

CONCLUSION

It is they who must set the tone and expectations for how the two should work together and for civil servants to respond supportively. And as they do this, ministers should ask themselves, 'What do I want to accomplish in government? How will I build trust and communicate with civil servants to make that happen? What are my indicators that those two things are being achieved? What will I do if they are not?'

It is the answers to those questions that will determine how government moves forward and serves its citizens. The future of the country will be determined in the mind of the minister.

APPENDIX

LIST OF INTERVIEWEES

MINISTERS

The Rt Hon. Dr Vince Cable was Secretary of State for Business, Innovation and Skills in the coalition government between 2010 and 2015. He spent a period of his early career as both a civil servant and a political adviser. He was never a junior minister and, very unusually, served for a full term of five years. The department had a single Permanent Secretary, Sir Martin Donnelly, for the entirety of that period.

Worked with: Andrew Lansley (in Cabinet) and Philip Rutnam (Director General of Business and Skills, Department for Business, Innovation and Skills)

The Rt Hon. David Gauke spent nine continuous years in government, before resigning on principle, citing that he could not serve Boris Johnson as Prime Minister and run the risk of pursuing a no-deal exit from the European Union. Over those nine years, he served in the Treasury as Exchequer Secretary to the Treasury (2010–14), Financial Secretary to the Treasury (2014–16), Chief Secretary to the Treasury (2016–17), Secretary of State for Work and Pensions (2017–18) and Secretary of State for Justice (and Lord Chancellor) (2018–19). Over his nine continuous years in government, Gauke was never demoted or sacked.

Worked with: Rory Stewart (junior minister in Ministry of Justice)

Caroline Flint served as a junior minister in five different departments: Parliamentary Under-Secretary of State for Home Affairs (Home Office 2003–05), Minister of State for Public Health (Department of Health 2005–07), Minister for Yorkshire and the Humber (2007–08), Minister of State for Employment (Department for Work and Pensions 2007–08), Minister of State for Housing and Planning (Department for Communities and Local Government 2008) and Minister of State for Europe (Foreign and Commonwealth Office 2008–09). Flint's time as Housing Minister was one of the twenty-five times the occupant of that role changed between 1997 and 2024.

The Rt Hon. Robert Halfon was Minister without Portfolio (Cabinet Office 2015–16), Minister of State for Apprenticeships and Skills (Department for Education 2016–17) and Minister of State for Skills, Apprenticeships and Higher Education (Department for Education 2022–24), effectively occupying the same role twice. In the intervening period, he was chair of the Education Select Committee. He is a rare example of someone who not only had a second chance to implement his learning from his first experience, in the same role, but also became a subject matter specialist in government.

Worked with: Jonathan Slater (Permanent Secretary at Department for Education)

APPENDIX: LIST OF INTERVIEWEES

The Rt Hon. Rory Stewart OBE was Parliamentary Under-Secretary of State for Water, Forestry, Rural Affairs and Resource Management (Department for Environment, Food and Rural Affairs 2015–16), Minister of State for International Development (Department for International Development 2016–18), Minister of State for Africa (Foreign and Commonwealth Office 2017–18), Minister of State for Prisons (Ministry of Justice 2018–19) and Secretary of State for International Development (2019). In his early career, Stewart was a diplomat and has therefore been both a civil servant and a minister. There are very few examples of this in the modern era.

Worked with: David Gauke (junior minister in Ministry of Justice), Simon McDonald (Permanent Secretary at Foreign and Commonwealth Office) and Clare Moriarty (Permanent Secretary at Department for Environment, Food and Rural Affairs)

The Rt Hon. Andrew Lansley (The Lord Lansley) CBE was Secretary of State for Health (2010–2012) and Leader of the House of Commons and Lord Privy Seal (2012–2014). In his early career, Lansley was a civil servant and is one of a very small number of people to have occupied roles on both sides of the relationship.

Worked with: Una O'Brien (Permanent Secretary at Department of Health)

CIVIL SERVANTS

Dame Clare Moriarty DCB was Permanent Secretary of the Department for Environment, Food and Rural Affairs (DEFRA) (2015–19) and Permanent Secretary of the Department for Exiting the European Union (DExEU) (2019–20). Moriarty spent most of her time at DEFRA navigating the department's response to Brexit, as working with the EU affected the vast majority of its activity. She also was in charge of DExEU through to its conclusion and wound down the department.

Worked with: Rory Stewart (Parliamentary Under-Secretary of State for Water, Forestry, Rural Affairs and Resource Management)

Sir Philip Rutnam KCB was Permanent Secretary at the Department for Transport (2012–2017) and Permanent Secretary at the Home Office (2017–20). After Rutnam resigned in 2020, he began legal action against the Home Office for constructive dismissal, making clear that his dismissal followed concerns he had raised about ministerial conduct towards staff. A subsequent inquiry by the Independent Adviser on Ministers' Interests (Alex Aiken) found Priti Patel had breached the Ministerial Code by her behaviour, which could be 'described as bullying'. In 2021, the Home Office settled out of court with a payment of more than £370,000 to Sir Philip.

Worked with: Vince Cable (Secretary of State for Business, Innovation and Skills)

Jonathan Slater was Permanent Secretary at the Department for Education (2016–20) and previously Director General of the Economic and Domestic Secretariat at the Cabinet Office. Following the exams algorithm fiasco in 2020, he was forced to resign after Boris Johnson 'concluded that there is a need for fresh official leadership' in the department. Slater's sacking was widely seen as a way to shield then Education Secretary Gavin Williamson over the exam chaos. Slater received a £278,000 loss-of-office payment.

Worked with: Robert Halfon (Minister of State for Apprenticeships and Skills)

APPENDIX: LIST OF INTERVIEWEES

Dame Una O'Brien DCB was Permanent Secretary of the Department of Health (2010–16). She was previously the Department of Health's Director General of Policy and Strategy, and prior to that the department's Director of Provider Reform Policy. O'Brien was rare as a Permanent Secretary as she had more than twenty years' experience of health policy and leading and managing change in health services, making her a subject matter specialist.

Worked with: Andrew Lansley (Secretary of State for Health)

Dame Sue Owen was Permanent Secretary of the Department for Digital, Culture, Media and Sport (2013–19). Prior to this she was Director General of Welfare and Wellbeing, Department for Work and Pensions (2009–11). During Owen's six years as Permanent Secretary, the department had six different Secretaries of State.

Simon McDonald, Baron McDonald of Salford (The Lord McDonald of Salford) GCMG KCVO was Permanent Under-Secretary at the Foreign and Commonwealth Office and head of the Diplomatic Service (2015–20). He had previously served as British ambassador to Germany and to Israel. Having previously agreed to oversee the merger of the Department for International Development with the Foreign and Commonwealth Office, McDonald was forced to take early retirement in autumn 2020 after Boris Johnson decided he wanted a new leader of the combined department.

Worked with: Rory Stewart (Minister of State for Africa)

Philip Rycroft CB retired from the civil service having been Permanent Secretary of the Department for Exiting the EU (2017–19). Prior to this, he had served as head of UK Governance Group and Director General of the Deputy Prime Minister's Office within the

Cabinet Office. He also held several senior roles in the Scottish government. Over his career, Philip worked with thirteen Cabinet ministers in various capacities.

Worked with: Clare Moriarty (handing over Permanent Secretary role at Department for Exiting the EU)

NOTES

INTRODUCTION

1. 'Philip Rutnam resignation: His full statement', *The Guardian*, 29 February 2020, https://www.theguardian.com/politics/2020/feb/29/philip-rutnam-resignation-his-full-statement
2. 'How Office boss quits over "campaign against him"', BBC News, 29 February 2020, https://www.bbc.co.uk/news/uk-politics-51687287
3. 'Is government fit for purpose? The Kakabadse Report', Public Administration and Constitutional Affairs Committee, Civil Service Effectiveness Inquiry, https://www.civilservant.org.uk/library/2018-Kakabadse_Report.pdf
4. Edward Malnick, 'Top civil servants on Tories' "hit list"', *Telegraph*, 22 February 2020, https://www.telegraph.co.uk/politics/2020/02/22/top-civil-servants-tories-hit-list/
5. Martin Stanley, 'Dismissal: Permanent Secretaries,' Understanding the Civil Service, https://www.civilservant.org.uk/information-dismissal-permanent_secretaries.html
6. Rajeev Syal and Rowena Mason, 'Inside Boris Johnson's Whitehall: "A poisonous, horrible atmosphere"', *The Guardian*, 25 February 2020, https://www.theguardian.com/politics/2020/feb/25/inside-boris-johnsons-whitehall-a-poisonous-horrible-atmosphere
7. Jill Rutter, 'Civil service–ministerial relations: Time for a reset', Institute for Government, 19 December 2022, https://www.instituteforgovernment.org.uk/publication/civil-service-ministerial-relations
8. According to the Ministerial and Other Salaries Act 1975
9. Douglas Wass, 'The Privileged Adviser', Reith Lecture, 23 November 1983, https://downloads.bbc.co.uk/rmhttp/radio4/transcripts/1983_reith3.pdf

PART ONE: SETTING THE SCENE

1. Martin Stanley, *Civil Servants, Ministers and Parliament*, 2024, p. 11
2. Dave Richards and Martin Smith, 'Wanted: A Haldane fit for the 21st century', University of Manchester, 16 December 2013, https://blog.policy.manchester.ac.uk/featured/2013/12/wanted-a-haldane-fit-for-the-21st-century/; and Dave Richards and Martin Smith, 'HC 842: The role and powers of the Prime Minister', Parliament, 7 March 2011, https://publications.parliament.uk/pa/cm201011/cmselect/cmpolcon/writev/842/pm12.htm
3. 'Chapter 2: Ministerial Responsibility for the Civil Service', Parliament, https://publications.parliament.uk/pa/ld201213/ldselect/ldconst/61/6105.htm#note9

4. 'United Kingdom profile – Timeline', BBC, 10 August 2018, https://www.bbc.co.uk/news/world-europe-18028620
5. Tim Durrant and Alice Lilly, 'Amber Rudd', Institute for Government, 1 December 2020, https://www.instituteforgovernment.org.uk/ministers-reflect/amber-rudd
6. G. Jones, 'The Prime Ministers' Men', *Whitley Bulletin*, April 1978, No. 4, pp. 66–8
7. Stephen Hanney, 'Special Advisers: Their Place in British Government', PhD thesis, Brunel University, 1993
8. 'The Cabinet Manual', Cabinet Office, October 2011, https://assets.publishing.service.gov.uk/media/5a79d5d7e5274a18ba50f2b6/cabinet-manual.pdf
9. 'The Ministerial Code', Cabinet Office, December 2022, https://assets.publishing.service.gov.uk/media/63a4628bd3bf7f37654767f2/Ministerial_Code.pdf
10. Heather Stewart, 'No. 10 faces legal challenge to PM's support for Priti Patel on bulling claims', *The Guardian*, 12 November 2021, https://www.theguardian.com/politics/2021/nov/12/no-10-faces-legal-challenge-to-pms-support-for-priti-patel-on-bullying-claims
11. 'Governance Project', UK Governance Project, 2024, https://www.ukgovernanceproject.co.uk/our-report/
12. https://commonslibrary.parliament.uk/research-briefings/cbp-7483/
13. 'Times Past, Times Future', BBC Radio 4, 31 January 1996, https://genome.ch.bbc.co.uk/b322ea0bafc44b99ad2b2302012a3f83
14. Sir Geoffrey Holland, 'Alas! Sir Humphrey, I Knew Him Well', RSA Lecture, 3 May 1995
15. Vince Cable, *How to Be a Politician*, 2022, p. 78
16. 'Churchill and the Commons Chamber', UK Parliament, https://www.parliament.uk/about/living-heritage/building/palace/architecture/palacestructure/churchill/
17. Frances Frei and Anne Morriss, 'Begin with Trust', *Harvard Business Review*, May–June 2020, https://hbr.org/2020/05/begin-with-trust
18. Rowena Mason and Heather Stewart, 'Javid resigned after Johnson pushed him to sack advisers', *The Guardian*, 13 February 2020, https://www.theguardian.com/politics/2020/feb/13/javid-resigned-after-johnson-pushed-him-to-sack-advisers
19. Frei and Morriss, 'Begin with Trust'

PART THREE: THE MIDDLE
1. Transcript, David Davis, 22 September 2022, Ministers Reflect archive, Institute for Government, https://www.instituteforgovernment.org.uk/sites/default/files/2023-01/David%20Davis.pdf
2. 'UK Covid-19 Inquiry: Witness Statement of Helen MacNamara', UK Covid-19 Inquiry, 9 October 2023, p. 29, https://covid19.public-inquiry.uk/documents/inq000273841-witness-statement-of-helen-macnamara-dated-09-10-2023/
3. Ibid., p. 90
4. Jack Worlidge et al., 'Whitehall Monitor 2024', Institute for Government, January 2024, https://www.instituteforgovernment.org.uk/publication/whitehall-monitor-2024/part-1
5. Suzannah Brecknell and Josh May, 'Garden Bridge ministerial direction caused "frustration" at centre of government', *Civil Service World*, 11 October 2016, https://www.civilserviceworld.com/professions/article/garden-bridge-ministerial-direction-caused-frustration-at-centre-of-government
6. 'A sense of direction', *Civil Service World*, 28 March 2012, https://www.civilserviceworld.com/in-depth/article/a-sense-of-direction
7. Josh Harris, 'Future directions for the Accounting Officer system', Institute for Government, 3 September 2013, https://www.instituteforgovernment.org.uk/article/comment/future-directions-accounting-officer-system
8. 'UK Covid-19 Inquiry: Witness Statement of Helen MacNamara', pp. 94–5
9. 'InCiSE 2019', Blavatnik School of Government, 2019, https://www.bsg.ox.ac.uk/about/partnerships/international-civil-service-effectiveness-index-2019

NOTES

PART FOUR: THE END

1. 'UK Covid-19 Inquiry: Witness Statement of Helen MacNamara', p. 11
2. Ministers Reflect archive, Institute for Government, https://www.instituteforgovernment.org.uk/ministers-reflect
3. Transcript, Jeremy Hunt, 7 January 2020, Ministers Reflect archive, Institute for Government, https://www.instituteforgovernment.org.uk/ministers-reflect/jeremy-hunt
4. Transcript, Margot James, 8 January 2021, Ministers Reflect archive, Institute for Government, https://www.instituteforgovernment.org.uk/ministers-reflect/margot-james
5. Transcript, Nicky Morgan, 19 December 2016, Ministers Reflect archive, Institute for Government, https://www.instituteforgovernment.org.uk/ministers-reflect/nicky-morgan
6. Transcript, Chloe Smith, 15 August 2023, Ministers Reflect archive, Institute for Government, https://www.instituteforgovernment.org.uk/ministers-reflect/chloe-smith
7. Transcript, Robert Buckland, 5 June 2023, Ministers Reflect archive, Institute for Government, https://www.instituteforgovernment.org.uk/ministers-reflect/robert-buckland
8. Transcript, Amber Rudd, 1 December 2020, Ministers Reflect archive, Institute for Government, http://www.instituteforgovernment.org.uk/ministersreflect/amber-rudd
9. Transcript, George Young, 21 July 2015, Ministers Reflect archive, Institute for Government, https://www.instituteforgovernment.org.uk/ministers-reflect/george-young
10. Transcript, Margot James, 8 January 2021, Ministers Reflect archive, Institute for Government, https://www.instituteforgovernment.org.uk/ministers-reflect/margot-james
11. Transcript, Desmond Swayne, 25 October 2016, Ministers Reflect archive, Institute for Government, https://www.instituteforgovernment.org.uk/ministers-reflect/desmond-swayne
12. Transcript, Hazel Blears, 29 November 2021, Ministers Reflect archive, Institute for Government, https://www.instituteforgovernment.org.uk/ministers-reflect/hazel-blears
13. Transcript, Justine Greening, 1 May 2018, Ministers Reflect archive, Institute for Government, https://www.instituteforgovernment.org.uk/ministers-reflect/justine-greening
14. Transcript, Greg Clark, 27 February 2020, Ministers Reflect archive, Institute for Government, https://www.instituteforgovernment.org.uk/ministers-reflect/greg-clark
15. Transcript, David Lidington, 22 January 2020, Ministers Reflect archive, Institute for Government, https://www.instituteforgovernment.org.uk/ministers-reflect/david-lidington
16. Ibid.
17. Transcript, Damian Hinds, 19 September 2019, Ministers Reflect archive, Institute for Government, https://www.instituteforgovernment.org.uk/ministers-reflect/damian-hinds
18. Transcript, Eric Pickles, 12 January 2022, Ministers Reflect archive, Institute for Government, https://www.instituteforgovernment.org.uk/ministers-reflect/eric-pickles
19. Transcript, Matt Warman, 25 April 2023, Ministers Reflect archive, Institute for Government, https://www.instituteforgovernment.org.uk/ministers-reflect/matt-warman
20. Transcript, Chloe Smith, 15 August 2023, Ministers Reflect archive, Institute for Government, https://www.instituteforgovernment.org.uk/ministers-reflect/chloe-smith
21. Transcript, Hilary Benn, 10 May 2023, Ministers Reflect archive, Institute for Government, https://www.instituteforgovernment.org.uk/ministers-reflect/hilary-benn
22. Transcript, David Davis, 22 September 2022, Ministers Reflect archive, Institute for Government, https://www.instituteforgovernment.org.uk/ministers-reflect/david-davis
23. Transcript, Estelle Morris, 17 November 2021, Ministers Reflect archive, Institute for Government, https://www.instituteforgovernment.org.uk/ministers-reflect/estelle-morris

ACKNOWLEDGEMENTS

My first thank you is to my wife Jess, to whom much credit is due for the title of this book (a significant improvement on my previous ideas). I'm grateful to you for your support in trying to get this written but also in helping me to be myself. You are the best person in my life and I will forever be grateful to be with you.

I had never really planned on writing a book, but I'm thankful to James Stephens at Biteback Publishing for turning a passing conversation into the opportunity to produce something more lasting. Thanks also to (the ever-patient) Olivia Beattie for helping me navigate publishing a book for the first time and editor Ella Boardman for making this far more readable than I had managed on my own. They say you shouldn't judge a book by its cover. But if the book itself is anywhere near as good as Zoë Pearson-Coles's design, I will be very pleased.

Thanks to my friends Sam Dillon and Mike Hough for generously reading through the whole text and providing me with incredibly helpful feedback. Also to my oldest friend, Paul Pambakian, for your encouragement and support in the early days of getting this book off the ground and your honest feedback throughout. One day I will catch you in the Ealing Men's League.

Many of my colleagues at Total Politics have been immensely helpful to me, from inception of ideas to introductions to interviewees and also sense checking my assertions. Particularly thanks to Suzannah Brecknell for helping me with some of the early-stage thinking and Tony Shaw for reading through sections and helping to provide some further colour and accuracy to them.

I am very grateful to everyone I interviewed, in various capacities, for much of the content of this book. Several were off the record or wished to remain anonymous and many others helped me to understand some of the mentality and reality of life in government. My particular thanks goes to the former ministers and Permanent Secretaries who generously gave their time on the record. Without them, this book would have been far less valuable (and interesting). In no particular order, thank you to Caroline Flint, Rory Stewart, Lord Lansley, Sir Vince Cable, David Gauke, Robert Halfon, Sir Philip Rutnam, Dame Una O'Brien, Dame Sue Owen, Dame Clare Moriarty, Jonathan Slater, Philip Rycroft and Lord McDonald of Salford. If this book has any positive impact, it is they who deserve much of the credit.

Finally, thank you to you, the reader. If you have got this far, you really are committed to better government working. It is people like you who will make this country a better place to live. Or, like me, you are the type of person who finds it difficult to mark a book as finished until you have *completed all of it*. Either way, thank you for reading.